Textual Criticism and Qur'ān Manuscripts

Textual Criticism and Qur'ān Manuscripts

Keith E. Small

LEXINGTON BOOKS
Lanham • Boulder • New York • Toronto • Plymouth, UK

Published by Lexington Books
A wholly owned subsidiary of The Rowman & Littlefield Publishing Group, Inc.
4501 Forbes Boulevard, Suite 200, Lanham, Maryland 20706
www.rowman.com

10 Thornbury Road, Plymouth PL6 7PP, United Kingdom

First paperback edition 2012

British Library Cataloguing in Publication Information Available

Library of Congress Cataloging-in-Publication Data

The hardback edition of this book was previously cataloged by the Library of Congress as follows:

Small, Keith E., 1959–
Textual criticism and Qur'ān manuscripts / Keith E. Small.
p. cm.
Includes bibliographical references and index.

ISBN: 978-0-7391-4289-9 (cloth : alk. paper)
ISBN: 978-0-7391-7753-2 (pbk. : alk. paper)
ISBN: 978-0-7391-4291-2 (electronic)

1. Koran—Criticism, interpretation, etc.—History. 2. Koran—Hermeneutics. I. Title.
BP130.45.S58 2011
297.1'226—dc22 2010053776

™ The paper used in this publication meets the minimum requirements of American National Standard for Information Sciences—Permanence of Paper for Printed Library Materials, ANSI/NISO Z39.48-1992. Printed in the United States of America

Contents

Preface

Over the past ten years I have had the privilege of studying ancient manuscripts of the Qur'ān and the New Testament. Pursuing a PhD comparing textual features from both of these traditions brought me into contact with beautiful manuscripts and gifted scholars from both academic disciplines, allowed me to answer my own questions on issues of the textual histories of these respective texts, and also permitted me to investigate questions that have been put to me over the years in numerous conversations with friends and colleagues.

This book is a partial presentation of the material examined for my PhD thesis which applied methods of textual criticism to similar sized and themed sections of the New Testament and the Qur'ān.[1] This book presents the Qur'ānic side of the research which was the more original contribution to current scholarship and a neglected discipline in its own right.

I found that the New Testament textual tradition is a particularly useful one to use as a basis of comparison because it too is a sacred book of a major faith community, and like the Qur'ān's tradition, the New Testament manuscript tradition is extensive both in the number of available manuscripts and the span of centuries these manuscripts represent. Unlike the Qur'ān's tradition, though, the New Testament's tradition has been extensively studied, particularly in the last three centuries, and a consensus has been reached in academia and all major Christian denominations to base the text of the New Testament on a rigorous study of these manuscripts instead of relying only or mainly on traditional texts. Though the focus of this book will be on the Qur'ān, there are places where general reference to textual criticism in the

New Testament tradition and other literary traditions will be useful for additional clarification.

Textual criticism from manuscripts is a needed supplement to the extensive textual records and studies done by Muslims through the centuries. First, these kind of studies will put Qur'ānic manuscript studies on the same level as Hebrew Bible and New Testament manuscript studies. Second, they can provide necessary evidence for evaluating and increasing the precision of description for the history of the Qur'ān's textual development. Third, they will provide a body of material against which the extensive Qur'ānic variants literature can be checked. Fourth, they also provide a body of material to which Islamic historical records concerning the collection of the Qur'ān and the development of its orthography can be compared. New Testament textual criticism is a useful discipline from which to approach Qur'ānic manuscript studies in that it is perhaps the most developed discipline for these kinds of textual and historical questions. One noted Qur'ān scholar has concluded after his own comparison of manuscript features with the traditional history of the Qur'ān's text:[2]

> Thus, it is today evident that the real history of the fixation of the Qur'ānic text attested in early manuscripts differs in extremely serious fashion from the history preserved in the Muslim tradition. Only an analysis of manuscripts will allow us to reconstruct the true history of the canon's establishment.

As much as these studies are needed in Islamic Qur'ān scholarship, they are also needed to supplement Western Qur'ān studies. For too long, the theories of Qur'ān transmission have been developed in isolation from them. For instance, Wansbrough's and Burton's landmark studies were based on examinations of the wider Islamic literary tradition without reference to thorough study of the development of Arabic orthography in early Qur'ān manuscripts.[3]

The Russian Qur'ān scholar Efim Rezvan, in his article on the history of Qur'ānic scholarship in Russia, mentioned that an attitude that marks Russian scholarship is objectivity with respect.[4] This is the view that has guided the methodology of this research. True objectivity can only be approached if there is a willingness for self-criticism and openness to correction. Sympathetic respect can graciously acknowledge areas of commonality and difference, and allow them to stand for careful mutual scrutiny. These qualities are especially important when dealing with a book that is sacred to a significant proportion of the world's inhabitants. I hope this book is received with an acceptance of these intentions. With that said, I also invite criticism of the views and opinions contained in this book. I take full responsibility for any errors that are present, and I also take full responsibility for the opinions that are expressed.

NOTES

1. Keith E. Small, *Mapping a New Country: Textual Criticism and Qur'ān Manuscripts*. PhD thesis, Brunel, London School of Theology, 2008.

2. Efim A. Rezvan, "The Qur'ān and Its World: VI. Emergence of the Canon: The Struggle for Uniformity," *MO* 4:2:13–54, here 23.

3. John Wansbrough, *Quranic Studies*. Oxford: Oxford University Press, 1977, and John Burton, *The Collection of the Qur'ān*. Cambridge: Cambridge University Press, 1977.

4. His exact phrase is "objective information about Islamic beliefs and traditions as well as respect for them." Efim A. Rezvan, "The Qur'ān and Its World: VIII/2. West-Östlichen Divans," *MO* 5:1: 32–62, here 32.

Acknowledgments

Many people have contributed to this book, and I am very grateful for their generous help. First and foremost, my thanks go to my family for their sacrifice, patience, and steadfast encouragement to me throughout this research. Also, the following people have made significant contributions to my research.

Deep thanks go to Prof. Peter Riddell, former director of the Centre for Islamic Studies and Christian-Muslim Relations at London School of Theology and now at Victoria Bible College, Melbourne, Australia, and Dr. Steve Walton, senior lecturer in New Testament studies at London School of Theology, for their guidance, instruction, criticisms and constant encouragement. Also, thanks are due to students and colleagues at the Centre for Islamic Studies at the London School of Theology for friendship, excellent conversations, and penetrating questions. Andy Bannister, especially, helped me work through ideas of the relationship between oral and written literature theory. Rev. Dr. Tharwat Wahba, lecturer at the Evangelical Theological Seminary in Cairo, gave invaluable help obtaining sources and with many informative conversations while he pursued doctoral studies at LST; Drs. Peter Williams and Dirk Jongkind at Tyndale House, Cambridge, provided generous help with sources and understanding comparative issues between the New Testament, Old Testament, and Qur'ānic traditions.

Thanks are also due for hospitality, very generous help with sources, and personal instruction concerning Arabic script and early Qur'ān manuscripts to the late Prof. Sergio Noja Noseda of Lésa, Italy; Drs. Gerd-R. and Elisabeth Puin of Saarbrücken, Germany; Michael Marx, director of the Corpus Coranicum project in Potsdam, Germany; and Prof. Efim Rezvan of St. Petersburg, Russia.

I also want to thank the many scholars who were at the 2005 Corpus Coranicum Conference in Berlin, for their encouragement, criticisms, suggestions, and help with sources, especially Professors Angelika Neuwirth, Andrew Rippin, Ahmed Pakatchi, and Yasin Dutton. In addition, thanks are due to Dr. Alba Fedeli of Milan, Italy, and Dr. Elisabeth Puin of Saarbrücken, Germany, for their help developing my thinking concerning Qur'ānic palimpsests.

From the United States, to Joshua Lingel, asst. professor at Biola University, La Mirada, California, thanks are due for help with sources, introductions to scholars, and many stimulating and instructive conversations. Thanks are also due to Prof. Daniel Wallace of Dallas Theological Seminary for help with sources, instructive conversations, correspondence, and encouragement.

Photographs of the manuscripts are used according to permissions granted by the following people and organizations:

The manuscripts British Library Or. 2165, fol. 31b, Or. 12884, fol. 142r-142v, and Or. 70.a.31 are used with the permission of the British Library Board.

The manuscripts Bibliothèque nationale de France Arabe 325a, fol. 4r; Arabe 326a, fol. 3r, 3v; Arabe 328a, fol. 53r; Arabe 330a, fol. 3r, 3v; Arabe 331, fol. 23r, 23v; Arabe 332c, fol. 27v; Arabe 333c, fol. 41v, 42r; Arabe 334c, fol. 34r; Arabe 340c, fol. 36r, 36v; Arabe 343, fol. 102v; Arabe 370a, fol. 2v and 3r, are used with the permission of the Bibliothèque nationale de France.

The images from the Topkapi manuscript, fol. 172b and 173a, are used with the permission of IRCICA, the Organisation of the Islamic Conference Research Centre for Islamic History, Art, and Culture in Istanbul, Turkey.

The manuscripts IST TIEM SE54, fol. 11a and 11b are used with the permission of the Fondazione Ferni Noseda of Lesa, Italy.

The images of the Ṣan'ā' manuscripts 01-20.x, 01-28.1 and 01-29.1 are used with the permission of the private collector, "GRP."

The images of the Meknes manuscript, film05_03 and film05_04, are used with the permission of the Corpus Coranicum Project of the Berlin Brandenburgische Akademie der Wissenschaften.

The image of the Samarkand Kufic Qur'ān, fol. 206, is in the public domain. This image was obtained from the Imaging Services at Princeton University.

The quotation in the epigraph at the beginning of section 3 excerpted from *Nineteen Eighty Four* is used with the U.S. permission from the Houghton Mifflin Harcourt Publishing Company (excerpt from *Nineteen Eighty Four* by George Orwell, copyright 1949 by Harcourt, Inc. and renewed 1977 by Sonia Brownell Orwell, reprinted by permission of Houghton Mifflin Harcourt Publishing Company) and the UK permission from the A.M. Heath & Co. Ltd, London (*Nineteen Eighty Four* by George Orwell [Copyright © George Orwell, 1949]. Reprinted by permission of Bill Hamilton as the Literary Executor of the Estate of the Late Sonia Brownell Orwell and Secker & Warburg Ltd.).

Abbreviations and Misc. Conventions

A.H.	Anno Hijri, "in the year of the Hijra," the year according to the Islamic Calendar
BL	British Library, London
BNF	Bibliotheque Nationale de Français, Paris
BSOAS	Bulletin of the School of Oriental and African Studies
CBL	Chester Beatty Library, Dublin, Ireland
CE	Common Era; the year according to the Western Calendar
CUP	Cambridge University Press
EI2	Encyclopaedia of Islam, New Edition
EQ	Encyclopaedia of the Qur'ān
GDQ	Geschichte des Qorāns
HTR	Harvard Theological Review
JAAR	Journal of the American Academy of Religion
JAOS	Journal of the American Oriental Society
JQS	Journal of Qur'ānic Studies
Lane	E.W. Lane, An Arabic-English Lexicon. CD-ROM Version
MME	Manuscripts of the Middle East
MO	Manuscripta Orientalia
MW	Muslim World
OUP	Oxford University Press
S.	Surah

MANUSCRIPT DESIGNATIONS

Since no unified system of designating Qur'ān manuscripts is in use, abbreviated forms of their respective individual catalogue numbers are used. The full catalogue number for each manuscript is given in the descriptions of individual manuscripts in chapter 2. For example, British Library Qur'ān manuscript Or. 2165 is referred to as BL Or. 2165. Paris Bibliotheque Nationale manuscripts are referred to with the abbreviation BNF, as in BNF 328a and BNF 330a. If a number of manuscripts from the Paris collection are mentioned together, BNF is prefixed to the first number but not attached to the rest in the list; for example, BNF 328a, 330a, 331, 333c.

DATE CONVENTIONS

Dates pertaining to both the Western and Islamic calendars are given. For instance, if a general date according to century is required, it will be given in the form of the Western century followed by the Islamic century: seventh/first century. If a specific date is given, it will be given as follows: 936/324, meaning CE 936 and A.H. 324. Occasionally, the context will require just one date to be given and in those cases it will be made clear which dating system is being followed.

VERSE CITATION CONVENTIONS

For the purposes of this study, the individual verses of the Qur'ān are divided into sections of phrases that are smaller than verses. When a verse is cited, it will be referred to by its normal verse number and then a number designating the specific phrase within that verse. For example, Q. 14:37:4 refers to the fourth phrase of Surah 14 verse 37.

Arabic Transliteration System

Consonants

ء	'	ص	ṣ
ب	b	ض	ḍ
ت	t	ط	ṭ
ث	th	ظ	ẓ
ج	j	ع	'
ح	ḥ	غ	gh
خ	kh	ف	f
د	d	ق	q
ذ	dh	ك	k
ر	r	ل	l
ز	z	م	m
س	s	ن	n
ش	sh	ه	h

Long Vowels, Consonants, Short Vowels

ا	ā		َ	a
و	ū	w	ُ	u
ى	ā		ِ	i
ي	ī	y		

Diphthongs, Word Endings

وَ	aw	ً	an
يَ	ay	ٌ	un
يّ	ī	ٍ	in
		ة	t when in construct or after long *alif*

NOTE

1. This is the system used by the Journal of Qur'anic Studies with some minor modifications from the U.S. Library of Congress system.

I

INTRODUCTORY MATTERS

The world is generally governed by words.

—Sir Christopher Wren (d. 1723)[1]

Writing remains but stories disappear.

—Abdulrahman Ben Essayouti, Imam of Timbuktu's Great Mosque[2]

NOTES

1. Glorney Bolton, *Sir Christopher Wren*. London: Hutchinson, 1956, 59.
2. "Libraries in the Desert," *The Economist*, June 2nd, 2007, 63.

1

A Critical Text for the Qur'ān?

It is widely acknowledged that there has never been a critical text produced for the Qur'ān based on extant manuscripts, as has been done with other sacred books and bodies of ancient literature.[1] The current printed texts of the Qur'ān are based on medieval Islamic tradition instead of the collation and analysis of extant manuscripts. In other literary disciplines it is almost taken for granted that scholarly study of a text must start with a text based on the collation and analysis of the oldest and best manuscripts available for that text. Qur'ānic studies operates with an open knowledge of this lack concerning the Qur'ān, and as such methods and their results have had to be adapted to this fundamental deficiency.

Western scholars have often expressed the handicap they feel over the absence of such a text. The scholars Arthur Jeffery, Gotthelf Bergsträsser and Otto Pretzl worked on complementary projects from the 1920s into the 1930s, and Jeffery alone into the 1950s, to amass necessary source materials to begin the construction of a critical text of the Qur'ān. Rippin noted in 1982 of Jeffery's attempt,

> When Jeffery wrote this article ["The Present Status of Qur'ānic Studies," 1957], one of his major interests, and that of a number of other people at the time, was to construct a printed text of the Qur'ān complete with a critical apparatus of textual and orthographic variants and so forth. This project did not come to fruition, nor does it seem today very likely that it will, although the need for and the desirability of such is still there.[2]

This is still an accurate description of the situation more than twenty-five years later, although a significant step to remedy this is in progress with the Corpus Coranicum project.[3] Most attempts to construct a critical text of the Qur'ān were abandoned for various reasons after World War II.[4] Recently, interest in such a project has revived because of significant discoveries of early manuscripts in Yemen, the rediscovery of the Bergsträsser photo archive of ancient Qur'āns, and because of the development of computer software which can overcome some of the practical collation problems.[5] But even with this start, Neuwirth and Sinai are correct in describing the overall situation as a "veritable litany" of lacunae, with "no critical edition of the text, no free access to all of the relevant manuscript evidence, no clear conception of the cultural and linguistic profile of the milieu within which it [the Qur'ān] has emerged, and no consensus on the basic issues of methodology" just to name a few of the more glaring omissions.[6] Donner helpfully notes that in view of the many limitations preventing the production of a critical text, the greater need of the moment is for preliminary work developing tools and methods with the eventual goal of producing a critical edition of the Qur'ān.[7] This book seeks to contribute to this preliminary work by exploring what can be achieved through a careful collation of textual variants from extant manuscripts and early Islamic literature and using them to address questions of textual origins and history for the Qur'ān. If this exercise were extended to the remaining portions of text available in the earliest Qur'ān manuscripts, it would provide a better basis for approaching the wide spectrum of issues currently addressed in academic Qur'ānic studies.

THE PLAN OF THIS BOOK

This book contains four parts, each containing one or more chapters. Part 1 comprises introductory matters and in two chapters contains the introduction (chapter 1) and a description and pictures of the manuscripts used, together with a collation of their texts for Surah 14:35–41 (chapter 2). Part 2 concerns the textual variants observed in the manuscripts in six chapters. Chapters 3 through 8 present the kinds of variants found: orthographic variants (chapter 3), copyist mistakes (chapter 4), diacritical mark variants and variants affecting grammar (chapter 5), variants to the consonantal line of text (chapter 6: *Rasm* variants), verse marker variants (chapter 7), and physical corrections to the manuscripts (chapter 8). Part 3 contains evaluation of these variants in three chapters: how the variants in the manuscripts compare to Islamic records of textual variants (chapter 9), concerning intentionality and non-intentionality on the part of scribes (chapter 10), and the role of orality in the textual transmission of the Qur'ān (chapter 11). Part 4 is chapter 12 which is devoted to conclusions.

METHODOLOGY

The method of Reasoned Eclecticism is the method of textual criticism chosen for this study. It is the method that has been used by the majority of New Testament scholars for at least a century. It is the approach behind the main critical New Testament texts in use among Christian and secular Western scholars.[8] Holmes sets out the basic approach of Reasoned Eclecticism:[9]

> By "reasoned eclecticism" I mean an approach that seeks to take into account all available evidence, both external (i.e., that provided by the manuscripts themselves) and internal (considerations having to do with the habits, mistakes, and tendencies of scribes, or the style and thought of an author). Central to this approach is a fundamental guideline: the variant most likely to be original is the one that best accounts for the origin of all competing variants in terms of both external and internal evidence.

This particular method has proven to be useful in two important ways. First, it is grounded in an academic discipline that has existed for more than two centuries. Second, it is a well-tested method for examining textual variants in ancient manuscripts across many literary traditions. Third, this method has proven flexible enough to take into account the variety of features found in the Arabic scripts involved. Fourth, it is a method that is not controlled by a particular religious, political, or academic ideology. It is a suitable vehicle for treating ancient manuscripts with the respect that such significant religious artifacts deserve, while yet maintaining a critical and realistic attitude toward the human influences in ancient book production.

In addition to there being a need to apply textual criticism to Qur'ān manuscripts to establish the earliest possible form of the text, there were also other important orthographic and historical issues that textual criticism addresses.

In 1979, E. Hobbs noted that the emphasis of scholarly interest over many decades vacillated between the search for the original text and tracing textual transmission:[10]

> There is an ebb and flow in these tendencies, and today there is more interest again in establishing the *Urtext*; but this double interest tends to be reflected in textual criticism in many fields today: to recover the *Urtext*, but also (or instead if the first is impossible) to establish the history of the text as far as is feasible.

Thirty years later, the tendency in Qur'ānic studies is flowing to explore both of these issues with a renewed vigor. This work seeks to demonstrate how traditional methods of textual criticism can inform both of these goals.

WHAT IS THE "ORIGINAL TEXT" OF THE QUR'ĀN?

On the face of it, the question "What is the 'original text' of the Qur'ān?" may seem simplistic and even patently self-evident. However, when one is dealing with the complexities of ancient book production, it becomes a multifaceted issue deserving precise definition. This is especially true when one is dealing with a literary tradition that operates with a mixture of oral and written literary conventions. For ancient books produced in cultures that preserved, maintained, and distributed their cultural and religious literatures through predominantly written means, the original text can be viewed as the state of the text when the document left the author's desk to be published and circulated. When oral dynamics are introduced, one may have a variety of oral performances preserved and distributed through oral and written means that could all vie for status as "originals."

One major discussion in Qur'ānic studies has centered on the search for an *Urtext* of the Qur'ān. Donner helpfully summarizes the search for this form of text to date and outlines many of the outstanding questions regarding it.[11] Islamic tradition has usually identified the Qur'ān as we know it with this *Urtext*, and this view has achieved a status of religious orthodoxy. In contemporary popular Islamic discourse, it is an assertion oft stated as established fact that the text of the Qur'ān has been preserved perfectly since it was given to Muḥammad. To the contrary, early and medieval Islamic scholarship was quite free in its recognition of textual variation and missing portions of the Qur'ān, and did not tend to make claims of perfect transmission. Also, study of ancient Qur'ānic manuscripts confirms the flexibility described in the earlier ages of Islamic scholarship.

In 1999 Eldon Epp explored how the term "original text" has been used in New Testament studies and pointed out that it has been used with a variety of meanings and a general lack of precision. He demonstrated that the process of an oral or written text becoming a published book was not a single event but instead involved discrete stages. Rippin makes the important point that illumines the scope of these stages that in these discussions, there needs to be clarity on what exactly is meant by the words "the Qur'ān."[12] He states that three elements must be kept in mind: a fixed body of text, the fixed body of text available in a written form, and that written form acquiring a measure of authority among a group of people. Each of these three elements implies processes whereby fixedness, written form, and consensus of authority were obtained. Any definition and explanation of an original text of the Qur'ān must clearly acknowledge and delineate these processes. Also, differing views of the history of the Qur'ān's textual history will vary in their views of the processes and length of time that it took the written text of the Qur'ān to acquire all three of these facets.

A useful scheme is a modified form of one developed by the New Testament scholar Eldon Epp. His scheme describes the process of book production by delineating four categories which this writer has expanded to five:[13]

1. *Predecessor text-form*: the oral or written sources the author used.
2. *Autographic text-form*: the form the author wrote as it left his desk.
3. *Authoritative text-form*: a form of text that acquired a degree of local geographic consensual authority.
4. *Canonical text-form*: a form of the text that acquired a degree of wide geographic consensual authority.
5. *Interpretive text-form*: any later intentional reformulation for stylistic, practical, or dogmatic reasons.

This scheme will be used throughout this book with these terms used as technical terms for various stages in the history of the development of the text. Also, with the state of early extant materials for the Qur'ān, one is at a loss for documenting the earliest recorded oral and written portions. This is because what comes down to us are early edited portions of just some of the material attributed to Muḥammad. With this limitation in mind, the emphasis of this book will be the examination of available written material, but with the recognition that there was an oral tradition in the background to which the written transmission was intimately related, and that what can be recovered is closely related chronologically to earlier versions of the text.

Original Text Issues for the Qur'ān

These categories are useful in determining which form of text of the Qur'ān is the appropriate goal for text critical study. For thorough reviews of the Islamic traditions concerning the initial collection of the Qur'ān the reader is invited to consult the standard Western academic critiques as well as Islamic treatments.[14] For the purposes of this book and considering the issue of the original text to be sought through textual criticism, some comments on traditional views of the Qur'ān's collection would be useful.

According to some Islamic traditions, within Muḥammad's lifetime his recitations were recorded in both writing and by memorization, but not in a complete, organized collection.[15] There are traditions that assert Muḥammad did leave a complete collection, but there are many reasons which make this unlikely, and this view has not gained acceptance in many scholarly circles.[16] These portions of material from within Muḥammad's lifetime, either written or oral, are equivalent to Epp's Predecessor text-form. They made up a loose collection of autographic material, though it had not been put in a single autographic text-form. One could legitimately speak of autographic text forms.

After Muḥammad's death, there were collections of this material in use among his Companions that became authoritative versions in their own right. This is seen in that they were recited and used in the different geographic locations where these Companions went in the early Islamic conquests. These can be considered Authoritative text-forms, each authoritative in its own right and in its own geographical sphere. It was the use of these different versions that allegedly caused conflicts so severe they threatened the unity of the empire and prompted 'Uthmān to create a single version. The traditions recount that 'Uthmān did this using for a basis one Companion's version, 'Umar's, but after 'Umar's death it was in the care of his daughter Ḥafṣa. 'Uthmān had this version edited, possibly including additional material as well as removing some material. This version of 'Uthmān's then became the Canonical text-form. Any later versions that improved the orthography, such as by al-Ḥajjāj and Ibn Mujāhid, and any others that added consonantal pointing or vocalization notation systems, could be termed Interpretive text-forms. If this action was taken by 'Uthmān, it prevented the possibility of fully recovering either the authoritative text-forms of the Companions, or the autographic predecessor text-forms of the Qur'ān.

If Islamic tradition is correct, then a relatively early Canonical text-form can be recovered if the dates given to the earliest Qur'ān manuscripts are correct and are as early as suggested. Western Qur'ān scholarship from the last century has generally confirmed this part of Islamic tradition, in that no manuscripts with forms of the text that could clearly be considered an Authoritative text-form or an Autographic Predecessor text-form have been discovered. Most extant Qur'ān manuscripts contain forms of the Canonical text-form and later Interpretive text-forms, with the possible exception of the few existing Qur'ānic palimpsests. The study of these manuscripts is still in the beginning stages. The ones studied so far show a text-form related to the Canonical text-form, but with more significant textual variants than any other known Qur'ān manuscripts. Western scholarship has also exposed some difficulties in reconstructing the Authoritative text-forms of the Companions, in that the secondary records for these are inadequate for the scope of the task,[17] and also, such reconstruction is undermined by a lack of consistency in the Islamic records of these variants. This has led to doubts in their authenticity.[18] Though these records may provide a basis for a partial reconstruction of Qur'ān material that was available after Muḥammad's death, that basis is a tentative one.

Is the pursuit of a critical text which reconstructs the Autographic text-form of the Qur'ān a fruitless exercise, then? By no means. In view of the two main purposes of textual criticism, there is a great need for collating the materials that are available. Though an exhaustive critical text of the Qur'ān documenting the very earliest forms of the text is not possible yet, a start toward one can be made by collating the manuscripts and inscriptions that are extant, and this exercise would go a long way toward remedying the generally acknowledged lack of resources available for this kind of Qur'ānic study.[19]

ILLUMINATING TEXTUAL HISTORY ISSUES

Though the Qur'ān tradition is hampered in regard to the earliest forms of text that can be recovered, there is great scope for studying how the Canonical text-form was edited further and gave rise to various Interpretive and Canonical text-forms. The history of the development of Arabic orthography in Qur'ān manuscripts is a major area for exploring this. The orthography was developed over Islam's first three centuries in order to be able to represent a precise pronunciation and interpretation of the text. The manuscripts chosen for this study amply demonstrate the complexity and inventiveness required to effect this transformation of the orthography.

Also, historical events intersect the textual tradition on possibly three occasions in the first three Islamic centuries where strong centralized religious and political authority intervened and authorized specific forms of the text. There are features in the texts of these manuscripts that probably demonstrate the application of intentional ideological shaping of the text.

Thirdly, with the backdrop of the strong historic orality of the Qur'ān in recitation, memorization, and preservation, these manuscripts contain information that can be used to chart a significant shift within Islam. This is a shift from a culture dependent on norms of oral literature to maintain religion, history and culture to one operating according to norms reflecting a dependence on written literature. The manuscripts chosen provide significant windows into this shift, and to the strengths and weaknesses of oral transmission in its relationship to written transmission of the text.

In order to pursue the two fundamental aims of textual criticism for this book, the following questions informed the analysis:

1. Concerning the recovery of the original text, what is the earliest text for the Qur'ān that can be attained through textual criticism on manuscripts?
2. What kinds of textual variants does the Qur'ān manuscript tradition contain? What elements of intentionality do they present? How did the orthography of the text develop? How do the variants in manuscripts compare to those recorded in Islamic literature?

3. Can elements of standardization of the Qur'ān text be discerned in the manuscript tradition?
4. Can the idea of one precise version of the Qur'ān going back to Muhammad be supported from the manuscript evidence?
5. Are there elements related to oral transmission of the text evident in the manuscripts?

These questions are discussed throughout the book, and in the concluding chapter are discussed in summary fashion.

LIMITATIONS OF THIS STUDY

This book is an exploration of textual criticism applied to Qur'ān manuscripts and as such it is selective in many respects. For instance, the brief history of the text of the Qur'ān that will be given in the conclusion is not the product of an intensive analysis of Islamic historical traditions. Rather, it is intended to be a summary account which highlights how manuscript studies can inform further historical study. Because of this intention, when Islamic traditions are cited, they will be mainly cited from secondary sources and translations.

This book is also not intended to be a general introduction to the text of the Qur'ān.[20] Instead it is much more limited in scope with the narrower focus of applying methods of textual criticism to extant Qur'ān manuscripts, and exploring how the results of such study can inform Qur'ānic studies.

A third limitation is in regard to the most important early Qur'ān manuscripts that are only just becoming available to Western Qur'ān scholarship. These are the few Ḥijāzi script palimpsest manuscripts folios in Yemen and that have come through European auction houses in recent years. The portion of text chosen for this study is not represented in any known palimpsests. The included references to palimpsests might then be regarded by some as irrelevant or distracting. However, when one compares the kinds of variants found in the surveyed manuscripts to the kinds found in the palimpsests, legitimate and significant observations can be made. It is hoped that as they become more available for study, the methods used in this study will prove useful for further analysis of the textual variants they contain.

With the limitations and possibilities of this book in mind, the reader is encouraged to enjoy the elegant economy and beauty of the ancient manuscripts, and to wrestle intellectually with the fascinating complexities of the production and dissemination of ancient books. The transmission of knowledge through the ages via handwritten manuscripts is a marvelous enterprise, and it is a privilege to be able to obtain glimpses of minds and hearts from the past as scribal practices are examined. May you find this a rewarding journey.

CONCLUSION

The methods of textual criticism which have been developed over the last three centuries for sacred texts, the Greek and Latin classics, and other ancient literary traditions have proven that they can substantiate the historical authenticity of ancient texts, as well as document stages and changes in textual transmission of these bodies of literature. As a rule, manuscripts of the Qur'ān have not been submitted to this kind of study. The methods Muslims rely on for establishing their views of the emergence and development of their Scripture's text were developed in the early centuries of Islam, and, while they provide a degree of evidential value, they do not take into account current methods of textual criticism or extant ancient Qur'ān texts. Because of this, much of their value is difficult to quantify, in comparison to the more substantial evidence that contemporary methods of textual criticism have proven they can provide. Without textual criticism being done on early manuscripts of the Qur'ān, claims for the preservation of the Qur'ān are difficult to evaluate and in some respects are both unverifiable and unfalsifiable; that is, they can't be proven to be either reliably or unreliably transmitted.

NOTES

1. See for instance B. M. Metzger, "Recent Trends in the Textual Criticism of the Iliad and the Mahabharata," B. M. Metzger, *Chapters in the History of New Testament Textual Criticism*. Grand Rapids: Eerdmans, 1963, 142–54 and Wendy Doniger O'Flaherty, ed., *The Critical Study of Sacred Texts*. Berkeley: Berkeley Religious Studies Series, 1979. A standard New Testament guide to textual criticism is Kurt Barbara Aland, *The Text of the New Testament*. Leiden: Brill, 1989 and one for the Hebrew Scriptures is Emanuel Tov, *Textual Criticism of the Hebrew Bible*. Minneapolis: Fortress Press, 1992.

2. Andrew Rippin, "The Present Status of *Tafsīr* Studies," *MW* 72 (1982) 224–38, here 224.

3. Corpus Coranicum can be contacted at Am Neuen Markt, 14467 Potsdam, Germany, www.corpuscoranicum.de.

4. Alford T. Welch, "al-Kur'ān," *EI2*. Leiden: Brill, 1960, 400–29, contains a brief history of why the project was abandoned.

5. The Corpus Coranicum conference in Berlin in November 2005 and the continuing project that has come out of it in Potsdam have revived the project of transcribing and collating the texts of early Qur'ān manuscripts. The photo archive

mentioned is part of the one amassed by G. Bergsträsser and O. Pretzl in the 1920s and 1930s. It is now held in the collection of the Freie Universität in Berlin and forms part of the basis of the Corpus Coranicum project.

6. Angelika Neuwirth and Nicolai Sinai, "Introduction," Angelika Neuwirth and Nicolai Sinai, *The Qur'ān in Context.* Leiden: Brill, 2010, 1–24, 1.

7. Fred M. Donner, "The Qur'ān in Recent Scholarship: Challenges and Desiderata," Gabriel Said Reynolds, ed., *The Qur'ān in its Historical Context.* London: Routledge, 2008, 29–50, 44.

8. Metzger, *Commentary*, Second edn., 11*–14*. B. M. Metzger and Bart D. Ehrman, *The Text of the New Testament.* New York: Oxford University Press, 2005, 300–43. This is the chief textbook that outlines this method for New Testament studies.

9. Michael W. Holmes, "The Case for Reasoned Eclecticism," in David A. Black, (ed.), *Rethinking New Testament Textual Criticism*, Grand Rapids: Baker Academic, 2002, 77–100, here 79.

10. Edward Hobbs, "Prologue: An Introduction to Methods of Textual Criticism," Wendy Doniger O'Flaherty, ed., *The Critical Study of Sacred Texts.* Berkeley: Berkeley Religious Studies Series, 1979, 1–27, here 2.

11. Donner, "Qur'ān," 31–41.

12. A. Rippin, "Foreword," in John Wansbrough, *Quranic Studies.* Amherst: Prometheus, 2004, ix–xix, here xiv–xv.

13. Eldon Jay Epp, "The Multivalence of the Term 'Original Text' in New Testament Textual Criticism," *HTR*, 92:3:245–81. "Authoritative text-form" is a category added by this writer.

14. The major Western treatments are: Richard Bell, *Introduction to the Qur'an.* Edinburgh: Edinburgh University Press, 1953; Régis Blachère, *Introduction au Coran.* Paris: Besson & Chantemerle, 1959; John Burton, "The Collection of the Qur'an," Jane Dammen McAuliffe, ed., *Encyclopaedia of the Qur'an.* Leiden: Brill, 2001, 351–61; Michael Cook, *The Koran: A Very Short Introduction.* Oxford: Oxford University Press, 2000; Theodor Noldeke, Friedrich Schwally, G. Bergsträsser, and O. Pretzl, *Geschichte des Qorāns.* Hildesheim: Georg Olms Verlag, 2005; W. M. Watt and R. Bell, *Bell's Introduction to the Qur'ān.* Edinburgh: Edinburgh University Press, 1970. Some current Islamic treatments that interact with Western scholarship are: Labib as-Said, *The Recited Koran.* Princeton, New Jersey: Darwin Press, 1975; M. M. Al-Azami, *The History of the Qur'anic Text.* Leicester: UK Islamic Academy, 2003; Ahmad Von Denffer, *'Ulūm al-Qur'ān.* Leicester: The Islamic Foundation, 1994; Farid Esack, *The Qur'an: A Short Introduction.* Oxford: Oneworld Publications, 2002, Ingrid Mattsen, *The Story of the Qur'an.* Oxford: Blackwell, 2008; Yasir Qadhi, *An Introduction to the Sciences of the Qur'aan.* Birmingham: Al-Hidaayah Publishing and Distribution, 1999; and Abdullah Saeed, *The Qur'an, An Introduction.* London: Routledge, 2008.

15. For instance, al-Bukhārī, *Sahih,* Kitāb 61, Bāb 3.

16. There are reports that the Qur'ān was collected into a definite form before Muḥammad's death, but if that were the case, then there would have been no need for 'Uthmān forming a committee to edit it and then have variant versions destroyed. Von Denffer, *'Ulūm*, 34–45, presents an example of contemporary Islamic views that assert Muḥammad left a single text of the Qur'ān at the time of his death.

17. This can be seen in what would need to be documented: the eighty separate known canonical oral recitations of the Qur'ān, the many known and as yet undocumented uncanonical oral recitations, the discrepancies in the Islamic records of the thousands of variant readings among many of these recitations, and the lack of actual manuscript evidence of these textual variants. The eighty recitations are explained in as-Said's book *The Recited Koran.*

18. Welch, in his *EI2* article, "al-Kur'ān" (*EI2*, V:400–429, here 407) observed that confidence in the authenticity of the variants declined during the 1930s as they were being collected and analyzed from early Islamic literature.

19. Rippin, "Foreword" in Wansbrough, *Studies*, ix, gives a pertinent description of the comparison of what is available to Biblical studies.

20. See note 14 for some suggested introductions.

2

Descriptions and Pictures of the Manuscripts

This chapter will present the manuscripts used for this study. Each manuscript is described and pictures of the pages used of each are provided in this chapter. The texts of these manuscripts for the portion Surah 14:35–41 were collated in order to discover the textual variants that were used in this study.[1] The choice of this portion and these particular manuscripts came about in the following manner.

The catalogues of Qur'ān manuscripts available in Western European collections were examined to see what portions of text were available across multiple numbers of manuscripts. Qur'ān manuscripts from Islam's first four centuries were highlighted in order to obtain the earliest possible texts, as well as to obtain manuscripts with orthographic features that spanned the development of Arabic script from a partially pointed consonantal script to a fully vocalized script able to reproduce in writing the precise phonetic values of each Arabic letter. The initial target was portions shared by ten manuscripts and this was later extended to twenty-two manuscripts, nineteen from Islam's first four centuries and three from within the last two centuries. A chart listing these manuscripts has been included after their descriptions.

Within the available portions represented across multiple manuscripts, Surah 14:35–41 was chosen in that it was a narrative portion of a very manageable length and which also had reference to three familiar scriptural figures, Abraham, and his sons Ishmael and Isaac (Ibrāhīm, Ismā'īl, and Isḥāq). This story is set in the Qur'ānic context of Ibrāhīm's' settling his son Ismā'īl in Mecca. This portion, though relatively brief, was found to contain representative variants for its respective textual tradition.

THE MANUSCRIPTS

1) Istanbul

This manuscript is a previously unpublished manuscript. It is mentioned by Professor Noja Noseda in his article concerning Ḥijāzī manuscripts.[2] Color digital pictures of the portions of this manuscript containing Surah 14 were obtained from the Fondazione Ferne Noseda. The catalogue designation of this manuscript is IST TIEM SE 54, f. 11A and B. It is housed in Istanbul at the Turk ve Islam Eserleri Muzesi.

The pages are approximately 280 x 370 mm with the writing area being approximately 270 x 350 mm. It is vertical in format and has twenty-four lines of text per page. There are single verse markers (four to six dots arranged vertically), five verse markers (small circles), and ten verse markers (small circles surrounded by dots), but these all appear to have been added later than the original transcription of the manuscript. The manuscript page has a torn edge and two holes.

This manuscript has an early Ḥijāzī style script most similar to Déroche's H I style and it can be dated to the early eighth/first century. It has partial diacritical marks and some red dots designating vowels. These were possibly added later. One facet of the consonantal diacritics is notable in that it uses a system similar to that used today in the Warsh text, one dash underneath to designate *fā'* and one dash above for *qāf*. In its regularity and fineness of line it is closest in style to the Ḥijāzi scripts found in manuscripts BNF 326a and BNF 328a, also used in this study, and probably dates to the eighth/first centuries. It is also similar to the manuscript Islamic Arabic 1572 found in the Mingana collection at the University of Birmingham.[3]

2) Topkapi

This manuscript is housed in the library of the Directorate of the Topkapi Palace Museum, Istanbul, catalogue number 44/32. It has recently been published in a color photographic facsimile and photos from this facsimile were used.[4]

The pages of this manuscript are 410 x 460 mm. The writing area is not recorded in the introductory notes of the facsimile. Originally, there were 18 lines per page, but on some of the paper pages that are replacements for earlier parchment ones the lines vary between sixteen and nineteen lines at the front of the codex and between thirteen and seventeen at the end.[5] The pages with surah 14:35-41 (folios 162b and 163a) are complete except for some small holes in the 10 verse marker decorations and from the surah divider decoration on the reverse side of fol. 163a.

The script style is a monumental Kufic script similar to Déroche's B II and CI styles. It is very similar to the script in the Samarkand Kufic codex used in this study, the Cairo Muṣḥaf pictured in the facsimile,[6] Paris BNF 324 and some other manuscripts.[7] This script style dates to the late seventh/early eighth century and was used well into the ninth century. Some of the consonants have slashes for diacritical marks and there are red dots representing a voweling system which was possibly added at the time of the manuscript's initial inscription. Like the Istanbul manuscript mentioned above, it uses a system similar to that used today in the Warsh text, one dash underneath to designate *fā'* and one dash above for *qāf*.

The next three manuscripts are from the manuscript discoveries made in Ṣan'ā', Yemen, in 1972. Pictures of two of them and a photocopy of a third were provided by a European collector. They have not been published or described in the literature.

3) 01-20.x

A photograph of this manuscript was obtained from a private collection. The original is located in Ṣan'ā', Yemen, in the keeping of the Yemeni Organization of Antiquities and Libraries at the Dār al-Makhṭūṭāt.

The page size is approximately 260mm x 200mm with the writing area being approximately 200mm x 140mm. In a departure from manuscripts with such an early script style, the page orientation is horizontal, perhaps as a precursor of the great majority of Kufic manuscripts from the Abbasid era. Of the two pages used for this study, the recto page has nineteen lines of text and the verso twenty. There are no single or five verse markers. The ten verse markers consist of a circle with a dot in the middle, and they look as if they were written at the same time as the text was transcribed.

It contains an early Kufic script which uses a heavier pen stroke than 01-28.1. It is most similar to Déroche's category B I and of the manuscripts in this study most resembles manuscript BNF 370a and the Meknes manuscript. This script style, however, gives the impression of being an earlier version of the script used in those two manuscripts because it is not as crisp or regulated in its execution. This manuscript is unique in this study for being the only one containing absolutely no consonantal diacritical marks. These factors, taken with the ones that follow, indicate a date from the mid- to late eighth/early second century.

4) 01-28.1

This manuscript is located in Ṣan'ā', Yemen, in the keeping of the Yemeni Organization of Antiquities and Libraries at the Dār al-Makhṭūṭāt.

The page size is 409mm x 294mm. The recto side of the two pages used in this study has twenty-five lines of text. The verso side has twenty-six. There are single verse markers in patterns of three dots arranged vertically. These appear to have been inserted at the time of the original transcription of this text. There are only enough though to break up the text into forty verses, compared to the standard verse count of fifty-two. There are ten verse markers which are circles with two encircling bands of dots. These appear to have been added later after the text was originally transcribed. There are portions of the manuscript missing from the top and bottom of the pages and there appears to have been some water damage at some point.

This manuscript contains a very early form of Kufic script similar to Déroche's category B Ib. It is closest in style to manuscript BNF 325a used in this study. It is very similar to the Ḥijāzī script style except that the script is consistently vertical in its orientation to the line. Diacritical marks are used on consonants. They are partially applied and seem to be according to the system currently in use with one exception. The small difference is that the two dots designating *qaf* are applied vertically not horizontally. It is probably from the early eighth/late first century. There is a picture of a page from this manuscript in the book, *Heavenly Art, Earthly Beauty.*[8]

5) 01-29.1

A photograph of this manuscript was obtained for this study from a private collection. The original is located in Ṣan'ā', Yemen, in the keeping of the Yemeni Organization of Antiquities and Libraries at the Dār al-Makhṭūṭāt.

The page size is 300 x 420 mm. The writing area is approximately 260 x 390 mm. The page orientation is vertical. The recto side has twenty-nine lines of text. The verso side has thirty. There are single verse markers that are patterns of between three and eight dots arranged vertically at the end of verses. These were possibly added in later because they are often squeezed into the small portion of existing space between two words. A complete verse count for Surah 14 was not possible with the available manuscript pages. There are no five or ten verse markers. The page has a corner missing and some tears and water damage which at times obscure the reading.

This manuscript has a form of the Ḥijāzī script similar to Déroche's category H I and the script found in BNF 328a. There are many diacritical marks on the consonants, more so than many of these early manuscripts, but not all of the consonants that could be designated by dots are dotted. Many of the diacritical dots appear to have been added after the original transcription of the text. This manuscript uses one dash above to designate *fā'* and one dash below the letter to designate *qāf*. This system matches Leemhuis's category

3 which is opposite to the systems found in the Istanbul and Topkapi manuscripts described above. It is also a new manuscript to add to Leemhuis's list of manuscripts and inscriptions using this convention of the Dome of the Rock; Saray, Medina 1a; Dār al-Makhṭūṭāt, Inv. No. 01-29.2; St. Petersburg, Inv. No. E-20; and Vienna, Cod. Mixt. 917.[9] Four further pages of 01-29.1 are found on the UNESCO CD, manuscript numbers 132.1–132.4, but these are mislabelled on the CD as belonging to manuscript 15-27.1.

6) BL Or. 2165

This is the British Library's oldest Qur'ān. This manuscript was examined using the color photographic facsimile produced by Drs. Déroche and Noseda[10] as well as color digital images obtained from the British Library.

Pages in this manuscript are approximately 220mm x 320mm. The writing area is approximately 200mm x 300mm. The approximations are due to the margins of the pages having been trimmed, leaving variable page sizes and writing areas. The manuscript has between twenty-one and twenty-seven lines of text per page. The page used in this study has twenty-four lines. It has single verse markers at the end of each verse which consist of six dashes aligned horizontally to the line of text. It also has ten verse markers, but in the portion of text used for this study no five verse markers. The single verse markers were included when the text was written, but the ten verse markers look as if they were added later because they occasionally obscure prior verse markers or letters of the text. Rabb argues that the ten verse markers were added later by someone trying to adjust the manuscript to read according to a different recitation system from the system enshrined with the single verse markers.[11]

Its Ḥijāzī script is held to be the prototypical example of the subscript, *al-Mā'il*. This uses a heavier penstroke than the other Ḥijāzī manuscripts used in this study. It is a partial text of the Qur'ān dated by most scholars from the late first century of Islam[12] to the late second century.[13] Recently, an argument has been put forward that it is Umayyad, and might be as early as AD 650-704/30-85 A.H.,[14] though the most recent study published concerning it retains the more conservative dating of seventh/first century or eighth/second century.[15] Additional pages possibly from this same manuscript are catalogue number LNS CA[ab], held in the Kuwait National Museum.[16]

7) The Samarkand Kufic Codex

The original is currently in Tashkent, Uzbekistan. A full-size facsimile was produced in 1905 by the Russian scholar S. Pissaref.[17] This study used a microfilm version of the facsimile[18] which was then checked against the 1905 facsimile held at the British Library.

The page size of the original is 530mm x 620mm. The writing area is 440mm x 500mm. This is similar to other monumental Qur'ans like BNF 324. This manuscript is partial, and it has single verse markers[19] and ten verse markers, but none for five verse divisions. Jeffery suggests that the ten verse markers were added later,[20] but the single verse markers were written contemporaneously with the text.

Two ranges of date have been ascribed to this manuscript. Many Muslims think it is one of the copies of the Qur'ān that 'Uthmān himself had prepared to be sent out to metropolitan centres of the new Islamic empire. It is even claimed that 'Uthmān's blood stains are on the original manuscript, held in Tashkent, Uzbekistan.[21] The consensus of Western scholars, however, puts its date later to the late eighth/early second century.[22] This later date is suggested by the developed script style, ornamentation, and the large format of the manuscript. The script style is similar to Déroche's categories B II and C I which are also the categories for the Topkapi manuscript described above. There is a picture of a page of the Samarkand manuscript which is taken from a new facsimile that has been produced in Tashkent, Uzbekistan, which was recently on display at the Sacred Exhibition at the British Library.[23]

8) BNF Arabe 325a

This manuscript is in the collection of the Bibliothèque Nationale de Français in Paris. Color images of the manuscript pages were obtained from the Bibliothèque Nationale.

The pages of this manuscript are 232mm x 309mm and the writing area is 205mm x 265mm. It has eighteen lines per page.[24] This manuscript has many diacritical marks and colored dots to mark some of the short vowels and *ḥamza*. It has single, five and ten verse markers. These all appear to have been written contemporaneously with the text, except perhaps the five verse markers, which sometimes are inserted into places that appear to contain inadequate space.

Déroche identifies this manuscript as containing the script style B I b eighth/second century.[25] Déroche also notes that this script style is very similar to Ḥijāzī and may be considered a form of it, though he prefers it to be grouped under the Abbasid/Kufic styles.[26] This script style is similar to that found in BNF 335 and two manuscripts in the Khalili collection.[27]

9) BNF Arabe 326a

This manuscript is in the collection of the Bibliothèque Nationale de Français in Paris. Color images of the manuscript pages were obtained from the Bibliothèque Nationale.

The page size is 178mm x 270mm, the writing area is 143mm x 242mm, and there are twelve lines per page. The pages used for this study had a small portion missing. It has some diacritical marks and no short vowel markings. It has single and ten verse markers, the ten verse ones apparently added later.

Déroche dates this manuscript to the second century A.H. He designates its script style (H I) in the same category as BNF Arabe 328a.[28] As such, it could date into the first century A.H. Blachère dated it in the second century A.H.[29] Unlike BNF 328a, the main manuscript cited as an example of this script style, this manuscript is oriented in a horizontal format, like the later Abbasid Qur'āns. A picture of this manuscript may be seen in Blachère's *Introduction*.[30]

10) BNF Arabe 328a

This manuscript is in the collection of the Bibliothèque Nationale de Français in Paris. A color image of the manuscript page used was obtained from the Bibliothèque Nationale. Also used was the color photographic facsimile produced by Drs. Déroche and Noseda.[31]

The page size is 240mm x 330mm and the writing area is variable and goes between 205/210mm x 300/310mm. There are between 21–28 lines per page. The page used in this study has 26.[32] It has single verse markers following the verses which consist of six dots arranged horizontal to the line in two rows of three. It has five verse markers consisting of a backwards Arabic letter *alif* (ا) contained within a dotted circle. There are also ten verse markers which consist of the Arabic letter *hā* (ه) encircled by dots. These five and ten verse markers appear to have been put in after the time of the transcription of the text because they sometimes obscure the verse markers.

This is one of the oldest Qur'ān manuscripts in the collection of the Bibliothèque Nationale de Français in Paris. It is held to date to the same era as BL Or. 2165, and a recent argument has been put forth moving its date back into the early to mid first century A.H.[33] Déroche cites this as the best known example of Ḥijāzī script and it is one of two prototypes listed for his Ḥijāzī I category,[34] the oldest of the Ḥijāzī style scripts. Other portions of this manuscript are found in the National Library in Russia in St. Petersburg, the Vatican Library, and the Khalili Collection in London.[35] Déroche has reunited these portions and analyzed them exhaustively in his recent work, *La transmission écrite du Coran dans les débuts de l'islam: Le codex Parisino-petropolitanus*.[36]

11) BNF Arabe 330a

This manuscript is in the collection of the Bibliothèque Nationale de Français in Paris. Color images of the manuscript pages used were obtained from the Bibliothèque Nationale.

The page size is 280mm x 370mm and the writing area is 270mm x 340/345mm. There are twenty-five or twenty-six lines per page with the pages used for this study containing twenty-five. This manuscript is oriented in a horizontal format, like the later Abbasid Qurʿāns. It has some diacritical marks and no short vowel markings. It has single verse markers and two systems of ten verse markers. The ten verse markers in the chosen portion are apparently contemporaneous with the inscription of the text.

Déroche dates this script style (H III) into the C.E. 800s, after the other two earlier Ḥijāzī subscripts, and after the rise in use of the early Abbasid scripts in the Abbasid era, possibly putting this manuscript into the late second century A.H.[37]

12) BNF Arabe 331

This manuscript is in the collection of the Bibliothèque Nationale de Français in Paris. Color images of the manuscript pages used were obtained from the Bibliothèque Nationale.

The page size is 348mm x 413mm with a writing area of 284mm x 342mm and nineteen lines per page. This manuscript has some diacritical marks and no short voweling marks. It has single and ten verse markers, the ten verse markers apparently being inserted after the initial transcription. Déroche dates this script style to the early second century A.H.[38] Déroche also notes that this script style (B I a) is very similar to Ḥijāzī and may be considered a form of it.[39]

13) BNF Arabe 332

This manuscript is in the collection of the Bibliothèque Nationale de Français in Paris. A color image of the manuscript page used was obtained from the Bibliothèque Nationale.

The page size of this manuscript is 350mm x 428mm with a writing area of 310mm x 357mm and twenty-one lines per page. This manuscript has few diacritical marks and no voweling marks. It has single and ten verse markers, which were written at the same time as the text. Déroche dates the use of this script style (C I a) to the late eighth/early second century.[40] Another example of this script style is KFQ 15 in the Khalili Collection.[41]

14) BNF Arabe 333c

This manuscript is in the collection of the Bibliothèque Nationale de Français in Paris. A color image of the manuscript page used was obtained from the Bibliothèque Nationale.

The page size of is 202mm x 268mm with a writing area of 119mm x 200mm and fifteen lines per page. This manuscript has only ten verse separators, which were written at the same time as the text. Déroche dates this script style (C III) to the tenth/third century.[42] This manuscript has few diacritics and some colored dots for vowels. Examples of this style can be found in manuscripts KFQ 63, KFQ 45, KFQ 57, and KFQ 63 in the Khalili Collection.[43]

15) BNF Arabe 334c

This manuscript is in the collection of the Bibliothèque Nationale de Français in Paris. A color image of the manuscript page used was obtained from the Bibliothèque Nationale.

The page size is 270mm x 330mm with a writing area of 221mm x 290mm and twenty-one lines per page. It has single, five, and ten verse markers, all included at the time of the text's transcription.

Déroche dates this script style (H IV) to the early ninth/late second century A.H. as a transitional script, incorporating the slant of the Ḥijāzī style with other features of the Abbasid styles.[44] Another example of this script is found in KFQ 59 in the Khalili Collection.[45]

16) BNF Arabe 340c

This manuscript is in the collection of the Bibliothèque Nationale de Français in Paris. Color images of the manuscript pages used were obtained from the Bibliothèque Nationale.

The page size is 140mm x 210mm with a writing area of 100mm x 155mm and sixteen lines per page. It is horizontal in format. It has single, five, and ten verse markers, the five verse markers possibly being added later.

Déroche dates its script style (B II) to the early to mid-ninth/late second to early third century, with it being the first script traceable to clearly dated samples in the Abbasid period.[46] It has few diacritical marks and some colored dots to represent voweling. Other examples of this script style can be observed in the Khalili collection, manuscripts KFQ 13, KFQ 14, QUR 48, and QUR 80,[47] and in a recent Sotheby's auction catalogue.[48]

17) Meknes

This is a previously uncatalogued and un-described Qur'ān that was photographed by Dr. Götthelf Bergsträsser for his photo-archive of early Qur'ān manuscripts. Permission was obtained to include a portion of this text, the only one from the collection yet to be digitally preserved.[49] In the catalogue of this archive, this manuscript is described as "Film Meknes.-10. Film Privatbibliothek Cherifen Abdarrahman b. Zidan sehr alter kufischer Codex."[50]

The page size is approximately 205mm x 275mm with a writing area of approximately 160mm x 210mm and seventeen lines per page. It has single, five, and ten verse markers, the five and ten verse markers possibly added later.

The script in this manuscript is closest to Déroche's category B II, dating to the early to mid-ninth/late second to early third century. It has few diacritic marks and some colored dots for voweling. Its script style is like that found in BNF Arabe 340c and the other manuscripts mentioned with its description above.[51]

18) BNF Arabe 343

This manuscript is in the collection of the Bibliothèque Nationale de Français in Paris. A color image of the manuscript page used was obtained from the Bibliothèque Nationale.

The page is 131mm x 194mm with a writing area of 85mm x 165mm and sixteen lines per page. It has only ten verse markers which appear to have been added to the text at a later time.

Déroche classifies its script as D commune, a category for manuscripts with general characteristics of this category but which defy more precise sub-categorization.[52] Déroche dates this general script style into the tenth/third and eleventh/fourth centuries.[53] It has few diacritics and colored dots for vowels and *ḥamza*.

19) BNF Arabe 370a

This manuscript is in the collection of the Bibliothèque Nationale de Français in Paris. A color image of the manuscript page used was obtained from the Bibliothèque Nationale.

The page size is 138mm x 211mm with a writing area of 97mm x 172mm and thirteen lines per page. It has only ten verse markers which appear to have been added to the text at a later time.

Déroche describes the script style as Abbasid general class C,[54] and it resembles most closely the script of plate XV in his catalogue, which is a picture of BNF Arabe 333c which he categorizes as C III. This would date it well into the tenth/third century.[55] It has few diacritics and some colored dots for vowels and *ḥamza*.

20) BL Or. 12884

This manuscript is in the collection of the British Library in London. Pictures of the pages were obtained from the Library and also the manuscript was examined first-hand. All of the Qur'āns described before this one were parchment. This is a paper Qur'ān, and the earliest one in the collection of the British Library. This manuscript was chosen because it represents a manuscript from the next era of the development of the text of the Qur'ān, after the standardization of the seven reading systems of Ibn Mujāḥid, after the introduction of paper as a material for manuscripts, having more fully vocalized texts, and reverting to the vertical page format. It is at this point that the Qur'ān's text starts to look like its modern text. Rather than the Qur'ān being a mysterious book that only specialists could read, at this point the emphasis turns to present a clear, precise, readable text that can be produced more easily for a more literate population.[56]

The pages are 215mm x 283mm and the writing area is 155mm x 215mm. There are seventeen lines per page. While containing single, five and ten verse separators that conform to the system used in the 1924 Cairo Qur'ān,[57] it also contains a second system of single verse separators indicated by gold rectangles, which divide Surah 14 into sixty-five verses rather than the current count of fifty-two verses. The basic verse counting system that contains fifty-one verses works with Tabbaa's hypothesis for other Qur'ān's of this era that their unified verse numbering system represents a new level of standardization designed to reinforce the newly achieved supremacy of Sunni dogma concerning one eternal Qur'ān.[58]

Concerning its date, the acquisition catalogue listing its entry into the British Library's collection says this:[59]

> On the back of the fly-leaf to which this has been pasted is an inscription stating that the manuscript was written in 340 (951 A.D.). Although this inscription is presumably not that of the original scribe, it might well have been copied from his colophon, in which this would be the oldest known bent Kufic Ḳur'ān and the oldest known paper Ḳur'ān. There is a bent Kufic paper Ḳur'ān in Istanbul University Library, A 6778, which is dated 361, and which has hitherto been considered the oldest in both respects.

If this colophon is correct, this Qur'ān predates the Qur'ān at Istanbul University Library, which Blair also mentions as the earliest dated paper Qur'ān.[60] Even if this colophon is wrong, the script style matches styles from this period. Déroche chronologically labels this the "New Style" of script in its relation to the older Kufic styles. Sheila Blair, following Whelan, descriptively labels it "Broken Cursive."[61] The earliest examples of this style can by traced to the early tenth/late third century, at the turn of the fourth century A.H. It continued in use for a further two centuries.[62] This script style goes by many names, Eastern Kufic perhaps being the most common.[63] This style represents a break with prior Qur'ān manuscript conventions in a number of ways. For instance, it has an almost fully vocalized script, both with diacritical marks for consonants and marks representing the short vowels and *ḥamza*. Unlike modern texts, however, it does not have *ḥamza* as a separate letter on the same line of text as the other consonants. It does use an "s" symbol for *ḥamza* so that it is clearly indicated, but it does not have the full letter *ḥamza* on the consonantal line. Baker provides a picture of part of a page of this manuscript.[64] Other manuscripts of this style, both fully pointed and partially pointed, can be observed in various collections and sources.[65]

21) Muṣḥaf Sharīf

This is a small facsimile edition of a 1682/1093 Qur'ān published in Istanbul.[66] It is listed as "A facsimile edition of the Qur'ān from the Istanbul manuscript of Ḥāfiẓ 'Uthmān, dated A.H. 1093." The text of this Qur'ān was chosen as an example of a Turkish Qur'ān text in use before the 1924 Cairo edition. Photos were obtained from the British Library and the manuscript was examined at the Library.

The page size is 110mm x 183mm with a writing area of 69mm x 115mm. There are eleven lines per page. It is beautifully decorated in vivid colors. The verse separators are in gold leaf, and gold leaf is used in many of the decorations. It has exactly the same kind of verse separators and script style as a Turkish Qur'ān in the Chester Beatty collection, manuscript 1475, which dates to 1339–1340/740–741.[67] There are single and ten verse markers with a total of fifty-four verses for Surah 14. This text is the reading attributed to the Qur'ān reader Ḥafṣ, a version of the reading of 'Āṣim, the fifth of Ibn Mujāḥid's seven recitation systems.

22) Warsh

This text is a modern printed version of the text attributed to Warsh of the reading of Nāfi', one of the seven readings of the Qur'ān approved by Ibn Mujāḥid. This reading is used mostly in North Africa and Yemen.[68]

The page size is 175mm x 234mm with a text area of 135mm x 214mm. There are sixteen lines per page. The text is fully vocalized and printed in Maghribi script on cream paper. Following Maghribi conventions, the letter *qāf* is marked by one dot rather than two. There are single and ten verse markers with a total of fifty-two verses.

The Qur'ān text used as a basis for comparison with the consonantal line of text for all of these manuscripts is the Arabic text of the Qur'ān accompanying the English translation of Drs. Muhammad Taqī-ud-Dīn Al-Hilālī and Muhammad Muhsin Khān which is currently published and distributed from

Table 2.1

Manuscript[1]	*Date*[2]	*Script Style*[3]	*Manuscript Orientation*[4]	*Manuscript Material*	*Orthographic Features*[5]	*Verse markers*[6]
Istanbul[7] *Tiem SE 54*	*I*	*H I (H)*	*Vertical*	*Parchment*	*sd, nsv, cd*	*1,5,10*
Topkapi	*II*	*BII/CI?(K)*	*Horizontal*	*Parchment*	*sd,nsv*	*1,5,10*
01-28.1	*I*	*B Ia (K)*	*Vertical*	*Parchment*	*sd, nsv*	*1,5,10*
01-29.1	*I*	*H I (H)*	*Vertical*	*Parchment*	*sd, nsv*	*1*
01-20.x	*I*	*A/B Ia (K)*	*Horizontal*	*Parchment*	*nd, nsv*	*10*
Or. 2165	*I*	*H II (H)*	*Vertical*	*Parchment*	*sd, nsv*	*1, 10*
SamK	*II*	*BII/CI? (K)*	*Horizontal*	*Parchment*	*fd, nsv*	*1,10*
BNF 325a	*II*	*B Ib (K)*	*Horizontal*	*Parchment*	*nd, cd*	*1,5,10*
BNF 326a	*II*	*H I (H)*	*Horizontal*	*Parchment*	*sd, nsv*	*1,10*
BNF 328a	*I*	*H I (H)*	*Vertical*	*Parchment*	*sd, nsv*	*1,5,10*
BNF 330a	*II*	*H III H)*	*Horizontal*	*Parchment*	*sd, nsv*	*1,10*
BNF 331	*II*	*B Ia (K)*	*Vertical*	*Parchment*	*sd, nsv*	*1,10*
BNF 332	*II*	*C I (K)*	*Vertical*	*Parchment*	*fd, nsv*	*1,10*
BNF 333c	*III*	*C III(K)*	*Horizontal*	*Parchment*	*fd, cd*	*10*
BNF 334c	*III*	*H IV (H)*	*Horizontal*	*Parchment*	*sd, cd*	*1,5,10*
BNF 340c	*III*	*B II (K)*	*Horizontal*	*Parchment*	*fd, cd*	*1,5,10*
BNF 343	*IV*	*D c (K)*	*Horizontal*	*Parchment*	*sd, cd*	*10*
BNF370a	*IV*	*C (K)*	*Horizontal*	*Parchment*	*fd, cd*	*10*
Meknes	*III*	*B II (K)*	*Horizontal*	*Parchment*	*sd, cd*	*1,5,10*
Or. 12884	*IV*	*NS I*[8] *(K)*	*Vertical*	*Paper*	*fv*	*1,5,10*
Sharif	*XI*	*Naskh*	*Vertical*	*Paper*	*fv*	*1,10*
Warsh	*XV*	*Maghribi*	*Vertical*	*Paper*	*fv*	*1,10*

[1] This is the manuscript number used in their respective catalogues.
[2] These are the *hijri* (A.H.) dates given in the respective catalogues for these manuscripts as to the century according to the Islamic calendar. The dates should be taken as a general guideline.
[3] Generally, these are the categories devised by Déroche in Déroche, *Catalogue*, and Déroche, *Tradition*, unless noted otherwise. The more general categories of Ḥijāzi and Kufic are noted in parentheses as (H) and (K), respectively.
[4] This refers to the orientation of the page as to a vertical book format or a horizontal one.
[5] Abbreviations used are: nd- no diacritics, fd- few diacritics; sd- some diacritics; md- many diacritics; nsv- no short vowels; cd- colored dots for some vowels; fv- fully vocalized with diacritics and short vowels.
[6] These are verse separators, usually seen as single verse, 5 verse, and 10 verse separators.
[7] This manuscript will be referred to as the "Istanbul" manuscript for convenience.
[8] Déroche designates this style "New Style I" Déroche, *Tradition*, 136-137.

the King Fahd Complex for the printing of the Holy Qur'ān in Saudi Arabia.[69] This is the reading attributed to the Qur'ān reader Ḥafṣ, a version of the reading of 'Āṣim, the fifth of Ibn Mujāḥid's seven recitation systems.

NOTES

1. The collation of these manuscripts, except for the Topkapi manuscript, can be found in Keith E. Small, *Mapping a New Country: Textual Criticism and Qur'ān Manuscripts*, PhD thesis, Brunel University, 2008, Appendix J, 340.

2. Sergio Noja-Noseda, "Note Esterne in Margine Al 1° Volume Dei 'Materiali per un Edizione Critica Del Corano,'" *Rendiconti*, 134:1:3–37.

3. http://vmr.bham.ac.uk/Collections/Mingana/Islamic_Arabic_1572/table/.

4. Tayyar Altikulac, *Al-Muṣḥaf al-Sharif, Attributed to 'Uthmān bin'Affān* (Istanbul: IRCICA, 2007).

5. Folios 1b, 2ab, 4ab, 6b, 11b, and the folios with the short surahs. Altikulac, *Al-Mushaf*, 75.

6. Altikulac, *Al-Mushaf*, 98.

7. BNF 324 is pictured in François Déroche, *Le livre manuscrit arabe* (Paris: Bibliothèque nationale de France, 2004), 105. Other manuscripts with a similar script can be seen in Colin F. Baker, *Qur'an Manuscripts* (London: British Library, 2007), 19; Yasin Dutton, "An Umayyad Fragment of the Qur'an and its Dating," *JQS*, 9:2:57–87, 59–60; Sam Fogg, *Islamic Manuscripts* (London: Sam Fogg, 2000), 8–9; Sam Fogg, *Islamic Calligraphy* (London: Sam Fogg, 2003), 12–13; Marcus Fraser and Will Kwiatkowski, *Ink and Gold: Islamic Calligraphy* (London: Museum für Islamische Kunst, Berlin, 2006), 18–19; Martin Lings and Yasin Hamid Safadi, *The Qur'ān* (London: British Library, 1976), 22; and Bernard Quaritch, *The Qur'an and Calligraphy* (London: Bernard Quaritch, no date), 52.

8. Mikhail B. Piotrovsky, ed., *Heavenly Art, Earthly Beauty* (Amsterdam: Lund Humphries, 2000), 99.

9. Frederick Leemhuis, "From Palm Leaves to the Internet," in Jane Dammen McAuliffe, ed., *The Cambridge Companion to the Qur'ān* (Cambridge: Cambridge University Press, 2006), 145–62, 148.

10. François Déroche and Sergio Noja-Noseda, *Sources de la Transmission Manuscrite du Texte Coranique* (Lesa, Italy: Fondazione Ferni Noja Noseda Studi Arabo Islamici, 2001), f. 31b.

11. Intisar A. Rabb, "Non-Canonical Readings of the Qur'an: Recognition and Authenticity (the Himsī Reading)," *JQS*, VIII:2:84–127, 98.

12. Adrian Alan Brockett, *Studies in Two Transmissions of the Qur'ān*. PhD thesis, University of St. Andrews, Department of Arabic Studies, 1984, 76.

13. Lings and Safadi, *Qur'ān*, 20.

14. Yasin Dutton, "Some Notes on the British Library's 'Oldest Qur'an Manuscript' (Or. 2165)," *JQS*, VI:1:43–71, 66.

15. Rabb, "Non-Canonical," 84.

16. These are pictured in Huon Mallalieu, "The Al-Sabah Collection in the Kuwait National Museum," *Arts of the Islamic World*, 1:2, Spring 1983, 7–12, 8–9. Two pages are displayed at www.islamic-awareness.org/Quran/Text/Mss/Kuwait.html.

17. S. Pissaref, Samarkandskii kuficheskii Koran, St Pétersbourg: l'Institut Archéologique de St. Pétersbourg, 1905.

18. This was purchased through their Library's Photographic Services under the title, Samarkanskii Kuficheskii Koran, Microfilm 674, http://catalog.princeton.edu/cgi-bin/Pwebrecon.cgi.
19. M. M. Al-Azami, *The History of the Qur'anic Text* (Leicester: UK Islamic Academy, 2003), 111, is incorrect in asserting that this manuscript is devoid of *āyah*, or verse, separators. They are evident upon inspection of the full-sized facsimile or the microfilm copy.
20. Arthur Jeffery and Isaac Mendelsohn, "The Orthography of the Samarqand Qur'an Codex," *JAOS,* 62:175–95, 179.
21. Jeffery and Mendelsohn, "Orthography," citing 175. Al Azami, *History*, 111, 128. It can also be seen at http://news.bbc.co.uk/2/hi/asia-pacific/4581684.stm.
22. Efim A. Rezvan, "Mingana Folios: When and Why," *Manuscripta Orientalia*, 11:4. Obtained from the author. Jeffery dated it to the third century A.H. Jeffery and Mendelsohn, "Orthography," 195.
23. John Reeve, *Sacred* (London: British Library, 2007), 91. The Sacred Exhibition was from 27 April–23 September 2007.
24. François Déroche, *Catalogue des Manuscrits Arabes* (Paris: Bibliotheque Nationale, 1983), 68.
25. François Déroche, *The Abbasid Tradition* (London: Nour Foundation, 1992), 36.
26. Déroche, *Tradition*, 35.
27. Déroche, *Tradition*, 48, 52; KFQ 50 and 20, respectively.
28. Déroche, *Catalogue*, 61.
29. Régis Blachère, *Introduction au Coran* (Paris: Besson & Chantemerle, 1959), 88.
30. Blachère, *Introduction*, figure 1 after page 88.
31. François Déroche and Sergio Noja-Noseda, *Sources de la Transmission Manuscrite du Texte Coranique* (Lesa, Italy: Fondazione Ferni Noja Noseda Studi Arabo Islamici, 1998), vol. 1.
32. Déroche, *Tradition*, 28.
33. Yasin Dutton, "An Early *Mushaf* According to the Reading of Ibn 'Āmir," *JQS,* III:1:71–90 citing 84.
34. Déroche, *Catalogue*, 35.
35. Folder Marcel 18 in St. Petersburg, Vat. Ar. 1605/1 at the Vatican, and KFQ 60 in the Khalili Collection.
36. François Déroche, *La transmission écrite du Coran dans les débuts de l'islam: Le codex Parisino-petropolitanus* (Leiden: Brill, 2009), 171.
37. Déroche, *Tradition,* 28–29.
38. Déroche, *Tradition,* 36.
39. Déroche, *Tradition,* 35.
40. Déroche, *Tradition*, 36.
41. Déroche, *Tradition*, 59.
42. Déroche, *Tradition*, 36.
43. Déroche, *Tradition*, 64–66.
44. Déroche, *Catalogue,* 64.
45. Déroche, *Tradition,* 32 picture 3.
46. Déroche, *Tradition,* 36.

47. Déroche, *Tradition,* 54–57.
48. Sotheby's, *Arts of the Islamic World* (London: Sotheby's, 2010), 10.
49. The Seminar für Semitistik und Arabistik at the Freie Universität Berlin provided the digitized photographs of this manuscript.
50. Photocopied catalogue obtained from the Seminar für Semitistik und Arabistik at the Freie Universität Berlin.
51. Déroche, *Tradition,* 36.
52. Déroche, *Catalogue,* 45.
53. Déroche, *Tradition,* 36–37, citing 42.
54. Déroche, *Catalogue,* 149.
55. Déroche, *Tradition,* 36.
56. Yasser Tabbaa, "The Transformation of Arabic Writing: Part I, Qur'ānic Calligraphy," *Ars Orientalis,* 21:119–48, citing 130, 141–43. Yasser Tabbaa, "Canonicity and Control: The Sociopolitical Underpinnings of Ibn Muqla's Reform," *Ars Orientalis,* XXIX, 91–100 citing 98.
57. It does not have a single verse separator after السماء, the current ending word for verse 38.
58. Tabbaa, "Transformation," 130, 141–43. Tabbaa, "Canonicity," 98.
59. British Library, *List of Oriental Manuscripts 1948-1964, Or. 11820-12898.* London: British Library, 1964. This entry is in the 1963 section.
60. Sheila S. Blair, *Islamic Calligraphy* (Edinburgh: Edinburgh University Press, 2006), 151.
61. Blair, *Calligraphy,* 144.
62. Déroche, *Tradition,* 132–35.
63. Déroche, *Tradition,* 132.
64. Baker, *Manuscripts,* 26.
65. Arthur J. Arberry, *The Koran Illuminated* (Dublin: Hodges, Figgis & Co. Ltd., 1967), 10, plate 23; Blair, *Calligraphy,* 152, 155; Déroche, *Tradition,* 174–83; François Déroche, *L'art du livre arabe* (Paris: Bibliothèque nationale de France, 2001), 39; Déroche, *Livre,* 49; Fogg, *Manuscripts,* 12–13; Fogg, *Calligraphy,* 44–46, 50–51; Fraser and Kwiatkowski, *Ink,* 58–63; David James, *Qur'ans and Bindings from the Chester Beatty Library* (London: World of Islam Festival Trust, 1980), 30–31; Lings and Safadi, *Qur'ān,* 33–36; Quaritch, *Qur'an,* 67, Item 17; Reeve, *Sacred,* 90; Sotheby's, *Oriental Manuscripts and Miniatures* (London: Sotheby's, 1996), 14; Sotheby's, *Arts of the Islamic World* (London: Sotheby's, 2008), 20–21; Sotheby's, *Arts 2010.*
66. *Mushaf Sharif* (Istanbul: Dojan Kardes, 1967). It is listed as Or.70.a.31 in the British Library catalogue.
67. Arberry, *Illuminated,* Plate 60.
68. *Qur'ān Karīm* (Hodeida, Yemen: Matbaghut al-Najār, 1989). This copy was acquired by the author from Morocco.
69. *M. Taqi-ud-Din al-Hilali and M.M. Khan, Interpretation of the Meanings of the Noble Qur'ān* (Riyadh, Saudi Arabia: Darussalam, 2001).

II

OBSERVING THE TEXTUAL VARIANTS

> It must follow that any history of the book—subject as books are to typographic and material change—must be a history of misreadings.
>
> —D.F. McKenzie[1]

This section will examine the selected early Qur'ān manuscripts for textual variants, and then analyze the variants using established categories. One complication in this is that there is a possibility that the material available for examination is the product of formal suppression of variant material in the course of Islamic history. Jeffery commented about this after recounting many of the incidents in this history:[2]

> In other words, when we have assembled all the variants from these earlier Codices that can be gleaned from the works of the exegetes and philologers, we have only such readings as were useful for purposes of *Tafsīr* and were considered to be sufficiently near orthodoxy to be allowed to survive.

While Jeffery collected variants from Islamic literature and Bergsträsser and Pretzl collected photographs of actual manuscripts, a survey of which variants exist in extant manuscripts was not made. Since that time, the only manuscripts for which studies have been made that include at least some of the textual variants are for some Qur'ānic palimpsest pages, the Samarkand Kufic manuscript housed in Tashkent, the Topkapi manuscript in Istanbul, St. Petersburg manuscript E-20, Bibliothèque Nationale Français Arabe

328a, and British Library Or. 2165.[3] This situation of relatively unexplored Qur'ān manuscripts leaves some questions unanswered. For example, if this destruction and suppression did take place, what kinds and amounts of textual variants remain in the extant manuscripts? Did any significant variants escape detection and correction amidst the various efforts at textual standardization and improvement? How do the variants that can be found in manuscripts compare to those asserted to have existed in manuscripts and oral transmissions described in Islamic literature? These are some of the questions this analysis will explore.

In addition to the few surveys of variants in particular manuscripts, what has been written about Qur'ānic textual variants usually concerns the variants described in secondary Islamic literature and their relation to various recorded reading systems, or variants that demonstrate the development of Qur'ānic orthography in Islam's early centuries. Also, in Western language introductions to the Qur'ān there are very few discussions focused on exploring and classifying the variants that are actually found in manuscripts. Doubt has been openly expressed by Western scholars as to the usefulness of such an exercise in view of the history within Islam of the early destruction of variant texts, and that extant Qur'ān manuscripts and the Islamic literature concerning textual variants seem to have been similarly purged of controversial variants.[4] A survey of the major Western introductions to the Qur'ān and specialist books concerning Qur'ān manuscripts confirms this general attitude of doubt.[5] Some scholars have gone so far as to believe the textual variants described in Islamic literature were all invented to solve exegetical and philological problems with the text of the Qur'ān.[6] Welch probably speaks for most where he says that though this may be part of the problem with the Islamic records, the variants reported should not be rejected altogether.[7]

Some modern Muslim writers in English do not mention variants in manuscripts except either to acknowledge in a general way that unintentional copyist errors did sometimes occur,[8] or to assert vigorously that they are without significance and there is no need to examine early Qur'ān manuscripts.[9] This is ironic when medieval Qur'ān scholars openly acknowledged textual variants, even reportedly between early copies of the 'Uthmānic text.[10] Also, the medieval Islamic historian Ibn Khaldūn openly attributed problems in the text of the Qur'ān to the lack of writing skills among the Companions who recorded it.[11] But even with these acknowledgements, the official codices reported to have been prepared at 'Uthmān's command, play no part in the later Qur'ānic sciences literature, except for frequent and often contradictory mention of the Medina Codex referred to as *al-imām Muṣḥaf 'Uthmān*.[12] Bergsträsser noted that Qur'ān manuscripts seem to have played no part in Islamic Qur'ān studies since the eleventh/fourth century.[13] Many modern Islamic scholars are apparently following this example with the notable exception of the Topkapi Muṣḥaf facsimile.[14]

The result is that neither Western nor Muslim scholars have done an extensive comparison of variants from a representative sampling of extant Qur'ān manuscripts. This section will seek to contribute to this situation by analyzing the variants found in 19 early Qur'ān manuscripts and two later texts using a representative portion of text, S. 14:35–41. After the analysis, some summary remarks and preliminary conclusions will be presented from the findings, which will be further analyzed in the remaining chapters.

The manuscripts surveyed present a range of textual variants covering a spectrum of types. Represented are variants in orthography and spelling, variants that demonstrate the development of a precise Arabic orthography in the early centuries of Islam, and variants that affect the grammar of the passage examined. Variants involving short vowels will not be examined because the great majority of the manuscripts surveyed do not contain them.

NOTES

1. D. F. McKenzie, *Bibliography and the Sociology of Texts*. London: The British Library, 1986, 16.

2. Arthur Jeffery, *Materials for the History of the Text of the Qur'ān*. Leiden: Brill, 1937, 10.

3. Alba Fedeli, "Early Evidences of Variant Readings in Qur'ānic Manuscripts," Karl-Heinz Ohlig and Gerd-R. Puin, eds., *Die dunklen Anfänge*. Berlin: Hans Schiler, 2005, 293–316; Alba Fedeli, "A.Perg.2: A Non-Palimpsest and the Corrections in Qur'ānic Manuscripts," *MO* 11:1:20–27; Alphonse Mingana and Agnes Smith Lewis, *Leaves From Three Ancient Qur'āns, Possibly Pre-'Uthmānic*. Cambridge: Cambridge University Press, 1914; Arthur Jeffery and Isaac Mendelsohn, "The Orthography of the Samarqand Qur'an Codex," *JAOS*, 62, 175–95; Tayyar Altikulac, *Al-Mushaf al-Sharif, Attributed to 'Uthmān bin 'Affān*, Istanbul: IRCICA, 2007; Efim A. Rezvan, *The Qur'ān of 'Uthmān*. St. Petersburg: St. Petersburg Centre for Oriental Studies, 2004; François Déroche, *La transmission écrite du Coran dans les débuts de l'islam: Le codex Parisino-petropolitanus*. Leiden: Brill, 2009; Yasin Dutton, "An Early *Mushaf* According to the Reading of Ibn 'Āmir," *JQS*, III:1:71–90; and Intisar A. Rabb, "Non-Canonical Readings of the Qur'an: Recognition and Authenticity (The Himsī Reading)," *JQS*, VIII:2:84–127, respectively. Characteristic variants for the San'ā' manuscripts are described in Gerd-R. Puin, "Observations on Early Qur'an Manuscripts in San'ā'," Stefan Wild, *The Qur'an as Text*. Leiden: Brill, 1996, 107–11. Some variants from later in the manuscript tradition are described in Efim A. Rezvan, "Oriental Manuscripts of Karl Fabergé. I: The Qur'ān," *MO* 7:1:40–61. A general description of kinds of variants that can be found. Keith Small, "Textual Variants in the New Testament and Qur'anic Manuscript Traditions," Keith Small,

Schlaglichter. Berlin: Hans Schiler, 2008, 572–93 provides a summary of the kinds of variants found in most of the manuscripts in this study.

4. A. Fischer, "Grammatisch schweirige Schwur- und Beschwörungsformeln des Klassichen Arabisch," *Der Islam*, 28, 1–105, 6, note 4.

5. Colin F. Baker, *Qur'an Manuscripts*. London: British Library, 2007, Richard Bell, *Introduction to the Qur'an*. Edinburgh: Edinburgh University Press, 1953; Régis Blachère, *Introduction au Coran*. Paris: Besson & Chantemerle, 1959; Michael Cook, *The Koran: A Very Short Introduction*. Oxford: Oxford University Press, 2000; François Déroche, *The Abbasid Tradition*. London: Nour Foundation, 1992; François Déroche, "Manuscripts of the Qur'ān," Jane Dammen McAuliffe, ed., *Encyclopaedia of the Qur'ān*. Leiden: Brill, 2003, 254–75; Theodor Noldeke, Friedrich Schwally, G. Bergsträsser and O. Pretzl, *Geschichte des Qorāns*. Hildesheim: Georg Olms Verlag, 2005; Neal Robinson, *Discovering the Qur'an*. London: SCM Press, 1996; W. M. Watt and R. Bell, *Bell's Introduction to the Qur'ān*. Edinburgh: Edinburgh University Press, 1970.

6. Fischer, "Grammatisch," 5–6.

7. Alford T. Welch, "al-Kur'ān," *EI2*. Leiden: Brill, 1960, 400–429, 408.

8. M. M. Al-Azami, *The History of the Qur'anic Text*. Leicester: UK Islamic Academy, 2003, 151, 158. The following introductions do not mention even copyist errors: Ahmad Von Denffer, *'Ulūm al-Qur'ān*. Leicester: The Islamic Foundation, 1994, Ahmad 'Ali al Iman, *Variant Readings of the Qur'an*. Herndon, VA: International Institute of Islamic Thought, 1998, Yasir Qadhi, *An Introduction to the Sciences of the Qur'aan*. Birmingham: Al-Hidaayah Publishing and Distribution, 1999. None of these analyzes the texts of actual manuscripts.

9. Muhammad Mohar Ali, *The Qur'an and the Latest Orientalist Assumptions*. Suffolk: Jam'iat Ihyaa' Minhaaj Al-Sunnah, 1999, 8–12; Muhammad Mohar Ali, *The Qur'an and the Orientalists*, Suffolk: Jam'iat Ihyaa' Minhaaj Al-Sunnah, 2004, 267–71.

10. Al-Azami, *History*, 97–99. He states that there were not more than forty characters different between six of the eight copies of 'Uthmān's version that were sent out to major Islamic centers. He lists twelve variants that were differences between 'Uthmān's personal copy and the copy kept at Medinah (p. 98). He is citing Ad-Dānī, *al-Muqni' fī' rasm masāhif al amsār*. Cairo: Maktab al-Kulīāt al-'Azhariyat, 1978, 112–14.

11. Ibn Khaldūn, *The Muqaddimah*. New York: Bollingen Foundation, 1967, 2:382.

12. Noldeke, Schwally, Bergsträsser and Pretzl, *Geschichte*, 3:6.

13. Noldeke, Schwally, Bergsträsser and Pretzl, *Geschichte*, 3:249.

14. Altikulac, *Al-Mushaf*.

3

Orthographic Variants Involving Long Vowels

Orthography means literally "correct writing" and refers to standards of spelling and usage of words as well as the influence letters and spelling have on grammar.[1] Implied in this simple definition is the process by which such standards come to be established. Arabic orthography has passed through many stages of development and the Arabic used in the earliest extant manuscripts is widely thought to belong to one of the earliest periods of its development. Also, it is widely held that the inscription and canonization of the Qur'ān propelled the development of Arabic orthography from an originally partial system to a fully vocalized system which could precisely represent every phonetic value of a word. In early Qur'ān manuscripts, one of the clearest ways to observe this development is in the use of long vowels *alif*, *yā'*, and *wāw*. This chapter will examine the textual variants concerning these letters that were observed in the surveyed manuscripts.

SUBSECTION 1: ORTHOGRAPHIC VARIANTS FOR *ALIF*, *YĀ'*, AND *ḤAMZA*

It has long been recognized that *alif* and *yā'* were used in ways in the early manuscripts that are no longer practised in Qur'ānic orthography.[2] The usage of these letters is much more variable than any of the other letters of the *rasm*. They are omitted, added, and at times interchanged. The standardization of the usage of these letters is one phenomenon that can be observed in manuscripts spanning the first three centuries of Islam.

Also in this early period, various means for notating *ḥamza* were used culminating in the invention and inclusion of a consonantal form for the letter. At first it was omitted completely; later *alif*, *yā'*, or *wāw* were sometimes used to designate it. Also, dots, often green, were used in some manuscripts to note its pronunciation. Finally, purpose-specific signs were used to designate its position and use. This development can also be observed in the manuscripts under examination. Some of these orthographic variants can affect the meaning of the text. Where this is an issue, it will be discussed in view of the specific variant being considered.

Variants Involving *Alif*

Variants involving *alif* are the most common variants encountered in the early manuscripts surveyed.[3] The range of variants associated with *alif* is also indicative of the flexibility with which it was used in the earlier stages of Arabic script.

Medial alif missing

Beeston, Blau, and Thackston separately note that in early Qur'ānic orthography, *alif* as a rule is not used in the middle of a word.[4] Déroche and Noja-Noseda observed this for the manuscript, BL Or. 2165 and list many of the words for which this is the case.[5] In the passage examined for this study, the following words appear in the manuscripts surveyed without medial *alif*:

14:35:1 قال (قل) Istanbul, 01-28.1, BL Or. 2165, BNF 326a, BNF 328a.
14:35:3 الاصنام (الاصنم) Istanbul, Topkapi, 01-28.1, 01-29.1, 01-20.x, BL Or. 2165, BNF 325a, 326a, 328a, 330a, 331, 332, 333c, 334c, 370a.
14:36:3 عصانى (عصنى) Istanbul, 01-28.1, 01-29.1, BL Or. 2165, BNF 326a, 328a, 331, 334c.

However, contrary to Beeston, Blau, and Thackston, the omissions are mostly variable across these manuscripts, and there are words where *alif* is never omitted. For the words cited above, the exceptions are: Istanbul, Topkapi, 01-28.1, BL Or. 2165, BNF 326a and 328a. These agree in their omission of the *alif* in the words listed above. Also, the Ḥijāzī manuscript 01-29.1 agrees in two out of three of these. The Kufic Topkapi manuscript agrees with one of the omissions. Déroche cites this phenomenon as an indication of the early date of Ḥijāzī manuscripts.[6] The early Kufic manuscripts, Topkapi and 01-20.x, agree in one of three of these omissions, the one in 14:35:3. Déroche is also more accurate than Beeston, Blau, or Thackston in describing the omission as a frequent occurrence rather than a normative one.[7] A confirmation of this is seen in that all manuscripts surveyed kept the medial *alif* in these words:

> 14:36:1, الناس ; 14:36:2, فانه ; 14:36:3, فانك ; 14:37:2, بواد ; 14:37:5, الناس ; 14:41:2 الحساب.

Déroche also notes that a systematic manner of notating these *alifs* was not established until the late eighth/second century.[8]

In regard to the word قال (قل)

> 14:35:1 قال (قل) (*Alif* missing in Istanbul, 01-28.1, BL Or. 2165, BNF 326a, 328a. *Alif* present in Topkapi, 01-29.1, 01-20.x, BNF 325a, 330a, 331, 332, 333c, 334c, 340c, 343, 370a, Meknes, BL Or. 12884, Sharīf, Warsh.)

The first of the three observed instances of the omission of medial *alif* is the one of which the most has been written. Puin called attention to this common phenomenon asserting that an example such as 14:35:1 قال (قل) presupposes an established oral tradition of correct reading.[9] The implication is that in this written form, there could be confusion as to whether or not it was perfect tense or an imperative: 'He said' or 'Say'. In Surah 14:35, however, the context makes it clear that it is perfect in that it is a narrative portion concerning Ibrāhīm. Noja-Noseda offered this explanation for how the two forms could be distinguished when the *alif* was not present:[10]

> We may hazard a guess that Arab-speaking peoples in the first age of Islamic preaching distinguished the two forms through the presence of the *wāw* for the perfect tense, while the conjunction was absent in the imperative. A graphical distinction would not therefore have had any distinguishing function—discharged indeed by the *wāw*—within the autochthonous linguistic system.

Al-Azami asserts that this convention is one of shorthand abbreviation, believing there to have been an accompanying oral tradition to clarify the correct pronunciation and grammar. He states that the *alifs* were originally present, then dropped for abbreviation, and then reinstated in the reforms of Ubaydullāh b. Ziyād in the time of al-Ḥajjāj, circa the eighth/late first century.[11] Noja-Noseda also suggests omitting *alifs* may represent an example of abbreviation to save space on an expensive piece of parchment.[12] Intentional abbreviation of an understood pronunciation is a valid hypothesis for the omission, but there are some issues that need to be explored. First, there is no written evidence of a more fully written prior text that was then abbreviated. Instead, the earliest available manuscripts have the *alifs* missing. It seems a simpler explanation that omitting the *alif* was a normal convention within a flexible orthography that was later standardized, than that there was a fixed longer text that was abbreviated for economic or practical reasons. Fleisch goes further than regarding it as an existing convention to assert that the notation of the long vowel *ā* by *alif* was an Arab invention and that it was carried out irregularly in the early stages of the development of Arabic script.[13]

That there was some kind of oral tradition accompanying the text is probable, and many scholars assert that the phonetically incomplete text was more an aid to memory than a means to preserve a precise pronunciation in script.[14] However, it is impossible to determine if there was one authoritative oral version supporting this written text, for at least the reason that Ibn Mujāḥid, in the tenth/third century, was only able to limit a plethora of oral and written recitations of the Qur'ān in his time to seven versions. If one authoritative pronunciation was not known at Ibn Mujāḥid's time, there is little hope of someone today recovering one from an even earlier time. Also, there is every probability that once a written text was standardized, any existing oral traditions would be conformed to it and ones not supporting the new form of text would go out of use.[15] And in spite of Ibn Mujāḥid's attempt at standardization of oral and written recitations, because of the deficient nature of the script being used, many competing reading systems did in fact arise.[16]

Whether it was a convention reflecting a flexible orthography, or a deliberate abbreviation of an already standardized spelling, the net effect remains that in certain places, the omission of the *alif* allowed for later ambiguity of meaning and precise pronunciation.[17] Rippin explores the significance of this simple omission of *alif* in relation to the historical development of the text of the Qur'ān, Islamic dogma concerning the understanding of the Qur'ān as a strictly divine revelation as opposed to a more human production, and implications for the notion of a parallel oral transmission of the text:[18]

> Another different type of example may help to indicate what is at stake here. The very last verse (112) of sūra 21 starts "He said [qāla], 'My Lord, judge according to the truth. Our Lord is the All-Merciful.'" The reference to "My Lord" and "Our Lord" in the text indicates that the subject of "He said" cannot be God but is the reciter of the Qur'ān, in the first place understood to be Muḥammad. Such a passage, in fact, falls into a common form of Quranic speech found in passages normally prefaced by the imperative "Say!" (qul). The significant point here is that in the text of the Qur'ān, the word here translated as "He said" is, in fact, more easily read as "Say!" due to the absence of the long "a" marker (something which

> commonly happens in the Qur'ān, to be sure, but the word qāla is spelled this way only twice—the other occasion being in Qur'ān 21/4 and that only occurs in some of the traditions of the writing of the text). In the early Sana'a manuscripts, the absence of the long "a" in the word qāla is a marker of an entire set of early texts. But why should it be that this particular passage should be read in the way that it is? It really should read "Say!" to be parallel to the rest of the text. This opens the possibility that there was a time when the Qur'ān was understood not as the word of God (as with "Say!") but the word of Muḥammad as the speaking prophet. It would appear that in the process of editing of the text, most passages were transformed from "He said" to "Say!" in both interpretation and writing with the exception of these two passages in sūra 21 which were not changed. This could have occurred only because somebody was working on the basis of the written text in the absence of a parallel oral tradition.

The omission of the *alif* in the word قال (قل) most likely demonstrates that the orthography was sufficiently undefined so that the omission of *alif* was not regarded as an error. The omission could also reflect a dialectical difference of pronunciation that was permitted by the flexible orthography. The other two examples of the omission of *alif* can also be explained this way. They can also be indicative of a layer of editing.

In regard to the words الاصنام (الاصنم) *and* عصانى (عصنى)

14:35:3 الاصنام (الاصنم) 'the idols' (*Alif* missing in Istanbul, Topkapi, 01-28.1, 01-29.1, 01-20.x, BL Or. 2165, BNF 325a, 326a, 328a, 330a, 331, 332, 333c, 334c, 370a. *Alif* present in BNF 340c, Meknes, BL Or. 12884, Sharīf, Warsh.)

The singular form of this noun is صنم. The plural form[19] is marked by the addition of an initial *alif* and a medial *alif* preceding the last radical.[20] Since the variant form retains the initial *alif* and is clearly a noun form because of the prefixed definite article, and since no other contextual or grammatical explanation offers an alternative explanation for the omission, the omission of the second *alif* probably reflects the transcription of a normal variation of the pronunciation of this plural form, or represents a valid alternative spelling of this word within the allowances of dialectical differences and orthographic flexibility.

14:36:3 عصانى (عصنى) 'And whoso *disobeys me*, still You are indeed oft-forgiving' (*Alif* missing in Istanbul, 01-28.1, 01-29.1, BL Or. 2165, BNF 326a, 328a, 331, 334c, 340c. *Alif* present in Topkapi, 01-20.x, BNF 325a, 330a, 332, 333c, Meknes, BNF 343, 370a, BL Or. 12884, Sharīf, Warsh.)

This word is a verb with a pronominal suffix denoting the object of the verb. The verb is عصى, "to disobey"[21] with the first-person suffix -نى.[22] Wright notes that it is an old custom in Arabic to change the final *yā'* of a word to *alif* when a pronominal suffix is added.[23] Since there is no verb with the root عصن, and roots with alternative diacritics do not make sense in the context,[24] and since the *nūn* serves to join the first person pronominal suffix to the verbal root, the best explanation for the omission of the *alif* is that it represents a valid alternative spelling of this word from the time before such spelling was formally standardized. This could also reflect the transcription of a dialectical or regional pronunciation.

Jeffery states what is perhaps the majority view concerning the effect on meaning of this kind of variant where he says, "Other peculiarities . . . seem to be nothing more than the natural peculiarities of a scribe working at a time when the minutiae of orthography were not so firmly fixed as they later became."[25] It was mentioned earlier that the Muslim historian Ibn Khaldūn (d. 1406/809) recognized the existence of such orthographic inconsistencies, though he attributed them to the ignorance of the companions of Muḥammad who wrote down the Qur'ān and were not versed in the craft of proper Arabic orthography.[26] Though this is anachronistic in assuming a level of orthographic precision greater than is demonstrable for the seventh century, it is an acknowledgement of variable scribal practices in Islam's first century. The Iranian scholar Ahmad Pakatchi surveyed various explanations in early grammars to the orthographic differences and stated,[27]

> We can conclude apart from differences in the way of justification (symbolism, mystical causes), the (*sic*) most of classical Muslim scholars suggested that the writing of Qur'ānic codices could not be considered as a regular system and [is] supposed to be [the] result of a kind of chaoticity, either referring to transcendent meanings or referring it to illiteracy of the writers. Among the classical scholars, we rarely come across with [an] awareness about the pre-Islamic writing traditions [that] influenced the first writers of [the] Qur'ān.

He goes on to mention how these systems can account for many of the early orthographical irregularities. Here are other variants related to *alif* that can be regarded as examples of a flexible orthography.

The Dagger Alif

In printed Qur'āns and manuscript copies, the dagger *alif* is used to represent a received pronunciation that does not precisely match the *rasm*.[28] The stated reason for this alteration was that the editors of the 1924 edition wanted to represent more accurately what they thought was the canonical text-form of

'Uthmān as preserved in Islamic Qur'ān literature from the 3rd to 5th Islamic centuries.[29] There are other contemporary examples of this in that between the Ḥafṣ and the Warsh texts in print, there are instances of difference where one will have an *alif* as a full letter on the main line of text, whereas the other will have it represented as a dagger *alif*.[30]

An early manuscript that contains *alifs* which were added later in red is manuscript E 20 from St. Petersburg which has recently been reproduced in facsimile form.[31] Since the 1924 Cairo edition attempts to reproduce the original orthography of 'Uthmān's version, it is an instructive exercise to compare the *alifs* found in early manuscripts with those of the 1924 edition, to see which are in the *rasm* and which are found as dagger *alifs* in the same edition. When this is done, one finds that there are many places in the 1924 Cairo text where there is a dagger or small *alif* that is not represented in the early manuscripts as an *alif* on the line of text. However, occasionally, these dagger *alifs* are represented on the line of text in the early manuscripts. This exercise demonstrates two facts: that what is believed to be in the 1924 text as the 'Uthmānic text-form does not precisely match the earliest available manuscripts, and they and later manuscripts demonstrate a greater flexibility of usage than one might expect.

Dagger *alif* in the 1924 Text Where No Full *alif* is in the Manuscripts[32]

14:35:1 1924: ابرٰهيم	Manuscripts: ابرهم	(all manuscripts)
14:35:2 1924: هٰذا	Manuscripts: هدا	(all manuscripts)

This omission is a common one in the papyri.[33]

14:37:4 1924: الصلوٰة	Manuscripts: الصلوه	(all manuscripts)

This is also a common spelling in the papyri.[34]

14:37:6 1924: الثمرٰت	Manuscripts: الىمرٮ	(all manuscripts except BNF 340c, Meknes, BL Or. 12884, Sharīf)
14:38:2 1924: يخفىٰ	Manuscripts: ىحڡى	(all manuscripts)
14:38:2 1924: اللّٰه[35]	Manuscripts: الل ه	(all manuscripts)
14:39:1 1924: للّٰه[36]	Manuscripts: لل ه	(all manuscripts)
14:39:2 1924: اسمٰعيل	Manuscripts: اسمعل	(all manuscripts)
14:39:2 1924: اسحٰق	Manuscripts: اسحق	(all manuscripts except BNF 333c)
14:40:1 1924: الصلوٰة	Manuscripts: الصلوه	(all manuscripts except Istanbul)[37]
14:41:1 1924: ولوٰلدى[38]	Manuscripts: ولولدى	(all manuscripts except Istanbul, 01-29.1, BNF 343c, BL Or. 12884, Sharīf)

The issue of the dagger *alif* in Ibrāhīm, Ishāq, and Ismā'īl will be considered in more detail below in subsection 2, Orthographic Variants Involving Proper Names.

Full *alif* Present in Manuscripts Where Dagger *alif* is Used in the 1924 Text

14:37:6 1924 الثمرٰت	الثمرات BNF 340c, Meknes, BL Or. 12884, Sharīf
14:39:2 1924 اسحٰق	اسحاق BNF 333c
14:40:1 1924 الصلوٰة	الصلواة Istanbul
14:41:1 1924 ولوٰلدى	ولوالدى Istanbul, 01-29.1, BNF 343, BL Or. 12884, Sharīf

Full *alif* Present in Manuscripts Where No *alif* is Present in the 1924 Text

14:38:3 1924 شيء	ساى Istanbul, Topkapi, 01-29.1, BL Or. 2165, BNF 326a, 328a

This is also a frequent spelling variant in the early Arabic papyri.[39]

Full *alif* and Dagger *alif* Where Only Dagger *alif* is Present in 1924 Text

14:37:6 BL Or. 12884 الثمرات
14:41:1 BL Or. 12884 ولوالدي

Dagger *alifs* that are Present in the Manuscripts, but are not Present as Full *alifs* or Dagger *alifs* in the 1924 Text

In addition to those noted above, Or. 12884 and Sharīf have additional dagger *alifs* both above the consonantal line before full *alifs* and below the line before some *yā*'s used as long vowels. Or. 12884 has more of these than the Sharīf text. It has a dagger *alif* before almost every full *alif* and vowel *yā*'. The Sharīf text has far fewer of both, but there are some of each present.

Though this last section might seem a bit pedantic, mentioning these in such detail does point out that the first fully vocalized texts were at least sometimes vocalized with *more* symbols than are used in the present text, and that the use of the dagger *alif* was a sudden innovation in the manuscript tradition. This also demonstrates another confirmation that the 'Uthmānic text the editors of the 1924 Cairo edition had in mind was one based more on tradition and secondary literature than what one finds in the manuscript tradition.[40]

Alif where one expects a yā'

Another example of a variant concerning *alif* and *yā'* is where an *alif* is substituted for a *yā'*. Two types of this variant were observed. The first involves the placement of an *alif* where later there was *yā'* for a seat for *ḥamza.*

14:37:5 1924 افئدة	01-28.1, 01-29.1 افادة

Most of the manuscripts simply omit the *ḥamza* and the *yā'* seat and simply read افدة (Istanbul, Topkapi, 01-20.x, BL Or. 2165, BNF 325a, 326a, 328a, 330a, 331, 332, 333c, 334c, 340c, Meknes, BNF 343, 370a). Thackston notes that the dotless *yā'* seat is the normal form used for internal *ḥamza* if the *ḥamza* is preceded by a short vowel *i* or a *sukūn*.[41] Wright implies that this phenomenon is a development of the orthography, that the *yā'* seat for *ḥamza* was conversion from the use of *alif*.[42] Puin, citing these two particular manuscripts, goes further and asserts that once the *alif* became associated solely with the long "*ā*" sound in such instances it had to be changed into a *yā'*.[43] As such, it is an indication of the development of the orthography in the very earliest manuscript transmission period.

The second instance of this involves *alif maqṣūra*:

14:38:2 1924 على	Topkapi, 01-20.x, BNF 332, 333c علا
14:39:2 1924 على	BNF 332, 333c علا

This is a phenomenon that has been noted to occur in early manuscripts for this particular word with its final consonant, *alif maqṣūra*. Wright and Thackston both note that this variant form could be related to an Aramaic precedent.[44] The presence of the form علا could then be the preservation of an earlier graphical form of the word. Rather than presenting this as an archaic form, al-Azami attributes this to a regional difference of spelling. He also cites the existence of manuscripts where the two different forms are written on the same page of text, showing that they were used interchangeably by the same scribe.[45] This would indicate that there was a period where both forms were used concurrently and both were viewed as legitimate spellings of this word. This view is further supported by the fact that the manuscripts that contain this variant are in the Abbasid style script and date to the seventh-eighth/ second-third century. They are not found in the earliest manuscripts available in this particular section of text. It would be worthwhile to check early manuscripts for the occurrences of these forms. For instance, Gibson notes the use of perpendicular *alif* for all occurrences of *alif maqṣūra* in certain ninth and tenth century Arabic New Testament manuscripts.[46] Hopkins notes that in the papyri, both forms are common, sometimes within the same document.[47]

Another support to the idea that they are examples of flexible orthography is that in the context studied, because of their placement in relation to the other words in the sentence, they would be clearly understood as acting like prepositions and could not be confused for verb forms constructed from these same letters, nor for noun or adjectival forms that denote height or a high station.[48]

In conclusion, these variants are examples of flexible orthography before the precise consonantal line was standardized. There is also the possibility that some of these are vestiges from a transition from Aramaic characters to Arabic letter forms. Some possibly reflect differences of regional pronunciation but in view of the lack of solid evidence as to precise regional pronunciations from written sources of this period or from tracing the geographic provenance of extant manuscripts, this can be no more than a possibility to be kept for consideration as and when such evidence becomes available.

Variants involving *Yā'*

Another category of orthographic variant observed concerns the use of the letter *yā'*. Though the variations concerning its use are not as numerous as with the *alif*, they are more varied than any of the remaining Arabic letters. Hopkins notes concerning the papyri that "the shortening of long vowels other than *ā* is very rare."[49] Three types of variant were observed. Some of these are also interesting because of their relationship to *alif*.

Omission of yā'

14:35:1 ارهم (Ibrahim) for إبرهيم (Ibrāhīm)

This variant will be considered in detail in the following subsection concerning Orthographic Variants Involving Proper Names.

14:37:4 لقموا BNF 326a (ليقيموا) "in order that they may perform"

There is one other occurrence of an omitted *yā'* in the manuscripts surveyed, and it has two of them omitted in the same word, though the second one is possibly there but is indistinct. This is most likely a copyist mistake since the form without the *yā* would be a verb which does not make sense in the immediate context (لقم , *laqama,* "to gobble or eat quickly").[50] Also, it is not a normal practise to attach prepositions to imperatival forms. Further, the particle ل (*li*) when followed by a subjunctive verb expresses purpose, "in order that,"[51] and is what is required by the narrative Ibrāhīm is relating to

Allah. He had settled some of his offspring by the sacred house so that they could perform the ritual prayer.

Yā' inserted for alif

There is an instance of this in 14:35:1 with the *yā'* in Ibrāhīm. It will be examined in the following section concerning orthographic variants in proper names.

Alif maqṣūra dotted as yā'

In a section above *alif maqṣūra* was discussed where its pronunciation as ā in manuscripts is represented by an *alif*. This section discusses the opposite tendency, when its pronunciation is closer to ī and is then represented by a fully dotted *yā'*. This phenomenon occurs in only two of the manuscripts surveyed, BNF 325a and BL Or. 12884. In this portion of text it occurs five times, or at every instance of an *alif maqṣūra* in BNF 325a and one time in BL Or. 12884:

14:38:2 يخفىٰ على	BNF 325a يخفي علي
14:38:3 شىء	BNF 325a, BL Or. 12884 شي
14:39:2 على	BNF 325a علي

No explicit comments could be found in the grammars consulted concerning this phenomenon. Perhaps this was an early way of denoting the diphthong *ai*, often marked in later manuscripts by a *sukūn* (°) and inserted over letters of prolongation and *alif maqṣūra*.[52] Or, since it is found mainly in an eighth/second century manuscript, perhaps it reflects an early regional pronunciation that the scribe wanted to make explicit. A third possible explanation is that it represents a temporary orthographic convention that sought to attach dots to all *yā'*s in the text. A fourth hypothesis is that perhaps it is characteristic of a now lost form of recitation of the text. A fifth hypothesis is that a later scribe added the dots with more zeal than knowledge, but the dots seem to have been written at the same time as the main line of text using the same color ink and the same width of reed pen.

In view of the lack of conclusive evidence, perhaps the best hypothesis is that it represents a regional pronunciation at an early time when pronunciation, orthography, and grammar had not yet been standardized to a degree to prevent this. It cannot easily be regarded as a scribal error because of its consistent usage in the passage. The consistency of the occurrence of the dots argues for it to be an intentional and understood convention for the scribe who wrote the manuscript and possibly for his geographic location, wherever that may have been. Overall, it would seem to be another example of a higher level of flexibility in the orthography of the Qur'ān in this early period than came to be the case later.

Variants Involving *Ḥamza*

All of the earliest manuscripts featured in this study are notable for the complete absence of the consonantal letter *ḥamza*.[53] This is a distinctive feature of early Qur'āns in general,[54] and it is widely acknowledged that the letter *ḥamza* was an innovation to Arabic orthography well after the time of the earliest Muslims.[55] In the manuscripts surveyed for this study, *ḥamza* makes its first appearance as a distinct symbol in BL Or. 12884, which dates at the earliest to the late tenth/third century, and even here, it is a symbol added above the consonantal line, not a consonant in its own right.

It is often asserted that the omission is due to the early orthography being based on the Arabic dialect used in Mecca at the time of Muḥammad which had no glottal stops.[56] Fischer states that as a rule, *ḥamza* was not pronounced either within a word or in final position, but only at the beginning of a word.[57] When it occurred at the beginning of a word it was written with an *alif*.[58]

Fischer and others recognize, though, that occasionally it was represented by *wāw* and *yā'* in the medial and final positions.[59] Puin observes that medial and final *alif* sometimes represented the glottal stop,[60] and Wright also asserts that occasionally medial *yā'* acted as a *kursī*, or "chair" for *ḥamza*.[61] However, when compared with the modern text, not all places that currently have *ḥamza* are represented in the early texts as having it, even accounting for the places where it is represented by *alif* or *yā'* or *waw*.[62] Only two early manuscripts possibly represented it with an *alif* and one with a *yā'*. Most of the occurrences of the glottal stop in the passage surveyed involved initial *alif*.[63] A few that do not, however, are worth mention.

37:5	افـٔدة	Sharīf, Warsh, Cairo 1924
	افده	Istanbul, Topkapi, 01-20.x, BL Or. 2165, BNF 325a, 326a, 328a, 330a, 331, 332, 333, 334c, 340c, 343, 370a, Meknes
	افاده	01-28.1, 01-29.1
	افيده	BL Or. 12884

In the modern text, a *ḥamza* is inserted between the *fā'* and the *dāl* without there being a support, or *kursi*, for it. Or. 12884 is the earliest manuscript surveyed which includes a *ḥamza* at this point in the text. To do so, it has an inserted *yā'* (dotted as a *yā'*) as a *kursi*, and it has its symbol for *ḥamza*, a stylized "*s*" shape, positioned over the *yā'* (افئدة). The modern text uses the earlier orthography in omitting the *yā'-kursi* but it adds the *ḥamza* over a *tatwīl* (an elongation of the connecting line between the *fā'* and the *dāl*), which is in the place where the *kursi* would have been placed (افـٔدة). The Sharīf text uses the same convention as the modern text in omitting the *yā'-kursi*, and the Warsh does as well, though it marks the *ḥamza* under the *tatwīl* rather than over it. BL Or. 12884 has another peculiarity in that each occurrence of *yā'-kursi* is consistently pointed with two dots as a normal *yā'*, a phenomenon which is not normative in classical Arabic orthography,[64] nor does it occur in the modern text. This phenomenon does however appear in the ninth century papyri, which precede this particular Qur'ān text by a century.[65] Two very early texts (01.28-1 and 01.29-1) possibly denote *ḥamza* with an *alif.*

The next five usages occur as clarifications of pronunciation. Since the original pronunciation in the Meccan dialect did not have internal and final glottal stops, the later philologians, based on their analysis of other dialects, "restored" the glottal stop where they determined it should have been.'[66]

38:3	شىء	Sharīf, Warsh, Cairo 1924
	شاى	Istanbul, 01-29.1
	السماء	Sharīf, Warsh, Cairo 1924
	السمما	01-20.x
39:3	الدعاء	Sharīf, Warsh, Cairo 1924
40:2	دعاء	Sharīf, Warsh, Cairo 1924
41:2	وللمؤمنين	Cairo 1924

For شىء and السماء in 14:38:3, Istanbul and 01-20.x apparently used a final *alif* to represent *ḥamza*. 01-20.x also apparently uses a *yā'* for an *alif.* The more modern manuscripts all used the conventional symbol for *ḥamza*. In addition to the letters *alif* and *yā'* on the consonantal line sometimes being used in lieu of *ḥamza* before they were used for supports in classical Arabic orthography,[67] a convention was adopted in the late 700s/100s and early 800s/200s in some manuscripts of using various systems of red, yellow, orange, blue, gold and green dots to mark particular vowel patterns, variant readings and the placement of *ḥamzas*.[68] Dutton has observed that *ḥamzas* are notated with a variety of colored dots—red, green, yellow, blue, and with other added marks as well.[69] Wright also notes the conventions of using colored dots and other marks to denote *ḥamza* in early Qur'ān manuscripts.[70]

Dutton has made the most thorough study of these systems of dots to date, seeking to decipher the systems in use during this early period. Though he has demonstrated that these dots were used in systematic and ingenious ways to communicate a wide variety of information, he recognizes that there is still much study to be done to isolate and clarify the different systems of the usage of these dots.[71] The various systems of dots used in some of the manuscripts in this study have not been interpreted since they mainly use red dots used to mark short vowels.[72] Also, since the systems of the use of these dots are so varied, and because this study is mostly concerned with textual variants to the consonantal line of text, it is enough at this point to lay out the overall picture of the conventions for *ḥamza* in this period. This is, however, an important area for future study in Qur'ān manuscripts.

Hopkins helpfully summarizes the conventions surrounding the use and non-use of *ḥamza* in the earliest dated papyri, and on the basis of observations made in this study in especially the Ḥijāzī Qur'ān manuscripts they can be said to work within the same conventions. He states (CA standing for Classical Arabic):[73]

> For all practical purposes it can be stated quite plainly that in the language of the early papyri *ḥamza* , the glottal stop, barely exists, being weakened to such an extent as to be either disregarded completely (usually in those cases where in CA *ḥamza* has no *kursī*), or absorbed into the categories of words containing w or y. This is a phenomenon common to all non-Classical varieties of Arabic. Exceptions to this state of affairs are rare indeed; the sign for *ḥamza* is extremely uncommon in these texts, and as it occurs (so far as I have noticed) almost exclusively in the late or literary papyri, it seems not unreasonable to regard it mainly as an intrusion from the CA tradition. Accordingly, I tend to believe that the absence of *ḥamza* in these documents is better interpreted not as an innovation, but rather as an inherited feature, continuing the situation prevailing in those dialects of Old Arabic which formed the basis of the CA orthography. The latter, as is well known, reflects a variety of the language which had already lost the glottal stop. The few attempts to indicate the glottal stop by means other than the *ḥamza* sign are also either quite late, or confined to literary texts, again suggesting the influence of CA.

Concerning the different consonantal letters used to designate *ḥamza*, their use as a *ḥamza* can usually be easily discerned and so they do not affect the meaning of the text to a significant degree. They do, however, demonstrate an important issue in the historical development of the orthography of the text concerning the representation of the glottal stop. The use of various systems of dots or other marks, together with the invention and inclusion of *ḥamza* as a distinct letter achieved two things: 1) it made the text more precise phonetically so that a possibly understood pronunciation was made explicit, and 2) it institutionalized a particular dialect's pronunciation as the standard Qur'ānic pronunciation. The institutionalized pronunciation was the Eastern Arabian pronunciation, rather than the Western Arabian one. [74]

SUBSECTION 2: ORTHOGRAPHIC VARIANTS INVOLVING PROPER NAMES

Textual variants concerning the spelling of proper names are a recognized phenomenon in textual studies. In this survey, three names were found to have spelling variants, Ibrāhīm, Ismā'īl and Isḥāq. It is interesting to note that even the modern text contains the two consonantal spellings for Ibrāhīm that are found in the earliest manuscripts though the situation in the earliest texts is much more variable than the current text.[75] The variability of the spelling of Qur'ānic proper names is a relatively unexplored area of study.

Here are the variants observed for the three names from the sample passage:

14:35:1 ابرهم	Ibrahim Istanbul, BL Or. 2165, BNF 326a, BNF 328a,
14:35:1 ابرهيم	Ibrahīm Topkapi, 01-28.1, 01-29.1, 01-20.x, BNF 325a, 332, 333c, 334c, 340c, 343, BNF 370a, Meknes
14:35:1 إبرٰهيم	Ibrāhīm- dagger *alif* BL Or. 12884, Sharīf, Warsh
14:39:2 اسمعيل	Ismā'īl Topkapi, 01-28.1, 01-29.1, 01-20.x, BL Or. 2165, BNF 325a, 326a, 328a, 330a, 331, 332, 333c, 334c, 340c, 370a, Meknes
14:39:2 اسمعل	Ismā'īl- no *yā'* Istanbul
14:39:2 اسمٰعيل	Ismā'īl- dagger *alif* BL Or. 12884, Sharīf, Warsh
14:39:2 اسحق	Isḥaq Istanbul, Topkapi, 01-29.1, 01-20.x, Or. 2165, BNF 325a, 326a, 328a, 330a, 331, 332, 334c, 340c, 370a, SamK, Meknes
14:39:2 اسحاق	Isḥāq- full *alif* BNF 333c
14:39:2 اسحٰق	Isḥāq- dagger *alif* BL Or. 12884, Sharīf, Warsh

Variants involving Ibrāhīm

14:35:1 ابرهم (Ibrahim) and ابرهيم (Ibrahīm) for إبرٰهيم (Ibrāhīm)
14:35:1 BL Or. 2165, BNF 328a, BNF 326a, Ibrahim (ابرهم)
14:35:1 Istanbul, Topkapi, 01-28.1, 01-29.1, 01-20.x, BNF 325a, 332, 333c, 334c, 340c, Meknes, BNF 343, 370a, Ibrahīm (ابرهيم)
14:35:1 BL Or. 12884, Sharīf, Warsh, Ibāhīm- dagger *alif* إبرٰهيم)

These spellings raise two issues: the omission of the *alif* represented in the standard text by a dagger *alif*, and the omission of the *yā'*. Concerning the omission of *alif*, a question arises: was the pronunciation of *alif* as long "ā" understood but not written as the dagger *alif* implies, or was the original pronunciation a short "a" sound? Wright's view is that the long "ā" was understood but not written, and was later represented with a *fetha*, but with the *fetha* representing the long "ā" sound, not the short "a" as it normally does.[76] This, however, seems to be anachronistically assuming that the later pronunciation of Ibrāhīm must have been used during the period of these early manuscripts. Hopkins' work in examining the grammar observed in the early Arabic papyri and the Greek transliterations of Arabic words demonstrates that in the papyri at least, such an assumption cannot be made.[77] He makes the observation repeatedly that the Arabic in the papyri seems to have resembled the pronunciation of dialects rather than Classical Arabic.[78] Since the script of the Ḥijāzī manuscripts most closely resembles the script of the early papyri, it is reasonable to suggest that the same conventions of pronunciation reflected in the papyri applied to the early Qur'ān manuscripts as well.

Hopkins makes the observation that the omission of the medial *alif* in the names of Ibrāhīm, Isḥaq, and Ismā'īl occurs commonly in the early Arabic papyri.[79] This writer has observed that the medial *alif* was always omitted in these names in the early Ḥijāzī manuscripts used for this study. It is also noticeably added in later in some Ḥijāzī manuscripts and many of the early Abbasid manuscripts.[80] What does their addition signify? Are they corrections of copyists' mistakes? Are they representative of a regional pronunciation? Do they represent the act of making the script explicitly inscribe a pronunciation that was understood, perhaps for the convenience and instruction of nonnative Arabic speakers? Or do they represent efforts to impose one pronunciation whereas before there might have been flexibility for accommodating more than one pronunciation?

A theological/ideological reason has also been suggested that this represents the implementation of a distinctly "Islamic" pronunciation of these names in order to move their pronunciation away from Christian or Jewish precedents.[81] They are almost certainly not corrections of copyist mistakes because of the regularity of their occurrence. A final answer probably lies among the remaining options and possibly is a combination of them.

The second variant, the presence or omission of the *yā'*, also raises questions. Does the omission of *yā'* in Ibrāhīm's name represent a normal orthographic convention in early Arabic? Or is its inclusion or exclusion in the early manuscripts indicative of a flexible orthography? When it is present, is it also a possible marker of the transition from an Aramaic predecessor to an established Arabic spelling and pronunciation of this patriarch's name in that it was once considered an *alif*?

Haleem asserts that in Surah 2, where this omission occurs in every occurrence of Ibrāhīm's name in the currently accepted text,[82] it suggests a special reading that is an allowable convention when a noun has a weak third radical and is in the nominative or genitive case.[83] This however seems inadequate to explain why in the current text it occurs in every occurrence of the name in Surah 2 but in none of the other occurrences of Ibrāhīm in the Qur'ān. Also contrary to Haleem's reasoning, Von Denffer, referring to both as-Suyūṭī and Ibn Abī Dāwūd, mentions that in the *muṣḥaf* of Abū Mūsā al-Ash'arī in Surah 2, Ibraham was read rather than Ibrāhīm.[84] Also, it is insufficient since the omission occurs in early Qur'ān manuscripts in many locations outside of Surah 2. Haleem's argument is also insufficient in that in many of the early manuscripts, in Surah 2 the *yā'* is present. Some of the early manuscripts use both versions of Ibrāhīm's name, even within the same surah and even on the same line of text.[85]

If this convention of omitting the *yā'* in Ibrāhīm in Surah 2, while preserving it in the rest of the Qur'ān in the 1924 Cairo text, is thought to present the archaic spelling conventions of the 'Uthmānic *rasm*, it fails in that the earliest available manuscripts present a more variable situation than what is presented in the current text. There are not two standard archaic spellings observable only in certain surahs. Rather, there are two spellings which seem to have been used interchangeably. This is perhaps different from what was found in the papyri. Hopkins cites only one example of medial *yā'* being omitted and it is not in the name Ibrāhīm.[86] Perhaps the occurrences he observed of this particular name all included the medial *yā'*.

There is also evidence that in the earliest available manuscripts, the copyists were faithfully copying a variable spelling convention that at their time was not yet standardized to one spelling; that is, they were not using their own conventions of spelling but were preserving an existing variable situation from an earlier period of transcription. This is seen in that two of the very earliest manuscripts available, BL Or. 2165 and Paris BNF 328a, agree in their patterns of the variant spellings of Ibrāhīm across portions of the Qur'ān that they have in common.[87] This is significant in view of Dutton's assertions that these two manuscripts are of the same provenance: Umayyad Syria from the late seventh or early eighth century/late first or early second,[88] and representative of the same Qur'ān recitation of Ibn 'Āmr.[89] Both of these manuscripts, in presenting duplicate transcriptions of the variable spellings, present evidence that at least some of the texts at this early time were presenting an already fixed *rasm* which incorporated even these spelling peculiarities. Also, both spellings must have been considered acceptable since they were so carefully preserved. This is evidence at the very least for an acknowledged degree of flexibility of spelling of the name of Ibrāhīm in this early period. Since these two spellings also involve a change to the *rasm*, the possibility that they present evidence for flexibility of pronunciation cannot be discounted. Perhaps this variation represents a regional spelling and/or pronunciation issue since other early manuscripts do not agree at these points.[90]

Haleem's explanation also seems insufficient when one observes that a noun with a similar ending, الرحيم (14:36:3), appears in all the manuscripts surveyed as containing the *yā'*. Scholars in other disciplines have noticed that the spelling of proper names can be quite variable.[91] It is reasonable to speculate that in the transition from Syriac to Arabic, or across the various geographical and ethnic groupings within the early Islamic empire, there could have been a period of time when the pronunciation and spelling of this name was flexible to a small degree, and that this variability came to be represented in the earliest manuscripts.

Taking both variants together, Jeffery suggests an etymological development behind the Arabic form that recognized problems with the final Arabic form.[92] He cites Abraham's name and mentions the medieval Arabic hadith and *fiqh* expert, an-Nawawī (d.1278/676), as listing five variant spellings for the name: ابرهام (Ibrahām), ابراهيم (Ibrāhīm), ابرهم (Ibrahim), ابرهم (Ibraham), and ابرهم (Ibrahum). In the manuscripts surveyed for this book and the extra manuscripts consulted for this word study, none contained the first variation.[93] Only a very few of the extra manuscripts consulted contained the second example and many of them have the *alif* added later in red or black, and then later manuscripts by adding a dagger *alif* (BL Or. 12884, Sharīf and Warsh).[94] The last three variant spellings in an-Nawawī's list all share the same consonantal form as found in Istanbul, BL Or. 2165, BNF 328a, and BNF 326a. These three, depending on the respective grammatical contexts, could be equally legitimate ways of pronouncing the basic line of text.

One collection of textual variants for the Qur'ān taken from the secondary Islamic Qur'ān literature, the *MQQ*, confirms two of the spellings above and adds another: البراهم (Ibrāham), ابراهيم (Ibrāhīm), adding ابراهام (Ibrāhām).[95] One other collection, the *MQ*, in addition to the ones mentioned by the *MQQ*, mentions more variant forms: ابراهم (Ibrāhim), and ابراهم (Ibrāhum).[96] In effect, only two spellings of Ibrāhīm are present in the earliest available manuscripts, ابرهم (Ibrahim) and ابرهيم (Ibrahīm), and this second one does not seem to have been recognized by the early Islamic philologists cited by Jeffery. Perhaps this is an indication that their discussions were conducted with the oral transmissions of the text in view rather than by comparing the readings from multiple manuscripts.

In view of these disparities in the early manuscript tradition, Jeffery's assertion seems overly confident that, "The form (Ibrāhīm) would thus seem to be due to Muḥammad himself, but the immediate source is not easy to determine."[97] Perhaps an oral pronunciation of this form can be attributed to Muḥammad,[98] but the full written form which includes both the *alif* and the *yā'* does not appear in the manuscript tradition until at least the early tenth/third century and it does not become a regular feature of the manuscript tradition until the reforms of Ibn Mujāḥid in the mid-tenth/third century. Without this full form, various pronunciations are possible, and were evidently used.

Some scholars assert that the occurrence in the early manuscripts of variant forms of Ibrāhīm are scribal errors. Puin states that since the Islamic "readings" literature acknowledges these kinds of variants, the ones that appear in manuscripts are usually explained as scribal errors.[99] Al-Azami, a contemporary Muslim scholar, dismisses such variants by stating,

> But if any scrap of parchment falls into our inquisitive hands and, despite our best allowance for orthographic differences, fails to slip comfortably into the 'Uthmāni skeleton, then we must cast it out as distorted and void.[100]

Rippin cites another current example of this kind of thinking. It attributes such textual variants in the Ṣan'ā' manuscripts to be copyist errors which precipitated the manuscripts being discarded in the first place.[101] Though this is an explanation that cannot be dismissed out of hand, Rippin remarks that "the existence of a consistent pattern of the writing of Arabic as in this case of using the internal *yā'* to represent a long 'a' seems to suggest otherwise because of the very consistency of the usage in the manuscripts."[102] This is confirmed by the manuscripts which present multiple examples of the two different spellings. There are too many examples for them to be attributed to scribal mistakes when the surrounding portions of text in these manuscripts demonstrate such care in copying. This is also true for the consistency of the omissions of *alif,* and the few places where *alif* is added by a later scribal hand. Also, even though there are two main spellings of Ibrāhīm, and that both spellings occur sometimes in the same manuscripts, the frequency and patterns of their occurrences argue against scribal error and actually argue for scribal care in reproducing the early flexibility of orthography as regards the spelling of Ibrāhīm.

This writer found that the two spellings for Ibrāhīm encountered in these manuscripts are also found at various places in all of the Ḥijāzī manuscripts surveyed as well as some early Kufic manuscripts.[103] There are two explanations for this phenomenon. The first is that they point to a flexibility of pronunciation of the long vowels in early Arabic and an equally flexible orthography to represent them. The second is that, at least with some proper names, these variants are indicative of archaisms that survived from the transition from Syriac spelling and pronunciation to a distinctive Arabic representation and pronunciation of these names. Mingana asserted that many Qur'ānic names are traceable to Syriac rather than Hebrew or Greek precedents, especially mentioning Isḥāq and Ismāʻīl.[104] Rippin includes Ibrāhīm where he notes that,

> Examples can be provided, on the evidence of the early manuscripts, of instances in which words, because of the way they were written in the primitive script of the time, were likely mispronounced as a result of a misunderstanding of the script and in the absence of a firm oral tradition. Examples include the name Ibrāhīm, more easily and better understood in a version closer to the Hebrew, Abrāhām, and Shayṭān, once again closer to the Hebrew if read Ṣāṭān. Both of these developed readings depend upon the misunderstanding of the early writing of the long "a" sound in the middle of the word.[105]
>
> Over time, that tradition of writing was forgotten and its remnants are seen in the developed text of the Qur'ān only at the end of words with the writing of a long "a" as an *alif maqṣūra*. At some point, this *yā'* was read according to the rules of classical Arabic orthography and pronounced as a long "I" or the diphthong "ay" rather than the long "a" which it represented originally. One response to these observations has arisen which suggests that the manuscripts with such readings are, in fact, flawed and this is why they were discarded in the trash pile of Sana'a. . . . Of course, the claim cannot be denied outright, but the existence of a consistent pattern of the writing of Arabic as in this case of using the internal *yā'* to represent long "a" seems to suggest otherwise because of the very consistency of the usage in the manuscripts.[106]

Variants involving Ismāʻīl

14:39:2	Ismāʻīl (اسمعل) and Isma'il (اسمعل) for Ismāʻīl (اسمٰعيل)
14:39:2 اسمعل	Ismāʻīl 01-28.1, 01-29.1, 01-20.x, BL Or. 2165, BNF 325a, 326a, 328a, 330a, 331, 332, 333c, 334c, 340c, 370a, Meknes
14:39:2 اسمعل	Isma'il- no *yā'* Istanbul
14:39:2 اسمٰعيل	Ismāʻīl- dagger *alif* BL Or. 12884, Sharīf, Warsh

This was the most stable name observed in the manuscripts. Only one variant version of this name was found in the manuscripts surveyed. The Istanbul manuscript has Isma'il, without the *yā'* (اسمعل). This variant raises some interesting questions. Is it a copyist mistake? Supporting this idea is the fact that neither Jeffery nor the *MQQ* nor the *MQ* record such a variant from the later Islamic Qur'ān literature. Also, it seems to go against the idea of there being a Syriac derivation behind the word. Mingana observed that the normal Qur'ānic form of this name which includes the *yā'* is an exact equivalent of the Syriac form.[107] It is also a very rare variant, unique to the manuscripts and records used for this book.

Or perhaps it is a variant like the shorter version of Ibrāhīm where the internal *yā'* at one point represented long "a". If so, this version without the *yā'* might represent a pronunciation that did not have the long "a" or long "i" sound, hence Isma'il. A firm conclusion cannot be drawn unless other instances of this spelling are discovered. Explaining it as a copyist mistake is perhaps the best option at this time while keeping the others under consideration.

Variants involving Isḥāq

14:39:2 Isḥaq (اسحق)	Isḥāq (اسحاق)
14:39:2 اسحق Isḥaq	Istanbul, 01-29.1, 01-20.x, BL Or. 2165, BNF 325a, 326a, 328a, 330a, 331, 332, 334c, 340c, 370a, SamK, Meknes
14:39:2 اسحاق Isḥāq- full *alif*	BNF 333c
14:39:2 اسحٰق Isḥāq- dagger *alif*	BL Or. 12884, Sharīf, Warsh

Only one variant spelling of Isḥaq (اسحق) was observed in the manuscripts surveyed, and in the wider usage represented in available extant early manuscripts. This variant form is اسحاق , which includes a full *alif.* In the current text, this full *alif* is represented by a dagger *alif* which is thought to present the earliest pronunciation of this word. The manuscript in which this variant is found presents a pronunciation which in retrospect enshrines an Islamic pronunciation of the name. This raises a question: if the original pronunciation of Isḥaq contained the *alif,* then why was it not represented with the letter being written as part of the *rasm*? Mingana asserts that the form of this name was derived from the Syriac rather than the Hebrew.[108] In his transliteration of these forms, neither of them has an *alif* or its equivalent in the second syllable.

Also, none of the manuscripts surveyed used a *yā'* in this syllable to represent an *alif,* as was suggested concerning Ibrāhām. The normal spelling of the name carries this on, though the Islamic pronunciation asserts the presence of an implicit *alif.* All of the earliest occurrences in the Ḥijāzī manuscripts are spelled without the *alif.* This one occurrence is in a later manuscript, but one from before the reforms of the tenth century. It makes explicit what later became the standard Islamic pronunciation of the name.

Spelling Variations in Other Proper Names

These spelling variations for proper names also take place against a wider background of spelling variation in proper names in the Qur'ān. In early manuscripts, consonantal spelling variants can be observed for at least the following names: Ibrāhīm, Isḥaq, Tawraīt, Shaīṭān, Isrā'īl, and Dāūd. As mentioned earlier, Ibrāhīm and Isḥaq are found in two basic forms. Tawraīt can be found in two forms.[109] Shaīṭān can be found in three forms.[110] Isrā'īl can be found in two forms.[111] And Dāūd can be found in four forms.[112] Other names appear to be more stable, like Mūsā, Yūnus, Nūh, 'Īsā, and Iblīs. [113] No variant spellings were observed for these names.

As mentioned earlier by Rippin, some scholars view the *yā'* in Ibrāhīm in 14:35:1 as being originally interchangeable with *alif.* Puin views this as a holdover from Aramaic for which the original pronunciation was lost.[114] Mingana asserted a general rule for this: [115]

> The *yā'* [y] as a substitute for the *aliph* is written in all the ancient manuscripts of the Qur'ān in the cases under consideration (proper names and religious vocabulary), and is undoubtedly under Syriac influence.

Puin goes on to assert that if this is so, then in addition to the spelling Ibrāhīm, other anomalies of Qur'ānic Arabic are solved concerning the forms of the words for Satan (شيطان, Shaīṭān) and Torah (تورية , Tawraīt),[116] originally pronounced Sātān and Torāh, which was more in line with Hebrew pronunciation. Fischer also sees an archaic holdover from Aramaic in this phenomenon.[117] This loss of knowledge of the original pronunciation would then explain the distinctive Islamic pronunciations which are read according to the rules of Classical Arabic that developed later. Puin goes on to assert that originally *alif* was used for all of the short vowels and that *waw* and *yā'* were to a degree used interchangeably with it until rules were formalized to use all three letters exclusively for the values they now represent.[118] Fedeli also observes this phenomenon of the long "a" sound being written with *yā'* as a normal orthographic convention in some early Qur'ān manuscripts,[119] as also does Blachère.[120]

Barr coined the phrase "zone of variable spelling" for the situation where there are multiple apparently accepted variant spellings for the same word in a Hebrew Bible manuscript.[121] It would seem that these Qur'ānic names also represent some restricted, but accepted, zones of variable spelling in scribal practice in the earliest Qur'ān manuscripts at the times they were copied. The variations are found too frequently and consistently to be simple copyist mistakes, occurring often on the same page and sometimes even on the same line. They also sometimes make explicit what later came to be the accepted pronunciation of a name.[122] Whereas most of the consonantal text had been standardized by the time of the writing of the manuscripts surveyed, with these names some small zones of variability remained. And it was from among these variable forms that there emerged later precise and inflexible forms of orthography for all of these names. It has been observed that there are even later corrections made in some manuscripts where *alifs* are inserted in red by a later scribe.

NOTES

1. Efim Rezvan, "Orthography," in Jane Dammen McAuliffe, ed., *EQ* (Leiden: Brill, 2003), 3:604–8, 604.

2. A. Mingana describes variants involving these letters in, "Syriac Influence on the Style of the Koran," reprinted in Ibn Warraq, ed., *What the Koran Really Says* (Amherst, New York: Prometheus Books, 2002), 183–84. W. Wright, *A Grammar of the Arabic Language* (Cambridge: Cambridge University Press, 1986), 1:11, note †, also notes these conventions concerning *alif* and *yā'*.

3. Gerd-R. Puin, "Observations on Early Qur'an Manuscripts in San'ā'," in Stefan Wild, ed., *The Qur'an as Text* (Leiden: Brill, 1996), 107–11, 108. Puin observed this in the Ṣan'ā' manuscripts and it also holds true for the earliest Qur'ān manuscripts in Western collections.

4. A. F. L. Beeston, T. M. Johnstone, R. B. Serjeant, and G. R. Smith, *Arabic Literature to the End of the Umayyad Period* (Cambridge: Cambridge University Press), 1983, 13; Joshua Blau, *The Emergence and Linguistic Background of JUDAEO-ARABIC* (Jerusalem: Ben-Zvi Institute for the study of Jewish Communities in the East, 1999), 266, note to p. 124, 9f.b.ff. See also Wheeler M. Thackston, *An Introduction to Koranic and Classical Arabic* (Bethesda: IBEX, 2000), 274.

5. François Déroche and Sergio Noja-Noseda, *Sources de la Transmission Manuscrite du Texte Coranique* (Lesa, Italy: Fondazione Ferni Noja Noseda Studi Arabo Islamici, 2001), 2.1:XXIV, XXVIII–XXX.

6. François Déroche, "Manuscripts of the Qur'ān," in Jane Dammen McAuliffe, *EQ* (Leiden: Brill, 2003), 3:254–75, 257.

7. François Déroche, *The Abbasid Tradition* (London: Nour Foundation, 1992), 29.

8. François Déroche, *Le Coran* (Paris: Presses Universitaires de France, 2005), 39.

9. Puin, "Observations," 108.

10. Sergio Noja-Noseda, "Book Review," *Annali*, 58, 1–2, 289–91, citing 290.

11. M. M. Al-Azami, *The History of the Qur'anic Text* (Leicester: UK Islamic Academy, 2003), 133–34.

12. Déroche and Noja-Noseda, *BL Or. 2165 facsimile*. 2.1:XXVIII.

13. H. Fleisch, "Hamza," *EI2* (Leiden: Brill, 1960), 150–52, citing 150.

14. A. Jones expresses the opinion of many in asserting, "The defects of the script were of a nature that would be intolerable for a people relying strongly on the written word and placing little importance on oral tradition." A. Jones, "The Qur'ān - II," *Arabic Literature to the End of the Umayyad Period. Cambridge History of Islam* (Cambridge: Cambridge University Press, 1983), 242.

15. "Nevertheless the acceptance of an agreed written version greatly limited the range of accepted alternatives in the oral tradition. Variants had to fall within the possibilities allowed by the textual outline, otherwise they were *shādhdh*, 'peculiar.' Oral tradition thus became subordinate to the written text, despite the latter's imperfections." Jones, "Qur'ān," 242.

16. Alford T. Welch, "al-Kur'ān," *EI2* (Leiden: Brill, 1960), 400–29, 408: "During the Umayyad period (661–750/41–132) the 'U<u>th</u>mānic text tradition became more and more diverse, and new readings arose combining elements of the 'U<u>th</u>mānic and Companion oral and text traditions, especially those of Ibn Mas'ūd and Ubayy. By early 'Abbasid times there was such a confusion of readings that it became impossible to distinguish 'U<u>th</u>mānic from non-'U<u>th</u>mānic ones, or to recover with confidence the 'original' 'U<u>th</u>mānic text."

17. An example of this using the word قل occurs at S. 21:4 where contextually it could be read either as an imperative or a perfect tense verb. Ibn Mas'ūd viewed it as an imperative, whereas the Cairo text has it as a perfect. This example was obtained personally from Dr. Gerd R. Puin.

18. Andrew Rippin, *Muslims: Their Religious Beliefs and Practices* (London: Routledge, 2001), 30–31.

19. It is a "broken" internal plural form of a very common pattern. Peter F. Abboud and Ernest N. McCarus, *Elementary Modern Standard Arabic* (New York: Cambridge University Press, 1983), 1:267–70.

20. A. Arne Ambros and Stephan Procházka, *A Concise Dictionary of Koranic Arabic* (Weisbaden: Reichert Verlag, 2004), 164; Hans Wehr, *A Dictionary of Modern Written Arabic* (Beirut: Libraire Du Liban, 1974), 527.

21. Ambros and Procházka, *Dictionary*, 190; Wehr, *Dictionary*, 618.

22. Abboud and McCarus, *Arabic*, 1:219.

23. Wright, *Grammar*, 1:11C.

24. غصن, "to put forth branches," Wehr, *Dictionary*, 675; and غضن , "to fold, crease," Wehr, *Dictionary*, 676; neither of which is attested in the Qur'ān.

25. Arthur Jeffery and Isaac Mendelsohn, "The Orthography of the Samarqand Qur'an Codex," *JAOS*, 62:175–95, 195.

26. Ibn Khaldūn, *The Muqaddimah* (New York: Bollingen Foundation, 1967), 2:382.

27. Ahmad Pakatchi, "The Orthographic Traditions in Early Arabic Writing as Reflected in Quranic Codices," Corpus Coranicum, Berlin, 2005, 6–9 November 2005, 2. The words in brackets were added by this author.

28. Adrian Alan Brockett, *Studies in Two Transmissions of the Qur'ān*. PhD thesis, University of St. Andrews, Department of Arabic Studies, 1984, 10. Also, Fleisch, "Hamza," 150.

29. Brockett, *Studies*, 9–10.

30. Brockett refers to these dagger *alifs* as "vocal *alifs*" and gives examples of their use in Ḥafṣ and Warsh texts as well as between Egyptian, Indian, and Persian Qur'ān manuscript traditions in Brockett, *Studies*, 131–33, 206.

31. Efim A. Rezvan, *The Qur'ān of 'Uthmān* (St. Petersburg: St. Petersburg Centre for Oriental Studies, 2004). See p. 66 for the description of these *alifs* and p. 142 line 1 in table 11 for an example.

32. Note that the introduction of the dagger *alif* for all of these words starts in BL Or. 12884. The Warsh text and the Sharīf text both have the dagger *alif* on all of these words, with two exceptions: 1) at 14:37:6, العرب , Or. 12884 has both the dagger *alif* and a full *alif*, القرات and the Sharīf text has a full *alif*, and 2) that for the last word in 14:41:1, ولولدى , Or. 12884 has both the dagger *alif* and the full *alif*, and the Sharīf text adds a full *alif*: ولوالدى.

33. Simon Hopkins, *Studies in the Grammar of Early Arabic* (Oxford: Oxford University Press, 1984), 14.

34. Hopkins, *Studies*, 16.

35. Note that the introduction of the *shadda* with the dagger *alif* in the orthography for Allah first appears in these manuscripts with BL Or. 12884. The Warsh text has a horizontal *alif* over the *shadda*. The Sharīf text has the *shadda* with the dagger *alif*.

36. Note that the introduction of the *shadda* with the dagger *alif* in the orthography for Allah first appears in these manuscripts with BL Or. 12884. The Warsh text has no dagger *alif*, horizontal *fetha*, or *shadda* over this occurrence of Allah. The Sharīf text does have the *shadda* with the dagger *alif*.

37. Hopkins, *Studies*, §13 mentions that with this word the *wāw* is pronounced as *alif*.

38. At this word, BL Or. 12884 has both the dagger *alif* and the full *alif*.

39. Hopkins, *Studies*, 17–18.

40. The point can be made even further. Just in S. 14:35-41 BL Or. 12884 has a further 30 instances of dagger alif more than the 1924 text and the Sharif manuscript has a further 17. For details see the author's PhD dissertation, Keith E. Small, *Mapping a New Country: Textual Criticism and Qur'an Manuscripts* (Brunel, London School of Theology, 2008), 115–16.

41. Thackston, *Introduction*, 281.

42. Wright, *Grammar*, I:72, § 131.

43. Gerd-R. Puin, "Vowel Letters and Ortho-epic Writing in the Qur'an," Gerd-R. Puin, *TBA* (Saarbrücken: 2010), 32. This was obtained from the author.

44. Wright, *Grammar*, I:280, § 358 (c); Thackston, *Introduction*, 274.

45. Al-Azami, *History*, 131–32.

46. Margaret Dunlop Gibson, *An Arabic Version of the Epistles of St. Paul to the Romans, Corinthians, Galatians with part of the Epistle to the Ephesians from a Ninth Century MS. in the Convent of St. Catherine on Mount Sinai* (London: C.J. Clay and Sons, 1894), 6.

47. Hopkins, *Studies*, 14.

48. For instance, the verb علا, "to be high, lofty, exalted." John Penrice, *A Dictionary and Glossary of the Kor-ān* (London: Curzon Press, 1975), 100, or علاء, "high rank," or علا, "anvils" (plural form), these last two in Wehr, *Dictionary*, 640.

49. Hopkins, *Studies*, 16.

50. Lane, *Lexicon*, لقم . Penrice has "to obstruct," 132.

51. Abboud and McCarus, *Standard*, 1:384.

52. Wright, *Grammar*, 13, section 10.

53. All manuscripts prior in date to Or. 12884.

54. Régis Blachère, *Introduction au Coran* (Paris: Besson & Chantemerle, 1959), 152; Yasir Qadhi, *An Introduction to the Sciences of the Qur'aan* (Birmingham: Al-Hidaayah Publishing and Distribution, 1999), 141.

55. Jones, "Qur'ān," 243.

56. Chaim Rabin, "The Beginnings of Classical Arabic," in Ibn Warraq, ed., *What the Koran Really Says* (Amherst, New York: Prometheus Books, 2002), 211–27, citing 217; Thackston, *Introduction*, 275; Welch, "Kur'ān," *EI2*, 400; Wright, *Grammar*, I:72, note.

57. Wolfdietrich Fischer, *A Grammar of Classical Arabic* (London: Yale University Press, 2002), 6, 9.

58. Fischer, *Grammar*, 9.

59. Fischer, *Grammar,* 6.

60. Puin, "Observations," 109.

61. Wright, *Grammar*, I:72, note.

62. Régis Blachère, *Le Coran* (Paris: Universitaires de France, 1977), 151.

63. 18 occurences in Surah 14:35–41. An additional 18 are assimilated into *wasla* or *madda.*

64. Fischer, *Grammar*, 10.

65. Hopkins, *Studies,* 26.

66. Thackston, *Introduction,* 275.

67. Wright, *Grammar,* I:72–73, note.

68. Yasin Dutton, "Red Dots, Green Dots, Yellow Dots & Blue," *JQS*, 2000, II:I:1–24, here 11–14.

69. Dutton, "Dots II," 11–14.

70. Wright, *Grammar*, 17. Note however, that the convention Wright describes of *ḥamza* being represented by the doubling of vowel points was not observed in any of the manuscripts surveyed for this study.

71. See Yasin Dutton, "Red Dots, Green Dots, Yellow Dots & Blue: Some reflections on the Vocalization of early Qur'anic Manuscripts - Part I," *JQS*, 1999, I:I:115–40, and Dutton, "Dots II," 15.

72. These manuscripts contained systems of red colored dots of varying complexity: Istanbul, BNF 325a, 333c, 334, 340c, 343, and 370a. The Meknes manuscript also has colored dots but the colors can not be distinguished in the black and white photos obtained for this study.

73. Hopkins, *Studies,* 19–20.

74. Wright, *Grammar*, 72–73. Hopkins, *Studies,* 20, note 5, lists sources discussing the Eastern and Western dialectical differences. This correction of dialect is also the conclusion expressed in the article "Ḥamza," by H. Fleisch in *EI2*, III:152.

75. Surah 2 in the standard text has ابرهم . All other parts of the current text have ابرهيم .

76. Wright, *Grammar*, 9.

77. Hopkins, *Studies*, 1–2.

78. For example, see Hopkins, *Studies,* 4–5, how the pronunciation of *imāla* and *taltala* were more similar to modern dialects than to the formal rules of Classical Arabic.

79. Hopkins, *Studies,* 11–13.

80. The full *alif* can be found in the Surah 2 portion of BNF 343, at 26:69 in San'ā' manuscript: 01-18-10, 115.3, line 14; at 53:37 in San'ā' manuscript: 17-21-1, 93.2 line 4; and at 87:19 in San'ā' manuscript: 16-20-2, 96.4 line 10, and 87:19 in San'ā' manuscript: 12-16-1, 111.4, line 4, where both look as if the *alif* were added in black at a later time; and added in red at 3:33 in San'ā' manuscript: Showcase 32, 87, line 4–5. All of these occurrences of *alif* occur in either tenth/third century manuscripts or as later scribal additions to early manuscripts.

81. Hans-Caspar Graf von Bothmer, Karl-Heinz Ohlig and Gerd-R. Puin, "Neue Wege der Koranforschung," www.uni-saarland.de/mediadb/profil/veroeffentlichungen/ffmagazin/1-1999/Neue_Wege.pdf, 31 October 2005, 39.

82. Surah 2: 124, 125 (2x), 126, 127, 130, 132, 133, 135, 136, 140, 258 (3x), 260. All other instances of this name in the 1924 Cairo text contain the *yā'*.

83. M. A. S. Abdel Haleem, "Qur'ānic Orthography: the Written Representation of the Recited Text of the Qur'ān," *The Islamic Quarterly*, XXXVIII, Number 3, 1994, 171–92, citing p. 4 of the online version at www.islamic-awareness.org/Qur'an/Text/Scribal/haleem.html, accessed 7 June 2006.

84. Ahmad Von Denffer, *'Ulūm al-Qur'ān* (Leicester: The Islamic Foundation, 1994), 50. However, Arthur Jeffery, *Materials for the History of the Text of the Qur'ān* (Leiden: Brill, 1937), 211, cites Ibn Abī Dāwūd as listing Ibrahām for this variant.

85. The Samarkand Kufic Qur'ān has both spellings in the same manuscript, and has both spellings within Surah 2. BL Or. 2165 has both spellings within the same manuscript, though within surahs spellings are kept consistent. BNF 328a contains both spellings and has both within S. 6. BNF 331 has both spellings and has both within S. 2. UNESCO CD, manuscript 85, dated to the seventh–eighth/first–second century, has both spellings even on the same line of text: S. 11:69 and 74- *yā'* is omitted, 11:75, 11:76 *yā'* is present.

86. Hopkins, *Studies,* 16–17.

87. These are at S. 9:70 where *yā'* is present, 14:35 where *yā'* is omitted, and 15:51 where *yā'* is present.

88. Yasin Dutton, "Some Notes on the British Library's 'Oldest Qur'an Manuscript' (Or. 2165)," *JQS*, VI:1:43–71, citing 66; Yasin Dutton, "An Early *Mushaf* According to the Reading of Ibn 'Āmir," *JQS*, III:1:71–90, citing 84.

89. Dutton, "Notes," 43.

90. At 9:70, the Samarkand Ḥijāzi manuscript has *yā'*. At 14:35 BNF 325a, and 332, both dated to the second century A.H., contain the *yā'*. BNF 326a, an eighth/second century manuscript omits it. See the chart of the usage of medial *yā'* in Appendix L for more examples.

91. For a thorough investigation of this in the Hebrew Bible manuscript tradition, see James Barr, *The Variable Spellings of the Hebrew Bible* (Oxford: Oxford University Press, 1989).

92. Arthur Jeffery, *Foreign Vocabulary of the Qur'an* (Baroda: Oriental Institute, 1938), 45.

93. It was also not observed in any additional manuscripts consulted for their conventions for spelling Ibrāhīm.

94. The full *alif* can be found in the Surah 2 portion of BNF 343, at 26:69 in San'ā' manuscript: 01-18-10, 115.3, line 14; at 53:37 in San'ā' manuscript: 17-21-1, 93.2 line 4; and at 87:19 in San'ā' manuscript: 16-20-2, 96.4 line 10, and 87:19 in San'ā' manuscript: 12-16-1, 111.4, line 4, where both look as if the *alif* were added in black at a later time; and added in red at 3:33 in San'ā' manuscript: Showcase 32, 87, line 4–5. All of these occurrences of *alif* occur in either tenth/third century manuscripts or as later scribal additions to early manuscripts.

95. Abd al-'Āl Sālim Makram and Ahmad Muktār 'Umar, *Mu'jam al-Qirā'āt al-Qurānīyah, Ma'a Maqaddimah fī Qirā'āt wa Ashhar al-Qurrā'* (Cairo, Egypt: 'Ālam al-Kitab, 1997), I:254, no. 377; I:262, no. 414; and II:514, no. 4152, respectively.

96. Abd al-Latīf Al-Khatīb, *Mu'jam al-Qirā'āt* (Damascus: Dār Sa'd al-Dīn, 1422/2002), Surah 2:124, p. 186–87.

97. Jeffery, *Vocabulary*, 45.

98. Margoliouth makes the assertion that the rhyme in S. 21:20, 22 (S. 21:21, 23 Fluegel's numbering) requires Ibrahīm, rather than Ibraham. David S. Margoliouth, "Textual Variations in the Koran," MW, 15, 334–44, citing 342, reprinted in Ibn Warraq, *The Origins of the Koran* (Amherst, New York: Prometheus Books, 1998), 160.

99. Bothmer, Ohlig and Puin, "Neue Wege," 38.

100. Al-Azami, *History*, 205.

101. Andrew Rippin, *The Qur'an and its Interpretative Tradition* (Burlington: Ashgate, 2001), xvi.

102. Rippin, *Qur'an*, xvi.

103. See Appendices K and L in Small, *Mapping*, for charts listing the various spellings encountered in the manuscripts surveyed.

104. Alphonse Mingana, "Syriac Influence on the Style of the Koran," in Ibn Warraq, ed., *What the Koran Really Says* (Amherst, NY: Prometheus Books, 2002), 171–92, 175–78.

105. Rippin, *Muslims*, 30.

106. Rippin, *Qur'an*,. xv–xvi.

107. Mingana, "Influence," 176.

108. Mingana, "Influence," 175.

109. These forms are: توريه and توره .

110. These forms are: شيطن (normal form) , شيطن (San'ā' 01-32.1, line 13 at S. 2:36); and شيطان (CBL 1401, S. 16:63 at f. 5v, line 8, and S. 17:53 at f. 10r, line 5). Note that in CBL 1401 at 17:53, where Shaiṭān occurs twice, the first occurrence on line 4 has no *alif* but the second one on line 5 of the same page does have the *alif*. The other two occurrences in CBL 1401 at 17:64 (f. 12v, line 8) and 18:63 (f. 18r, lines 2–3) do not have the *alif*.

111. These forms are: اسريل and اسرايل .

112. These forms are: داود (D.ā.ū.d), دواد (D.ū.ā.d), دود (D.ū.d) , and داد(D.ā.d). They occurred in the following manuscripts: Dāūd (Or. 2165, CBL 1401, Sana 01-15.9), Dūād (SamH, Or. 2165, Sana 01-32.1), Dūd (SamH), and Dād (SamH). Wright, *Grammar*, 18, mentions three spellings of Dāūd, but none of them are Dūād.

113. These were observed in SamH, Or. 2165, BNF 328a, CBL 1401 and the UNESCO CD-ROM.

114. Bothmer, Ohlig, and Puin, "Neue Wege," 40.
115. Mingana, "Influence," citing 184.
116. Bothmer, Ohlig, and Puin, "Neue Wege," 40.
117. Fischer, *Grammar,* 7.
118. Puin, "Ortho-epic," 3.
119. Alba Fedeli, "Early Evidences of Variant Readings in Qur'ānic Manuscripts," in Karl Heinz-Ohlig and Gerd-R. Puin, eds., *Die dunklen Anfänge* (Berlin: Hans Schiler, 2005), 293–316, 12.
120. Blachère, *Introduction*, 91.
121. Barr, *Spellings,* 204.
122. This is true for Isḥāq with a full *alif* and Shaīṭān with a full *alif.*

4

Copyist Mistakes

All manuscript traditions have variants that are clearly the result of scribal carelessness and inattention.[1] In ancient manuscript traditions, scribal habits were usually very careful and precise, but occasionally there were lapses which resulted in mistakes. For this brief chapter, instances of negligence have been gathered from examples where letters were added, changed, or omitted. As such, some of the examples of haplography and diacritical mark variants are included here. Hopkins comments that collections of early Arabic material of all types display scribal lapses resulting in the omission of letters and even words.[2] This has proven true for the Qur'ān manuscripts surveyed as well as there being other kinds of mistakes. Below are the ones encountered. These do not include copyist mistakes that were caught by a scribe and physically corrected.

ADDITIONAL LETTERS

14:35:3 Meknes- there is an additional tooth letter: وسى instead of وٮى
14:38:3 01-20.x- there is an additional tooth letter: السمما instead of السما
14:39:1 Topkapi- there is an additional tooth letter: الذٮى instead of الذى
14:40:2 BNF 370a- letters are added: الادعا instead of دعا
14:40:2 Istanbul- added letter: درسى instead of درٮى

This last variant could conceivably contain a doubled *yā'*, as it is in the word when it is written in a fully pointed script. However, since this does not seem to be a normal feature in this manuscript, it is likely that this is a copyist mistake.

MISPLACED DIACRITICS AND SIMILAR LETTERS

After describing the phonetic deficiencies of the early Arabic script because of the partial use of consonantal diacritical marks and the absence of short vowel marks, Gilliot remarks helpfully:[3]

> Although the reader who was familiar with the language would, in most cases, have no difficulty ascertaining which pronunciation was intended, there were so many words which permitted quite different vocalisations that instances of dubious pronunciation were not infrequent.

This appears to be confirmed in the following instances of odd variable placement of diacritical marks. All of them can be taken as copyist mistakes.

14:37:1 Topkapi- *Nūn* for *tā* suffix: ذرينى instead of ذريتى
14:37:2 Topkapi- *bā'* for *yā'*: غبر instead of غير
14:37:2 BNF 334c- *zā'* for *rā'*: رزع instead of زرع
14:37:3 BNF 330a- *jīm* for *ḥā'*: المجرم instead of المحرم
14:37:6 01-28.1- *fā'* for *qāf* وارزفهم instead of وارزقهم

On two occasions a similarly shaped consonant is substituted for another:
Final *nūn* for *yā'*
14:35:3 BNF 328a- وبن instead of وبنى
14:37:5 BNF 334c- تهون instead of تهوى

An unpointed short stem for *lām*
14:40:1 01-20.x- احعمى instead of احعلى [4]

HAPLOGRAPHY

There were some letters missing from words that can safely be regarded as copyist mistakes.

14:36:2 BL Or. 2165- *bā'*: تعنى instead of تبعنى
14:37:4 BNF 326a- *yā'*: لقموا instead of ايقيموا
14:39:2 Istanbul- *yā'*: اسمعا instead of اسمعيا[5]
14:39:3 Istanbul- *yā'*: اسمع instead of اسميع

Haplography of Words

In most manuscript traditions, there are instances of omission that are of a larger size including words and phrases. If this survey provides an indication, the Qur'ān tradition has very few of these larger variants. There is only one instance of this kind of variant among the Qur'ān manuscripts surveyed. This is the omission of the small particle ذي from BNF 340c. Its omission does not change the meaning of the text.

There are omissions and scribal mistakes of this larger sort recorded in some manuscripts. Rezvan records some examples of copyist mistakes of omitted words in 15th and 18th century Qur'āns.[6] Mingana notes one instance of an omitted word in a palimpsest.[7] Fedeli notes three omissions in palimpsests, two of which are phrases, and an omission of a word in a normal manuscript.[8] E. Puin notes additional and missing passages in the *inferior* script of another palimpsest.[9] These larger omissions in the palimpsests, though, were probably not accidental. Instead they probably represent a different form of the text, possibly from before the basic standardization of the consonantal text.

These small numbers of variants across so many manuscripts demonstrate the level of care which scribes used in this manuscript tradition. Copyist mistakes were found in the earliest manuscripts as well as later ones. Since these were clearly mistakes, their effect on the meaning would be quickly discerned by the reader and corrected. It is significant that almost half of the Qur'ānic variants in this category involve the misplacement of diacritical marks. The diacritical points in Arabic, however, if they were being read with a memorized text in mind, might have been easy to pass over since they occur much more frequently, and so remained in these texts without detection or correction.

NOTES

1. A sample presentation of scribal errors for New Testament manuscript studies is Kurt and Barbara Aland, *The Text of the New Testament* (Leiden: Brill, 1989), 282–87.

2. Simon Hopkins, *Studies in the Grammar of Early Arabic* (Oxford: Oxford University Press, 1984), 60–61.

3. Claude Gilliot, "Creation of a Fixed Text," in Jane Dammen McAuliffe, ed., *The Cambridge Companion to the Qur'an* (Cambridge: Cambridge University Press, 2006), 41–58, citing 47.

4. The height of the letter which should be *lam* is higher than the letter to its left, but noticeably shorter than a normal *lam*.

5. This variant is discussed in more detail in the names section under Ismā'īl.

6. M. E. Rezvan, "Qur'ānic Fragments From the A.A. Polotsov Collection at the St. Petersburg Branch of the Institute of Oriental Studies," *MO* 7:2:20–35, 23.

7. Alphonse Mingana and Agnes Smith Lewis, *Leaves From Three Ancient Qur'āns, Possibly Pre-'Uthmānic* (Cambridge: Cambridge University Press, 1914), xl, item C.
8. Alba Fedeli, "Early Evidences of Variant Readings in Qur'ānic Manuscripts," in Karl Heinz-Ohlig and Gerd-R. Puin, eds., *Die dunklen Anfänge* (Berlin: Hans Schiler, 2005), 293–316, 300, 309–10, 312–13.
9. Elisabeth Puin, "Ein früher Koranpalimpsest aus San'ā' (DAM 01-27.1)," in Markus Groß and Karl Heinz-Ohlig, eds., *Schlaglichter* (Berlin: Hans Schiler, 2008), 461–93, 463.

5

Diacritical Mark Variants and Variants Affecting Grammar

Since the earliest Qur'ān manuscripts as a rule have very few diacritical points differentiating consonants, when they do occur they merit careful attention. In the manuscripts surveyed in this study, the great majority of diacritical marks that were designated are in accord with the current text. However, there were a number of occasions where their use departed from current norms. This, together with the variable pointing systems employed in the earliest stages of Qur'ānic manuscript transmission, lead to three phenomena needing to be explored: 1) the sporadic use of diacritics in what are considered to be their proper places, 2) the use of different systems of diacritics, and 3) when diacritics are used that make the letter a consonantal variant. This last category involves changes of grammar. These will be examined in turn.

First is the sporadic use of diacritics in what are considered to be their proper places. Gruendler and Grohmann have noted that in the earliest available manuscripts, there appears to be an established and full system of diacritics in use, though it is used selectively.[1] Gruendler also made the observation that there was a certain degree of fluidity in the application of this system.[2] This phenomenon was confirmed in the manuscripts examined. There are different patterns of which letters are dotted and which are not in the manuscripts which have partial systems of diacritics. For instance, BL Or. 2165 and Paris BNF 328a consistently dot the same kinds of letters above the letter, but not in the same words of the text. In BL Or. 2165, in S. 14:35-41, 18 of 27 initial *nūns* are dotted. In BNF 328a only 8 of the 27 are dotted. BL Or. 2165 has 5 of 9 of the initial *tā's* dotted, but BNF 328a does not have any of them dotted.

The second phenomenon is the use of differing systems of diacritics. Variable systems of the use of these diacritical points were developed.[3] Leemhuis has observed that added diacritical dots or strokes can be observed both above and below a letter.[4] As an example he cites three systems used in manuscripts to distinguish *fā'* and *qāf*.[5] He summarizes them as follows:

1) One dash above for the *fā'* and two above for the *qāf*.
2) One dash underneath for the *fā'* and one above for the *qāf*.
3) One dash above for the *fā'* and one below for the *qāf* (the opposite of number 2).

With this summary, Leemhuis states that the first became the standard in the Arab East and in printed forms of the Qur'ān. The second became the standard in the Arab West and is still found in lithographed Qur'āns from the Maghreb.[6] The third was in use for a short period in the Ḥijāz and Yemen. This third one is used in the inscriptions of the Dome of the Rock in Jerusalem and in two of the manuscripts surveyed in this study, the Topkapi manuscript and the Ṣan' ā' manuscript 01-29.1.[7]

In addition to the systems for *fā'* and *qāf* which Leemhuis observed, two other systems were observed in the manuscripts in this study. First, a variant to system 1) was observed in manuscripts BNF 330a, BNF 331, and BNF 334c that only *fā's* were dotted above the letter with a single dot or dash but no *qāfs* were dotted. Second, in manuscripts BL Or. 2165, BNF 328a, no *fā's* or *qāfs* were dotted at all. This could be regarded as a fourth system. Adjusting Leemhuis' system for these additional categories, the manuscripts used in this study can be grouped as follows:

1) One dash above for the *fā'* and two above for the *qāf*: BNF 325a, 326a, 01-28.1, Ḥafṣ, and Sharīf.
   1a) (only *fā's* dotted) BNF 330a, BNF 331, and BNF 334c.
2) One dash underneath for the *fā'* and one above for the *qāf*: Istanbul, Warsh.
3) One dash above for the *fā'* and one below for the *qāf*: Topkapi, 01-29.1.
4) Neither *fā'* nor *qāf* dotted) BL Or. 2165, 01-20.x, SamK, BNF 328a, 332, 333c, 340c, 343, 370a, Meknes.

It is interesting that manuscripts discovered in Yemen (01-28.1, 01-29.1, and 01-20.x) were found using three of the four systems (1,3,4). Also, the Istanbul manuscript, which is in an early Ḥijāzī script, has system 2). This confirms Leemhuis' conclusion that all systems seem to have been in use at as early a time as can be documented in extant Qur'ān manuscripts.

Manuscript 01-20.x is interesting in its complete lack of diacritics. Though this is an early Kufic-style text, it is similar in this regard to later Kufic texts (eighth-ninth/second-third century) that are more sparingly pointed than the earliest Ḥijāzī texts. But 01-20.x is even more sparingly pointed than any of the other manuscripts surveyed. Perhaps it bears testimony to those efforts of some scholars who resisted the introduction and development of such reading aids. The Caliph Ma'mūn (reigned 813-833/198-218) is said to have forbidden such aids,[8] though he reigned almost a century later than this particular manuscript was produced. Concerning the earlier period, Jeffery makes the important observation,[9]

> Again we have an imposing array of traditions against the putting of any points for distinguishing the letters, or for the marking of vowels or other reading signs in the Codices. In fact, it is recorded of Khalīl b. Aḥmad († 170 or 175) that it was one of his claims to fame that he successfully fought against this prohibition of putting in the diacritical points. This again agrees with the observed fact, for texts which on other grounds seem to be among the oldest are generally without these points. This criterion, however, cannot always be applied, and that for two reasons. In the first place it was not uncommon for later scribes to add the points to Codices which came into their hands, and it is frequently very difficult to decide whether the diacritical points are the work of the original scribe or have been added later. Secondly, it was somewhat of a fad in certain circles, as we learn from Ibn al-Mudabbar's Risālat al-'Adhrā', to omit all diacritical points, and so in some Codices of relatively late date they are omitted.

This kind of resistance is perhaps part of a larger resistance to the general reduction of the role of oral transmission of knowledge in these early Islamic centuries. Cook documents a similar resistance to putting hadīth into writing.[10]

Also, one manuscript presented a different convention for dotting most of the consonants that are currently distinguished through the placement of one dot over the consonant. Categories 1), 2), and 4) for the dotting of *fā'* and *qāf* occurred within the general convention of dots for the rest of the consonantal letters being placed above the letters, as is found in the current systems both East and West. In these systems, though, where there was variation with *fā'* and *qāf*, all of the other consonants that needed distinguishing followed the current system. One manuscript, 01-29.1, however, used a different system.

First, it should be noted that this manuscript has more consonants pointed than any other manuscripts surveyed of similar age and script style. Second, the system used for these dots places single dots above and below many letters, not just *fā'* and *qāf*. The single dots above match the letters that in the current system are dotted above: ف , ض , ذ , ز , خ. Letters with a single dot below match letters that have no dot: ص , د , ر. Exceptions are *qāf*, distinguished from *fā'* with one dot below; ح, with one dot to the right side; ط and ظ, which are not dotted and so not distinguished from each other; and ع and غ, which are not dotted or distinguished. In most of the other manuscripts, when a consonant other than *fā'* and *qāf* was dotted, it was done according to the current system using the bare consonant with a single dot above.

Concerning the second situation, when different systems of diacritics were used, the clarity of the text would have been improved for anyone reading the text familiar with that particular system. But if the text was read by someone familiar with one of the other systems the possibility was there to read a letter as the exact opposite letter it was supposed to distinguish. For example, in BNF 325a, 326a, and 01-28.1 the letter ف *(fā')*, was distinguished from ق *(qaf)* by having one dot over it instead of two. In the Istanbul manuscript ف *(fā')* goes undotted and ق *(qaf)* has one dot. In these early manuscripts, not every instance of a letter is distinguished from its look-alikes, so people using a particular system could have read the opposite of the letter intended by the diacritic. The concurrent use of these variant systems also highlights the degree of flexibility of diacritical mark systems being used in Qur'ān manuscripts at this time.

The third phenomenon is when diacritics are used making the letter a consonantal variant to the standard line of text.

DIACRITICS USED TO CLARIFY THE ORTHOGRAPHY

There was one instance observed where the orthography was overtly clarified through the intentional placement of diacritical points. At 14:38:1 in BNF 330a, four diacritical marks are added to the word نخفى to make each of its letters clearly understood, where the average use of diacritics in the part of the manuscript is only one or two per word. Also, the fourth diacritic is a dot after the *fā'* over the first part of the *yā'*, as if there were a *nūn* between the two, like a first person singular pronoun suffix. The stem for the *nūn* is not there, and such a suffix would not fit the context, so it is probably an extra dot that was accidentally placed there.

VARIANTS AFFECTING GRAMMAR

Many of kinds of grammatical variants would be designated by short vowel patterns which are only recorded on three of the manuscripts examined, BL Or. 12884, the Muṣḥaf Sharīf, and the modern Warsh text. Since the short vowels do not occur in the earlier manuscripts, grammatical variants related to them are not an object of study in this research.[11] However, some grammatical variants do involve the consonantal line, either through the variable placement of diacritical points on consonants or the addition of letters. Where these have occurred in the early manuscripts they have been noted and will be discussed.

Variants Affecting Grammar Due to Diacritical Marks

A few were observed related to the placement of diacritical dots which changed the basic grammatical function of the word.

A Synonym From Variant Diacritics:

Tā' for *thā'*?

14:37:6 BNF 334c- التمرت instead of الثمرت

The reason for the question mark in the title is the orthographic peculiarity of this letter in 14:37:6. The two dots used to designate the letter as a *tā'* which is written differently from the normal convention in this manuscript. Usually two slashes or strokes are used and they are written vertically, one on top of the other, either straight above the letter or diagonally up off and to the left. The marks over this letter, however, are two dots written side by side immediately over the letter. In this manuscript, only one *thā'* is marked with three dots, the word يثبت at 14:27. At that location it is marked with three dots in a triangle that points down to the left.

Gruendler notes that the early forms of these diacritics had distinctive forms and orientations.[12] The *tā*'s in epigraphic texts use two short strokes aligned vertically or diagonally above or next to the letter. BNF 334c follows this convention. The *thā*'s are distinguished by three points in a triangle that is oriented pointing to the lower left. BNF 334c at 14:27 uses this precise convention, but at 14:37:6 the two points are aligned horizontally and there is no sign of a third point. It seems to be a *tā'* not a *thā'*, and the *tā'* of a type of diacritic not used elsewhere in this text but known to have been used later. As such, the points could have been added by a later scribe.

Taken as a *tā'*, it could be an intentional addition to change the meaning of the word from the general "fruit" to the more specific "dates," تمرة.[13] This probably would have been a later addition because the word, تمرة , is not attested in the Qur'ān.

Change of Person

There were two places in the selected passage where manuscripts had variants of person indicated by diacritical points.

14:41:2 01-29.1- *Tā'* for *yā'* تقوم instead of يقوم

This variant is a change of person from third to second person: "And the believers in the day when *You* reckon the account" instead of "when the account is reckoned," changing the passage from narrative to direct discourse. This makes the invocation more internally consistent and personal between Ibrāhīm and Allah. It is also conceivable that it was made to heighten the drama of the narrative and to emphasize Allah as the final judge. This improves the clarity and sense of the text. Also, a change of person from third to second seems more likely than vice versa since if it were the second person originally there would not have been a good reason for changing it to the third person form. This makes the third person form the more likely earlier text-form if one of the two was specified originally. However, these are both legitimate interpretations of the unpointed consonantal text and either could conceivably have been interpretive text forms of an earlier and more ambiguous text form.

The second place affects the narration concerning Ibrāhīm, speaking on behalf of himself and his sons, and Allah concerning who reveals the secrets of the hearts of people:

14:38:2 Topkapi- *Ya'* for *nūn* يعلن for نعلن

"You know what we conceal and what *He revealed*," rather than the standard reading "You know what we conceal and what *we reveal*."

This does fit the overall narrative context and theology of the Qur'ān, though there is an awkward change of person in a direct address, and is possibly a copyist mistake. However, it was placed there with bold strokes in a text with few other letters so clearly designated. Two examples of this kind of variant are also present in the palimpsests.[14]

CONCLUSIONS

The presence of these kinds of variants points to the fact that scribes sometimes took it upon themselves to correct grammar that they thought was in some way deficient and to clarify ambiguities that were allowed by an unpointed text. The changes were small but important in their immediate contexts. Examples which would have a greater effect are also known.[15] It is also fair to say that none of the variants listed above violates the greater context of their respective passages and, though they were intentional changes to the text, their relative infrequency in relation to the incontestable portions of the text testifies to a strong desire of scribes to remain faithful to the perceived meaning of the text. Variants of this sort also achieved a special level of attention in the wider tradition as is recorded in works like the *MQQ,* the *MQ*, and Jeffery's *Materials*, where many of the listed variants consist of alternative ways of pointing the basic consonantal text.[16]

NOTES

1. Beatrice Gruendler, "Arabic Script," in Jane Dammen McAuliffe, ed. *EQ* (Leiden: Brill, 2001), 1:135–42, citing 139. Grohmann also observed this in the earliest Arabic papyri: Adolf Grohmann, "The Problem of Dating Early Qur'āns," *Der Islam*, 33:213–31, citing 226.
2. Gruendler, "Script," *EQ*, 1:140.
3. A. F. L. Beeston, T. M. Johnstone, R. B. Serjeant, and G. R. Smith, *Arabic Literature to the End of the Umayyad Period: Cambridge History of Islam* (Cambridge: Cambridge University Press, 1983), 13.
4. Frederick Leemhuis, "From Palm Leaves to the Internet," in Jane Dammen McAuliffe, ed., *The Cambridge Companion to the Qur'ān* (Cambridge: Cambridge University Press, 2006), 145–62, citing 147.
5. Leemhuis, "Palm Leaves," 147.
6. The Warsh text used in this study displays this system.
7. Leemhuis, "Palm Leaves," 148. These two are new manuscripts to add to Leemhuis' list of the four other manuscripts known to have this system.
8. David S. Margoliouth, "Textual Variations in the Koran," *MW,* 15:334–44, 339.
9. Arthur Jeffery, "Review of 'The Rise of the North Arabic Script and its Kur'ānic Development' by Nabia Abbott," *MW*, 30 (1940), 191–98, 195.
10. Michael Cook, "The Opponents of the Writing Tradition in Early Islam," *Arabica*, 44, Fascicle 4, 457–530.
11. Many of the variants listed in Abd al-'Āl Sālim Makram and Ahmad Muktār 'Umar, *Mu'jam al-Qirā'āt al-Qurānīyah, Ma'a Maqaddimah fī Qirā'āt wa Ashhar al-Qurrā'.* (Cairo, Egypt: 'Ālam al-Kitab, 1997), 2:514–17 are differences in short vowels. This is also true of Arthur Jeffery, *Materials for the History of the Text of the Qur'ān* (Leiden: Brill, 1937).
12. Beatrice Gruendler, *The Development of the Arabic Scripts* (Atlanta: Scholars Press, 1993), 42.
13. Lane, *Lexicon*, نمر.
14. Examples can be found in Alphonse Mingana and Agnes Smith Lewis, *Leaves From Three Ancient Qur'āns, Possibly Pre-'Uthmānic* (Cambridge: Cambridge University Press, 1914), no. 26, xxxix; and Alba Fedeli, "Early Evidences of Variant Readings in Qur'ānic Manuscripts," in Karl Heinz Ohlig and Gerd-R. Puin, eds., *Die dunklen Anfänge* (Berlin: Hans Schiler, 2005), 293–316, 311.
15. See Daniel A. Madigan, *The Qur'ān's Self-Image* (Oxford: Princeton University Press, 2001), 40, for a discussion on how the placement of diacritics affects the theological doctrine of abrogation as applied to the Qur'ān's text at S. 2:106.

16. For example, twenty-one out of one hundred and fifty-nine variants were strictly diacritical and vowel mark variants from the records of Ibn Mas'ūd's codex for S. 2 in Jeffery, *Materials*, 25–32.

6

Rasm Variants

Rasm variants are variations to the consonantal line of text. As a category, these can consist of anything from a single letter up to lengthy portions of text. Islamic literature and tradition list many of these as having existed for the Qur'ān in the early centuries of Islam. Modaressi and Gilliot provide extensive lists from Islamic tradition of large portions that were thought to have once existed for the Qur'ān but for various reasons did not become part of the current text of the Qur'ān.[1] Variants collections like *MQQ*, *MQ*, and Jeffery also contain many records of variant letters, words, and even phrases. While there is such a great amount of variants listed in the secondary literature, the lack of such variants in extant manuscripts has led to various hypotheses to explain the disparity.

As will be seen in this chapter, the manuscripts surveyed for this study had some word variants and added and omitted letters. The variants will be presented and categorized according to their size and effect on the *rasm*. Preliminary thoughts as to the reasons behind the size of these variants will be given with more discussion following in part 3 concerning evaluation.

CLARIFYING ORTHOGRAPHY

At 14:40:1 in the Istanbul manuscript, an *alif* is added in the small space between two letters and it partially obscures the final letter of الصلوه . Also, at 14:41:1 in the same manuscript, an *alif* is added between the second *wāw* and the second *lām* in ولولدى. In both of these cases, these added *alifs* are perhaps to make an understood pronunciation of the long "*a*" explicit, or it could be to make this part of the text conform to what was then a new orthographical practice that required the addition of *alifs*. Such a practice is said to have been ordered by the Umayyad governor Ziyād b. Abīhi (d. 684) when he ordered two thousand *alifs* to be added to the text of the Qur'ān.[2] The added *alif* at 14:41:1 is notable for another reason. It makes the reading of this particular word match what is reported to have been the reading of Ibn Mas'ūd at this point in the text.[3]

VARIANTS AFFECTING GRAMMAR DUE TO AN ADDED LETTER

14:39:2 01-29.1- الكبير instead of الكبر

The added tooth letter, if not a copyist error, is most probably a *yā'* since the word does not make sense with any of the other possible letters of *nūn*, *tā'*, *thā'*, or *bā'*. Only one word with this extra letter makes sense in this context: الكبير. This word can be translated "very old age" as a plural form of كبر "old age."[4] Wright describes how verbal adjectives can be in the genitive plural form to convey a superlative idea.[5] This is possibly an intentional variant which draws attention to Ibrāhīm's extreme old age and indirectly to the miraculous nature of Isḥāq's birth. It could also be a simple copyist error because this kind of duplication is a common mistake in manuscript traditions.

However, in this manuscript, the added letter is carefully written with a different height from the first one, which is a common way that these letters with the same basic form are written when immediately beside one another. The height of one of the two is made different to distinguish the letters.[6] This letter could have been, then, not a slip of the pen but an intentional addition or a careful transcription of what was in a prior text. It also could possibly be a feature of a prior text-form, considering the antiquity of this particular manuscript. It is also a form found in other parts of the Qur'ān for extreme old age concerning biblical figures at S. 12:78 (Jacob) and 28:23 (Moses).

14:40:2 01-29.1- دعان instead of دعا

The *nūn* here was added after the initial text and is squeezed in at the top of the line of text just before the verse separator. It is not a sign for *ḥamza* because this is not done elsewhere in the manuscript and using *nūn* is not a normal method for marking *ḥamza* in early manuscripts. Also, it is not a symbol written by a later scribe designating an indistinct word because the word is distinct, and there is no accompanying word in the margin.[7]

Perhaps it is an intentional addition to make the form دعان which Penrice states is a form of دعانى , which occurs at S. 2:186 and is translated there, "He prays to me."[8] But, instead of the form being used as the noun with an attached pronoun acting as the indirect object as in 2:186, this would use the same form as a first person common plural possessive pronoun. This would make it an intentional variant to improve the text grammatically by making the normal interpretive translation "my prayer" to "our prayer," making it more explicit and in agreement with 14:40:1 where Ibrāhīm includes his offspring in his invocation. Though the significance of this added letter is not certain, it cannot be viewed as a copyist mistake because the way it is added in purposefully where there was insufficient space demonstrates it must have been an intentional addition. This kind of variant with the interchange of singular and plural forms is also found in the Qur'ānic palimpsests. Fedeli records two instances at S. 5:54 in the Bonhams palimpsest.[9]

A DIFFERENT WORD THROUGH THE ADDITION OF LETTERS?

14:40:2 BNF 370a- الادعا instead of دعا

The three letters الا were squeezed into and above the space between the two words دعا and تقبل. It is difficult to satisfactorily explain why these letters were deliberately inserted. Did the scribe think دعا , "invocation" needed to be made more definite by adding the article? Then why add the extra *alif*? Was it an attempt to change the word to الادعيا, "the adopted son"[10] to make it a possible Jewish or Christian gloss to Ismā'īl's' being Ibrāhīm's "half-son"? A form of the negative لا does not fit the context.[11] Hopkins documents a rare use of الا in the Arabic papyri of "only" which would make some sense, but it is hard to grasp how it would affect the meaning enough to add it intentionally.[12] These options all seem very unlikely. The addition of the three letters creates no new word form, so it is very difficult to decipher why it was intentionally added to the text, except to say that it was a symbol which had a definite meaning for the copyist which was then lost for later generations of readers.

WORD VARIANTS

This category is restricted to single words. Groups of words and phrases will be discussed in a later category.

Synonym using a Different Conjunction: *wa-* instead of *fa-*

14:37:5 BNF 328a- واجعل instead of فاجعل

These two conjunctions have similar but distinguishable meanings. *Wāw-* (و) "joins equivalent sentences and clauses," whereas *fā'-* (ف) indicates sequential thought, "and then, and so, consequently, for."[13] At this point in the text it has a significant effect on meaning. As *fā'-*, the standard reading, it states the answer to prayer Ibrāhīm explicitly desired from Allah in reward for settling his offspring near the sanctuary: "*So* fill some hearts among men with love towards them." It is an explicit prayer request. As *wāw-*, the variant, it gives another reason for settling his offspring near the sanctuary, so that he can perform the *sālāt* prayers "*and* fill some hearts among men with love towards them," in other words, so that the people will be more inclined to Abraham's family if they pray at the sanctuary. It is a difference of emphasis and the direct action of Allah. The standard reading fits the context better, and this kind of variant is observed so infrequently that it could very well be a copyist mistake. The infrequency of this kind of variant can be seen in the fact that out of 76 occurrences of *fā'-* and 228 occurrences of *wāw-* in the selected verses of these combined manuscripts, only one occurrence of this variant was observed.[14]

However, this kind of variant is not unknown for other locations in the Qur'ān. Rabb and Dutton both observe that the reverse of this variant, substituting a *fā'-* for a *wāw-*, occurs in BL Or. 2165 at S. 26:217 with the word وتو.[15] They consider this to be a major textual variant indicative of Syrian and Medinan usage. The Topkapi Codex has at least two instances of this kind of variant. At 26:217, the same variant occurs that was mentioned by Rabb and Dutton for BL Or. 2165.[16] At S. 91:15 a *wāw-* is substituted for a *fā'-* in فلا .[17] The few palimpsests examined so far also present four of this particular substitution of conjunctions as well as recording the substitution of an additional conjunction.[18]

A Missing Word

14:37:2 BNF 340c- غير زرعى instead of غير ذى زرع

The word ذى is missing and the following word زرع has an added ى to make it زرعى. Concerning the missing word ذى, this word is the genitive form of the nominal demonstrative ذو, with the meaning of "the possessor of" or "endowed with,"[19] in this case specifying that the valley did not possess sown grain, that is, it was a barren valley. It is a particle that is always used in construct with a complement,[20] in this case, the word زرع. With it missing, the meaning of the sentence is not affected. Hopkins notes that by the time Classical Arabic was formalized, this word had already passed out of living speech, being used only in a small number of set expressions.[21] Perhaps in the region where BNF 340c was originally copied, it had passed out of living speech even in the stock expressions. Its omission would affect the oral recitation of this passage, and it is not listed as a variant in any of the Companions' versions as recorded in the major collections. It is also interesting that there is not a correction written in the margin beside the omission.

Concerning the attached *yā* on زرعى, it could be a first person singular attached pronoun and would give the meaning, "in a valley without *my* sown corn," or, "in a valley without *my* offspring." The first option does not make sense in the context. The second option is intriguing but awkward. It would make the verse mean, "I have made some of my offspring to dwell in a valley without my offspring." Perhaps this could serve to emphasize that Ibrāhīm was settling his offspring away from their tribal kinship relationships, or settling one son away from the other son. Though possible, these explanations seem unlikely. Also, it should be noted that "offspring" is not a normal meaning of زرع. Lane mentions it as one meaning of the noun form of this word with all of the others having reference to crops.[22] If this was meant as "offspring," it is an intentional variant, but it is more likely a copyist error, or a stylistic convention for writing final *'ayn.*

It is notable that this is the most significant occurrence of a missing word in all of the manuscripts surveyed and supports the general observation that the text in most extant manuscripts is remarkably stable. However, the Mingana palimpsest contains examples of added and omitted words.[23] The palimpsest pages that Fedeli examined had added and omitted words and different phrases as well.[24] Additional significance concerning the palimpsests can be seen in that these were not accidental omissions that were corrected but were texts with variants of much greater substance than can observed elsewhere in extant manuscripts. The existence of different words, including added and omitted words, can be found in the lists of what the Companions' collections reportedly contained. Some of these records also include different phrases, as for example Jeffery reports regarding Ibn Mas'ūd's version at S. 2:198, 213, 214, 229, 233, and 240.[25] Larger units of phrases and portions are also asserted to have existed for the Qur'ān prior to its reputed standardization under the Caliph 'Uthmān.[26]

In line with the observations just made, the following types of variants were not observed in the Qur'ān manuscripts surveyed in this study. They seem also to be rarely found in other Qur'ān manuscripts, even though they are common in other textual traditions and are reported to have existed in the Islamic secondary literature.[27] Even though they are absent from the portions of the manuscripts that were surveyed exhaustively, they are discussed here because of the possible significance of their conspicuous absence from the Qur'ān manuscript tradition.

TRANSPOSITION VARIANTS

Transpositions are words or phrases juxtaposed in a line or between lines of text. No transpositions were observed in the manuscripts surveyed. There are records that at one time they did exist in the Qur'ān. Jeffery records that a transposition of text was asserted to have existed in Ibn Mas'ūd's codex at 14:24.[28] Three examples of transposition can be observed in the Bonhams palimpsest at 5:41, 5:48, and 5:50.[29] One of the manuscripts in this survey did, however, have a sizable portion of a line that had been erased and rewritten.[30]

CONFLATION OF PHRASES

Conflation is the combining of particular parts of two different phrases into a new phrase. No examples of this kind of variant were observed in the manuscripts surveyed. However, one writer has observed an example of this in an early Islamic theological treatise quoting a verse of the Qur'ān attributed to the early Qur'ān scholar, Ḥasan al-Baṣrī.[31] At one point the author of this treatise mentions a verse that cannot be found in the current text of the Qur'ān as if it was part of the text of the Qur'ān. The supposed verse is:

> Thus the word of thy Lord is realized against the *ungodly* that *they are the inhabitants of the Fire.*

This appears to be a conflation of two other verses, S. 10:33 and S. 40:6.

> S. 10:33: Thus the word of thy Lord is realized against *the ungodly* that they believe not.
> S. 40:6: Thus the word of thy Lord is realized against the unbelievers that *they are the inhabitants of the Fire.*

This particular conflation is not found in an extant manuscript. Others like it are also reported in the works of the early grammarian Sībawayhi.[32] There are also examples to be found in Jeffery's collection attributed to Ibn Mas'ūd and Ubayy ibn Ka'b.[33] As to ones found in actual manuscripts, Brockett mentions two conflationary passages in Qur'ān manuscripts in the collections of St. Andrews and Edinburgh New College.[34] Brockett also mentioned that he had seen others in extant manuscripts, though he gave no details.[35] Fedeli documents a section of S. 5:44 in the Bonham's palimpsest that has different words and phrases from the standard text. This cannot be considered conflation strictly in that the different individual phrases cannot be clearly identified with other Qur'ānic phrases.[36] They do, however, demonstrate a more fluid text that retains phrases and wording that can be identified with portions of the standard text which is combined with other material.[37] The Qur'ān's text seems to have had an early point of intentional fixation which prevented the formation of conflationary readings arising in the course of later textual transmission. Rather than being the product of editing variants among written texts, Qur'ānic conflations from the early period are possibly vestiges of an early accepted flexibility from oral composition and transmission dynamics, which was not acceptable later on.

ADDITIONAL WORDS AND PHRASES

Among other textual traditions, this category has the potential for providing the greatest changes to the text and the greatest changes of meaning in the text. There is also wide scope for both intentional and unintentional variants. Through inattention, scribes have been known to omit entire lines and portions of text because of similar endings of words and lines. Also, there was the temptation to improve style and grammar, and perhaps even to strengthen a dogmatic belief by making the text say more clearly what it was understood to mean.[38]

It is significant to note that no variants of this type were observed in the Qur'ānic manuscripts surveyed. The longest variant of this type to exist in an extant manuscript known to this author is in the *scriptio inferior* of the Bonhams palimpsest, and it is a complete sentence found in a verse that also has an additional phrase.[39] The Mingana palimpsest contains examples of added and omitted words.[40] The Bonhams and Fogg palimpsest pages that Fedeli examined had added and omitted words and different phrases as well.[41] In the Mingana, Bonhams, and Fogg palimpsests alone twelve examples of different words can be observed, and three of those twelve in the Bonhams manuscript involve two phrases and an added sentence.[42] The palimpsest page E. Puin examined also has these kinds of additions and omissions.[43] Helali observes that the form of text found in the inferior text of the largest known Qur'ānic palimpsest does not match any known pattern of variants for any recitation system of the Qur'ān.[44]

The additional significance of the palimpsests can be seen in that these were not accidental omissions that were corrected by the original scribe but were texts with variants of major substance as part of basic form of the text.

The significant lack of omissions and additions of any size in the great majority of early Qur'ān manuscripts can be taken as another confirmation of an early and concerted program to establish a precise consonantal text for the Qur'ān, or at the least, a later historical impetus to preserve only manuscripts with a particular consonantal text. These provide further evidence that an early and extensive editorial project was made on the text of the Qur'ān, or at least major portions of what was early regarded as sacred material.

It is significant that these larger variant portions found only in the palimpsests match the kinds of variants that are reported in some of the literature and traditions concerning the collection of the Qur'ān. It is also significant that the exact variants they contain are greater in number and extent that what is reported in that literature to have once existed. The suggestion was made by Fischer in the 1940s that the variants in the Islamic records were pious fictions.[45] Though there is a degree of invention in the accounts of variants (as has been ably demonstrated by Rippin[46]), the testimony of the palimpsests, and especially the Fogg palimpsest that contains a variant that is also attributed to Ibn Mas'ūd, should instead be viewed as containing authentic memory of such variants, and also that the phenomenon was likely much more extensive and diverse than what has been preserved in the secondary records or extant manuscripts. This is also confirmed by Islamic tradition in that the other variants in collections that are known to have existed are said to have contained many more variants than are found in Ibn Abī Dāwūd's collection that Jeffery published.[47]

This is an indication that the literature as it stands is not a complete record of the variants once existing in the Qur'ānic manuscript tradition; that the tradition at one time did indeed contain many more variants than are now extant in the period just prior to the inferior texts of the extant palimpsests and also very possibly in Islam's first three centuries prior to Ibn Mujāhid (d. 934/323). There is the definite possibility that these kinds of variants were much more common during the earliest period of the transmission of the Qur'ān than was the case later on. Their disappearance from the later stages of the manuscript tradition is evidence that they represent an early stage in the editing and standardization of the text.

NOTES

1. Hossein Modarressi, "Early Debates on the Integrity of the Qur'an," *Studia Islamica*, 77:5–39; Claude Gilliot, "Un Verset Manquant du Coran ou Réputè Tel," Marie-Thérèse Urvoy, *En Hommage au Père Jacques Jomier, O.P.* (Paris: CERF, 2002), 73–100.

2. Efim A. Rezvan, *The Qur'ān of 'Uthmān* (St. Petersburg: St. Petersburg Centre for Oriental Studies, 2004), 68.

3. Arthur Jeffery, *Materials for the History of the Text of the Qur'ān* (Leiden: Brill, 1937), 52.

4. A. Arne Ambros and Stephan Procházka, *A Concise Dictionary of Koranic Arabic* (Weisbaden: Reichert Verlag, 2004), 234; Lane, under كبر; John Penrice, *A Dictionary and Glossary of the Kor-ān* (London: Curzon Press, 1975), 123.

5. W. Wright, *A Grammar of the Arabic Language* (Cambridge: Cambridge University Press, 1986), 2:218.

6. For example, manuscript 01-29.1 and Or. 2165, manuscripts with very different Ḥijāzī scripts, both do this with ربنا at 14:37:1 and 14:38:1.

7. Wright, *Grammar,* 1:26.

8. Penrice, *Dictionary,* 48.

9. Alba Fedeli, "Early Evidences of Variant Readings in Qur'ānic Manuscripts," in Karl Heinz-Ohlig and Gerd-R. Puin, eds., *Die dunklen Anfänge* (Berlin: Hans Schiler, 2005), 293–316, S. 5:54; 301.

10. Penrice, *Dictionary*, 48.

11. Penrice, *Dictionary*, 7.

12. Simon Hopkins, *Studies in the Grammar of Early Arabic* (Oxford: Oxford University Press, 1984), 259, §324.

13. Wolfdietrich Fischer, *A Grammar of Classical Arabic* (London: Yale University Press, 2002), 175–76.

14. Another confirmation is that only one occurrence of it is recorded in all of Surah 2 in Jeffery's materials concerning Ibn Mas'ūd 's text at S. 2:283. Jeffery, *Materials,* 32.

15. BL Or. 2165 f. 77a, l. 7. Intisar A. Rabb, "Non-Canonical Readings of the Qur'an: Recognition and Authenticity (The Himsī Reading)," *JQS*, VIII:2:84–127, 90; Yasin Dutton, "Some Notes on the British Library's 'Oldest Qur'an Manuscript' (Or. 2165)," *JQS*, VI:1:43–71, 45.

16. Dr. Tayyar Altikulac, *Al-Mushaf al-Sharif, Attributed to 'Uthmān bin 'Affān* (Istanbul: IRCICA, 2007), 88, 483, f. 240a.

17. Altikulac, *Al-Mushaf,* 89, 807, f. 402a.

18. Fedeli, "Evidences," S. 5:43; 301; Alphonse Mingana and Agnes Smith Lewis, *Leaves From Three Ancient Qur'āns, Possibly Pre-'Uthmānic* (Cambridge: Cambridge University Press, 1914), no. 2, xxxvii; no. 9, xxxviii; and no. 18, xxxix. Fedeli also records another interchange: *wa* for *'innā*: Fedeli, "Evidences," S. 5:44; 301.

19. Fischer, *Grammar,* 148–49; Penrice, *Dictionary,* 53.

20. Penrice, *Dictionary,* 53.

21. Hopkins, *Studies,* 160, note 1 for §164.

22. Lane, *Lexicon,* زرع.

23. Mingana and Smith Lewis, *Leaves,* xxxix, no. 30, xl, as verified by Alba Fedeli, "Mingana and the Manuscript of Mrs. Agnes Smith Lewis, One Century Later," *MO* 11, 3, September 2005, 3–77.

24. Fedeli, "Evidences," 300–305.

25. Jeffery, *Materials,* 29–30. This writer did a brief survey through Surah 2 and found 55 word variants, 6 of them involving phrases.
26. Modarressi, "Debates"; Gilliot, "Manquant."
27. Keith Small, "Textual Variants in the New Testament and Qur'anic Manuscript Traditions," in Markus Groß and Karl Heinz-Ohlig, *Schlaglichter* (Berlin: Hans Schiler, 2008), 572–93; Keith E. Small, *Mapping a New Country: Textual Criticism and Qur'an Manuscripts* (Brunel: London School of Theology, 2008).
28. Jeffery, *Materials,* 51.
29. Fedeli, "Evidences," 300.
30. This is at 14:39:2-3 in manuscript BN 370a. It will be discussed in detail in chapter 8 on corrections.
31. Michael Cook, *The Koran: A Very Short Introduction* (Oxford: Oxford University Press, 2000), 118–19.
32. Andrew Rippin, *Approaches to the History of the Interpretation of the Qur'ān* (Oxford: Clarendon, 1988), 32, note 5.
33. Jeffery, *Materials,* 97 for S. 56:10–12.
34. Adrian Alan Brockett, *Studies in Two Transmissions of the Qur'ān*. PhD thesis, University of St. Andrews, Department of Arabic Studies, 1984, 150.
35. Rippin, *Approaches*, 32, note 5.
36. Fedeli, "Evidences," 301.
37. Comparatively, in the New Testament textual tradition, conflations are particularly a mark of the later Byzantine text-type which came about as generations of Byzantine editors chose from available variant readings to form a smooth and more complete text. B. M. Metzger and Bart D. Ehrman, *The Text of the New Testament* (New York: Oxford University Press, 2005), 279. This was a more informal editing process that occurred especially in the ninth centuries and eleventh centuries C.E. to meet the practical requirements of the liturgical use of older New Testament manuscripts as they were adapted for use as lectionaries. Timothy J. Ralston, *The Majority Text and Byzantine Texttype Development: The Significance of a Non-Parametric Method of Data Analysis for the Exploration of Manuscript Traditions* (Dallas Theological Seminary, New Testament Studies, 1994), 289.
38. Examples of all of these phenomena were observed in New Testament manuscripts. Small, *Mapping*.
39. Fedeli, "Evidences," S. 5:44; 301.
40. Mingana and Smith Lewis, *Leaves,* xxxix, no. 30, xl, as verified by Fedeli, "Mingana," 7.
41. Fedeli, "Evidences," 300–305.
42. Mingana and Smith Lewis, *Leaves,* no. 3, xxxvii; no. 15, xxxviii; no. 17, xxxviii; no. 18, xxxix; no. 30, xxxix. Fedeli, "Evidences," 4x in S. 5:44; 1x in S. 5:46; 301–2; S. 2:222, 305.
43. Elisabeth Puin, "Ein früher Koranpalimpsest aus San'ā' (DAM 01-27.1)," Markus Groß and Karl Heinz-Ohlig, eds., *Schlaglichter* (Berlin: Hans Schiler, 2008), 461–93.
44. Asma Helali, "The Sanaa Palimpsest: Introductory Remarks to Philological and Literary Aspects," The Qur'an: Text, History & Culture, SOAS, University of London, 2009, 14 November 2009.

45. Fischer, "Grammatisch," 5–6, note 4.

46. See for instance Andrew Rippin, "Qur'an 21:95: 'A ban is upon any town,'" *JSS*, XXIV:43–53 Andrew Rippin, "Qur'ān 7.40: 'Until the camel passes through the eye of the needle,'" *Arabica*, XXVII:107–13/

47. Jeffery mentions four others that have disappeared. Jeffery, *Materials,* x.

7

Variant Verse Divisions

A notable feature of even the earliest extant Qur'ān manuscripts is that there are symbols designating division at the end of meaningful sense units. These sense units have for the most part come to be regarded as the individual verses of the Qur'ān and the symbols as verse separators.[1] These symbols usually consist of various clusters of dots or strokes, often in groups of three or more.

A common view is that the earliest Qur'ān manuscripts did not contain such verse divisions. However, if the Ḥijāzi manuscripts are the earliest extant Qur'ān manuscripts, this view is inaccurate.[2] Also, contrary to a common view, there is little evidence that their use was gradually added to the manuscript tradition. They are present in the earliest extant manuscripts.[3] All of the Ḥijāzi manuscripts used in this survey from the earliest period had them.[4] Even a Ḥijāzi palimpsest page has them on its *scriptio inferior*.[5] Of the early Kufic manuscripts surveyed for this study, one did not have them, 01-20.x, but other early Kufic manuscripts have them.[6] This is also borne out through a survey of the available pictures of Qur'ān manuscripts from Ṣan'ā'. On the UNESCO CD and in the manuscripts surveyed for this research, all of the vertical format first century A.H. manuscripts have single verse markers. On the UNESCO CD, most of the horizontal format manuscripts given a first century A.H. date do not have them, though many do.[7] There also seems to have been a movement, especially in the Kufic manuscript tradition, to discontinue their use after Islam's first century. The great majority of Qur'ān manuscripts from the first three centuries that do not have them are Kufic ones from the second and third centuries A.H.[8] Also, if the Ṣan'ā' manuscripts are an indication, the earliest Kufic ones often had them as well.

There are types of verse counting symbols that did gradually enter the entire manuscript tradition starting within the first century A.H. These were special symbols that were grouped roughly every five or ten verses. Also, sometimes these were added later to texts that did not originally have them. As the manuscript tradition progressed, these often became the objects of special artistic embellishment. Most of the manuscripts used in this study had individual verse separators. All of them had ten verse markers, and many of them also had five verse markers. Some of the manuscripts had all three types.

The Islamic tradition recognizes different systems of the placement of all three types of verse markers and associates them with regional metropolitan centers of Qur'ān recitation.[9] Spitaler compiled a survey of these from Islamic tradition and delineated 21 different systems that were supposedly in use during Islam's first three centuries.[10] An important task in Qur'ān manuscript studies is to attempt to match the system of a particular manuscript to one of the systems described in the literature. One scholar has based much of his argument that two of the earliest extant manuscripts which were used in this survey, BL Or. 2165 and BNF 328a, have the mutual provenance of Umayyad Damascus.[11] The numbering systems in these two manuscripts are closely aligned to a system that the literature asserts was in use in Syria during the Umayyad period.

Another factor that complicates the systems of verse division is that some manuscripts have multiple systems, usually the result of a later scribe correcting the initially inscribed system. In the manuscripts surveyed, BL Or. 12884 has the most easily discerned second system in that both of its verse counting systems are noted by gold illuminations, rosettes for one set, rectangles for the other. Déroche observes that in BNF 328a there are three systems, the initial one and then two systems imposed by later correctors.[12] Rezvan notes that for manuscript E 20, a later corrector added additional verse separators to those originally inscribed, including ones noting every ten, hundred, and two hundred *āyāt*.[13] The Topkapi Codex also has verse separators that were added in later.[14] Rabb notes that for BL Or. 2165, the initial system was corrected by two scribes who added in ten and hundred verse symbols according to a different verse numbering system. He also notes that it has a symbol for every seven verses.[15]

Close examination of the systems these manuscripts used bring out some important observations.[16] No two manuscripts had precisely parallel counting systems, and none of them exactly matched the systems described by Spitaler. BL Or. 2165, BNF 328a, and BNF 325a did have almost identical single verse systems to each other, and they were the closest to each other of any of the manuscripts. These three are close to Spitaler's Damascus category. Rabb asserts that overall BL Or. 2165 is closer to a system from Ḥims.[17] BNF 330a, 331, Meknes, and BL Or. 12884a follow the Kufan system of verse numbering most closely.[18] There were many manuscripts that did not follow any of the systems described in Spitaler. These were BNF 326a, 332, 333c, 340c, 343, and 370a. The relatively late manuscript, BL Or. 12884, appears to have two systems notated, one in rough agreement to the Kufan system, and the other very much out of step with all reported systems. There is even less agreement between the placement of five and ten verse markers. This lack of precise correspondence with recorded systems has been observed for other manuscripts as well. Rezvan notes that the verse division system in E 20 does not match any of the known systems.[19] The Topkapi manuscript, though similar to the current main system in use has its own peculiarities.[20] This phenomenon raises the question as to whether the systems collated by Spitaler were actual systems in use in specific geographic areas, whether they are testimony to tendencies of geographic practices, or whether they are a later attempt to project a hypothetical order back onto a period which in fact had no such formal organization of reading systems. If they are in fact hypothetical, then their use for identifying the original provenance of a manuscript is greatly diminished.

Some of the manuscripts had no single verse separators: 01-20.x, BNF 333c, 340c, and 343. The total number of verses varied widely. The Cairo text for S. 14 is divided into fifty-two verses according to the Kufan system in Spitaler's tables. BNF 326a had this same amount of text divided into forty-seven verses. BNF 328a, 330a, and 334c had fifty-six. BL Or. 12884b had the same portion of text divided into sixty-five verses, twenty-six of these in unique positions not shared with any of the other manuscripts. Surah 14:35–41 as a unit started anywhere from verse counts 14:31 to 38, and BL Or. 12884b had this portion starting at 14:48. The overall picture is that there was a great variety of counting systems in use, and a variety greater than the Islamic tradition recognizes. Puin also observed this phenomenon among the early Ṣan'ā' manuscripts.[21]

Also, if these separators are more than simple markers for designating sections of text but are also marking a pause in recitation, or their placement affects the rhyming pattern, then these varying systems represent various ways of reciting the text. These different systems would have had a very audible effect on the recitation of the text. A careful look through the chart of single verse separators shows that individual verses were of varying length between the systems. Almost always, the individual verse separators are placed at the end of a sentence, or at a place that semantically can function as the end of a sentence. Some of them are placed at the end of what are phrases in compound sentences, or even other locations that affect the meaning of the verse. Four such instances were observed in the manuscripts surveyed for all of S. 14, and only one of these was in S. 14:35–41. The four are as follows:

1. 14:14, manuscript BNF 332: This has a verse marker after the word ذلك, breaking up a phrase. This is perhaps a mistake in the placement of this marker, because there seems to be no grammatical, stylistic, or exegetical reason for breaking the verse at this point.
2. 14:25, manuscript BL Or. 12884b: Placed at the end of a phrase, if this marker denotes a new sentence, then the meaning of the text is changed slightly, placing more emphasis on Allah commanding a tree to bear its fruit.
3. 14:33, manuscript BL Or. 12884b: Placed at the end of a phrase, if this marker denotes a new sentence, then the meaning of the text is changed significantly. Instead of, "and He has made the sun and the moon, both constantly pursuing their courses, to be of service to you," it would read, "And He has made the sun and the moon constantly pursue their courses. And it is of service to you."
4. 14:39, manuscript BNF 331: Here a 10 verse marker is placed in the middle of a sentence, breaking a phrase. Here is how the sentence reads with the marker in it: "All the praises and thanks be to Allah, who has given me in old age (10VM) Ishmael and Isaac." There seems to be no grammatical function for its placement. If 10 verse markers were used to mark a pause in pronunciation, then it is also hard to discern an advantage for placing it at this point.

Though these variable placements do not change any rhyme patterns, the differences in verse endings would have an effect on pauses and reciting the text to make the meaning clear. Nelson remarks concerning one of the rules of correct recitation (*waqf wa l-ibidā'*):[22]

> The types of pauses are characterized by the syntactic and semantic completeness or incompleteness of the preceding phrase and determine whether the reciter is to stop, to continue with what follows, or to back up to bridge a break in meaning or syntax.

If the placement of these verse separators affects recitation, perhaps this is a confirmation of the assertions of Jeffery and Rabb, both citing al-Jazarī's *Nashr*, that before the Qur'ān recitation systems had been limited to the Seven during the time of Ibn Mujāḥid (d. 324/936), there were at least fifty different recitation systems in use.[23] The variety exhibited in these manuscripts of verse systems confirms this situation and would suggest that Qur'ān recitation, even based on the 'Uthmānic consonantal text, demonstrated a much more fluid and variable situation than the traditions report.[24]

NOTES

1. Gerd-R. Puin, "Observations on Early Qur'an Manuscripts in San'ā'," Stefan Wild, ed., *The Qur'an as Text* (Leiden: Brill, 1996), 107–11, 109.

2. Contrary to Azami, the very earliest Qur'ān manuscripts almost all contain these verse separators. He is mistaken in the assertion that the manuscript, the Samarkand Kufic manuscripts held in Tashkent, is devoid of them (M. M. Al-Azami, *The History of the Qur'anic Text* [Leicester: UK Islamic Academy, 2003], 111). They are readily apparent in the microfilm copy used for this study and in the photographic reproductions of the manuscripts produced in 1905.

3. Al-Azami, *History,* 111.

4. Istanbul, 01-28.1, 01-29.1, Or. 2165; BNF 328a, 326a.

5. Sam Fogg, *Islamic Calligraphy* (London: Sam Fogg, 2003), 9, visible between the و and ه in تحموه on line 12.

6. For example, SamK, BNF 325a, 330a, 331, 332.

7. This CD was searched using the indices prepared by Keith Small and Elisabeth Puin: Keith E. Small, "UNESCO CD of San'a' MSS: Qur'ān MSS Contents," *MO* 12:2:65–72; Keith E. Small and Elisabeth Puin, "UNESCO CD of San'ā' MSS: Part III," *MO* 13:2:59–71.

8. François Déroche, *The Abbasid Tradition* (London: Nour Foundation, 1992), 22.

9. Puin, "Observations," 109.

10. Anton Spitaler, *Die Verszählung des Koran* (München: Verlag der Bayerischen Akademie der Wissenschaften, 1935).

11. Yasin Dutton, "Red Dots, Green Dots, Yellow Dots & Blue: Some Reflections on the Vocalisation of early Qur'anic Manuscripts—Part I," *JQS*, 1999, I:I:115–40; Yasin Dutton, "Red Dots, Green Dots, Yellow Dots, Blue," *JQS*, 2000, II: I:1–24.

12. François Déroche, *La transmission écrite du Coran dans les débuts de l'islam: Le codex Parisino-petropolitanus* (Leiden: Brill, 2009), 78.

13. Efim A. Rezvan, *The Qur'ān of 'Uthmān* (St. Petersburg: St. Petersburg Centre for Oriental Studies, 2004), 65, 66.

14. Dr. Tayyar Altikulac, *Al-Mushaf al-Sharif, Attributed to 'Uthmān bin 'Affān* (Istanbul: IRCICA, 2007), 79.

15. Intisar A. Rabb, "Non-Canonical Readings of the Qur'an: Recognition and Authenticity (the Himsī Reading)," *JQS*, VIII:2:84–127, 99.

16. See the "Qur'ānic Verse Numbering Systems Charts," in Keith Small, *Mapping a New Country: Textual Variants and Qur'ān Manuscripts*, PhD thesis, Brunel University, 2008, Appendix M, 373.

17. Rabb, "Non-Canonical," 95, 99.

18. BL Or. 12884 seems to have two systems of numbering single verses. They are designated Or. 12884a and Or. 12884b in the chart.

19. Rezvan, *Qur'ān,* 68.

20. Altikulac, *Al-Mushaf,* 86.

21. Puin, "Observations," 110.

22. Kristina Nelson, *The Art of Reciting the Qur'an* (Austin, Texas: University of Texas Press, 1985), 19.

23. Arthur Jeffery, *Materials for the History of the Text of the Qur'ān* (Leiden: Brill, 1937), 2, note 3 citing *Nashr*, 1:90; Rabb, "Non-Canonical," 101, 124, note 114, citing *Nashr*, 1:34–37. Forty systems in addition to the canonical 10 are mentioned.

24. *Christopher Melchert disagrees with this suggestion and thinks that though it is a plausible guess that verse division was influenced by recitation conventions, it is actually a separate question and generated a separate literature—the literature of 'adad āy al-Qur'ān.* This was expressed in a written note to the author concerning this portion of text.

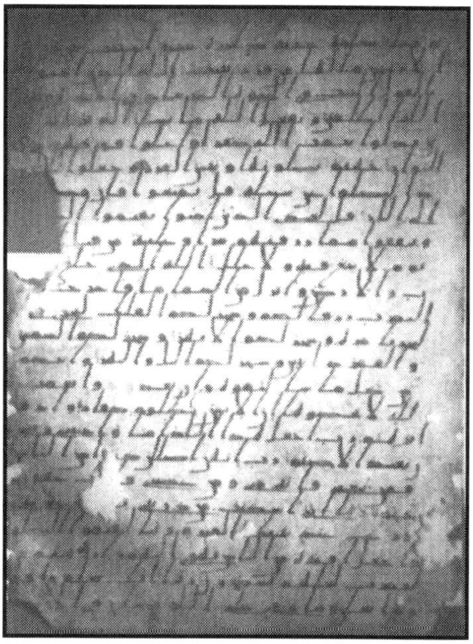

Figure 1. Istanbul Manuscript: IST TIEM SE 54, fol. 11A, 14:26-38. Used with the permission of the Fondazione Ferne Noseda.

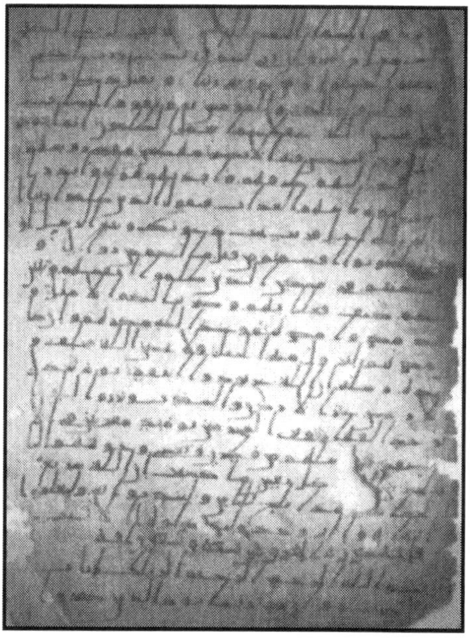

Figure 2. Istanbul Manuscript: IST TIEM SE 54, fol. 11A, 14:38-15:2. Used with the permission of the Fondazione Ferne Noseda.

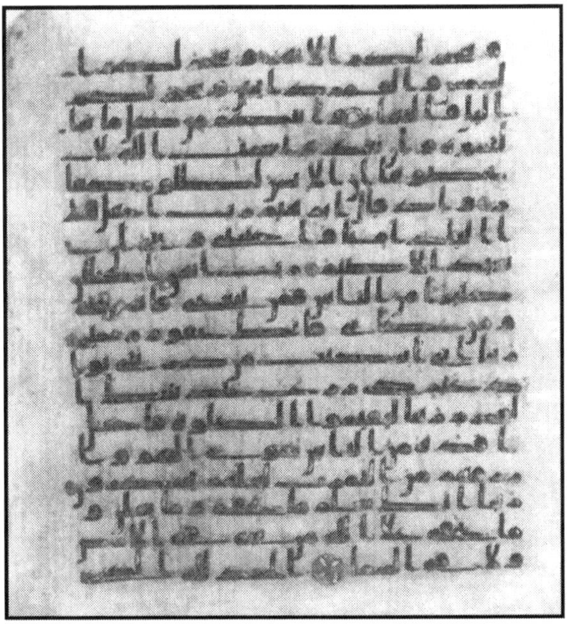

Figure 3. Topkapi Qur'ān, fol. 172b, S. 14:32-39. Used with the permission of IRCICA.

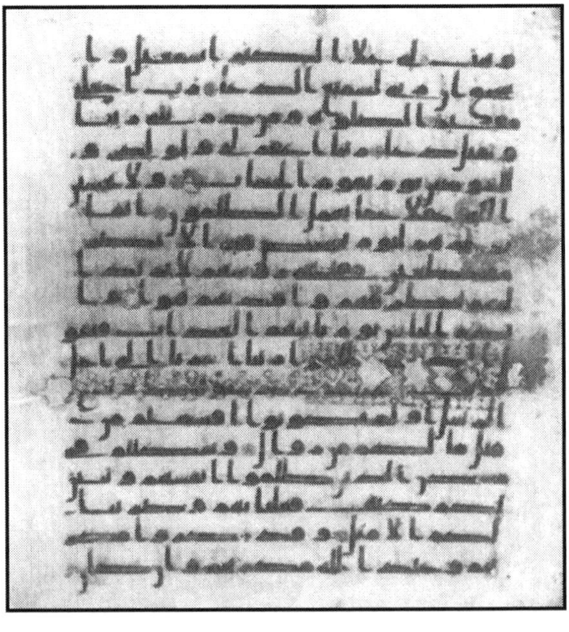

Figure 4. Topkapi Qur'ān, fol. 173a, S. 14:39-46. Used with the permission of IRCICA.

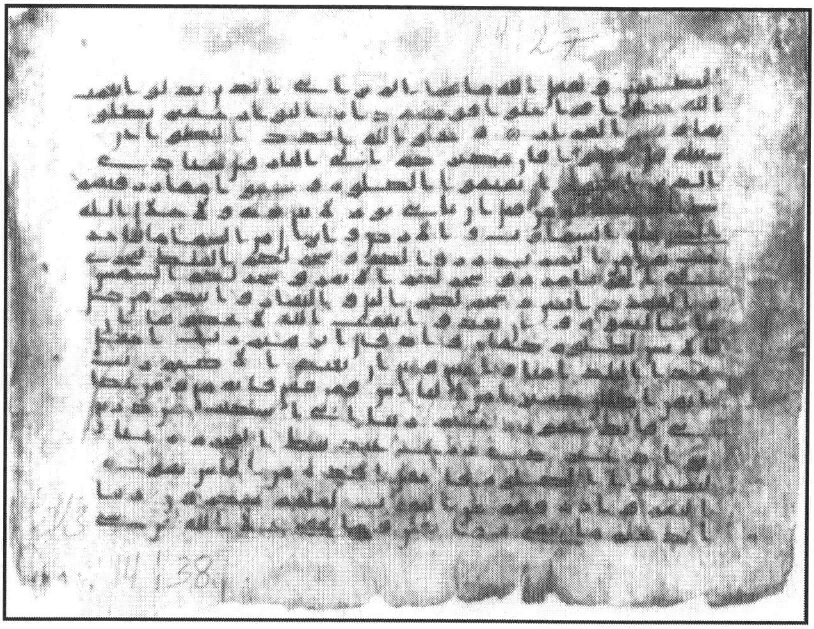

Figure 5. San'ā' Manuscript 01-20.x, S. 14:27-38. Used with the permission of GRP.

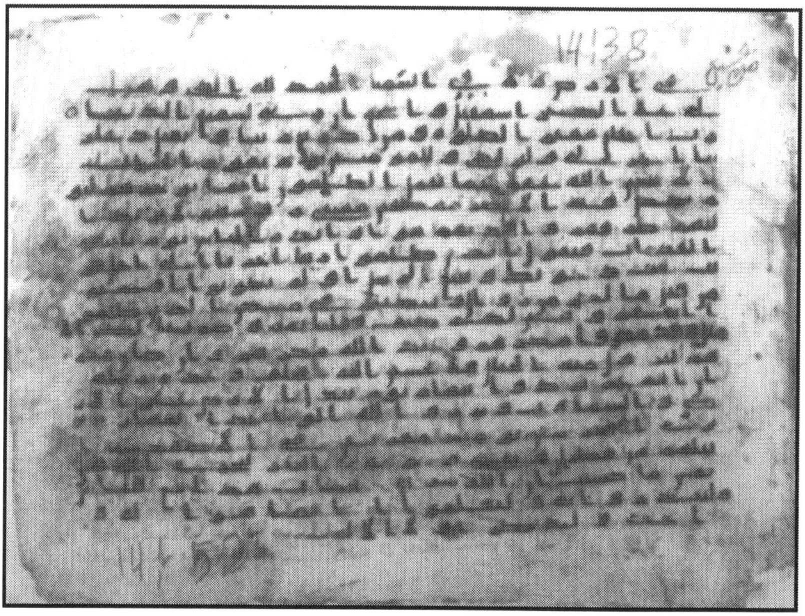

Figure 6. San'ā' Manuscript 01-20.x, S. 14:38-52. Used with the permission of GRP.

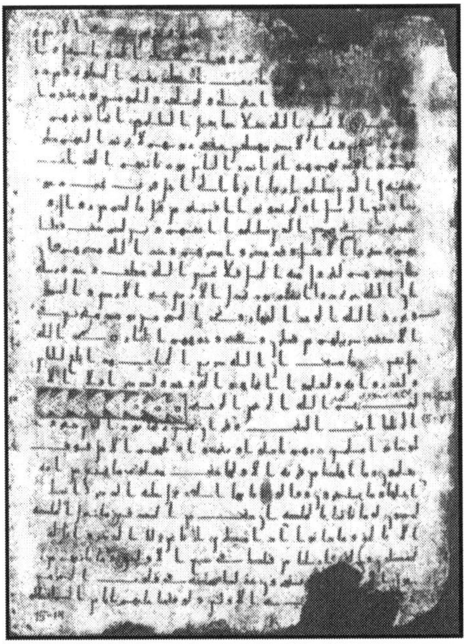

Figure 7. San'ā' Manuscript 01-28.1, S. 14:21-37. Used with the permission of GRP.

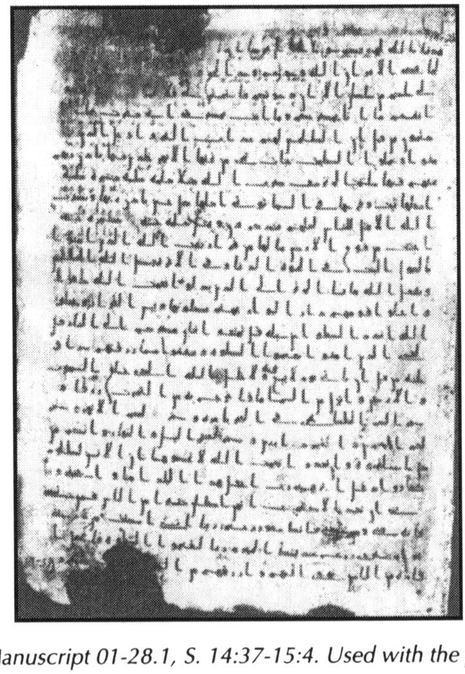

Figure 8. San'ā' Manuscript 01-28.1, S. 14:37-15:4. Used with the permission of GRP.

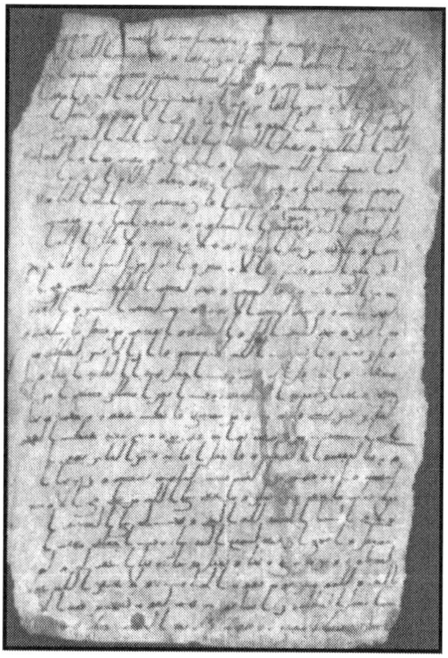

Figure 9. San'ā' Manuscript 01-29.1, S. 14:24-43. Used with the permission of GRP.

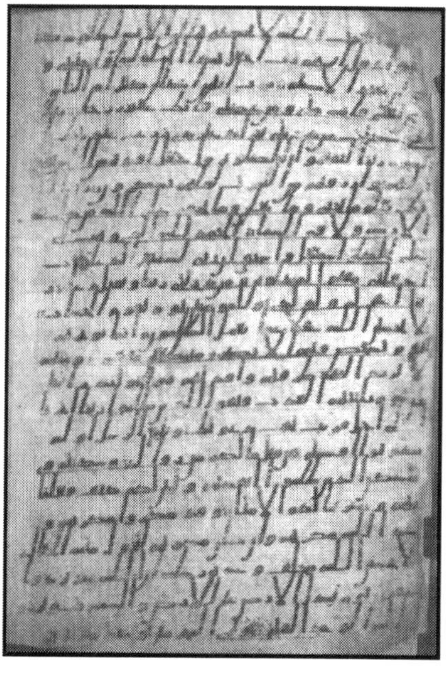

Figure 10. BL Or. 2165, fol. 31b, S. 14:34-49. © The British Library Board.

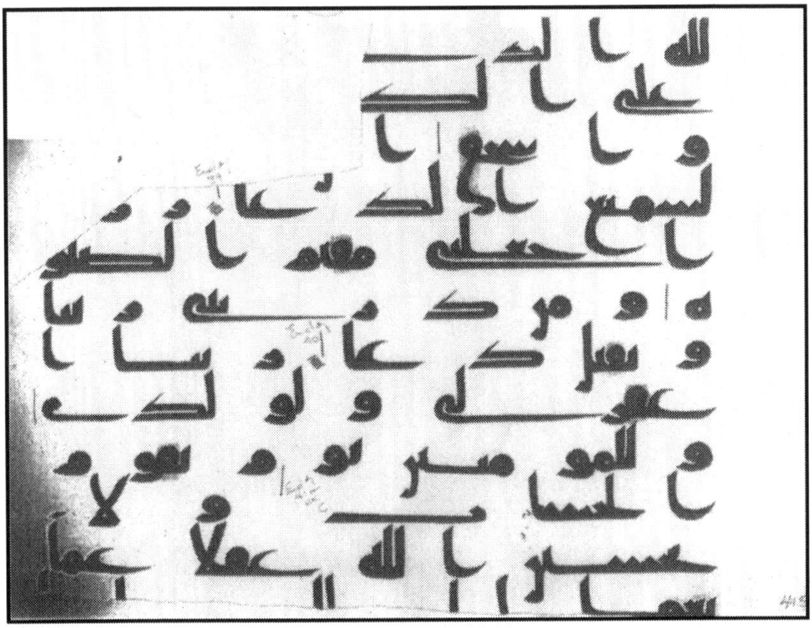

Figure 11. Samarkand Qur'ān, fol. 206, S. 14:39-42. Public Domain.

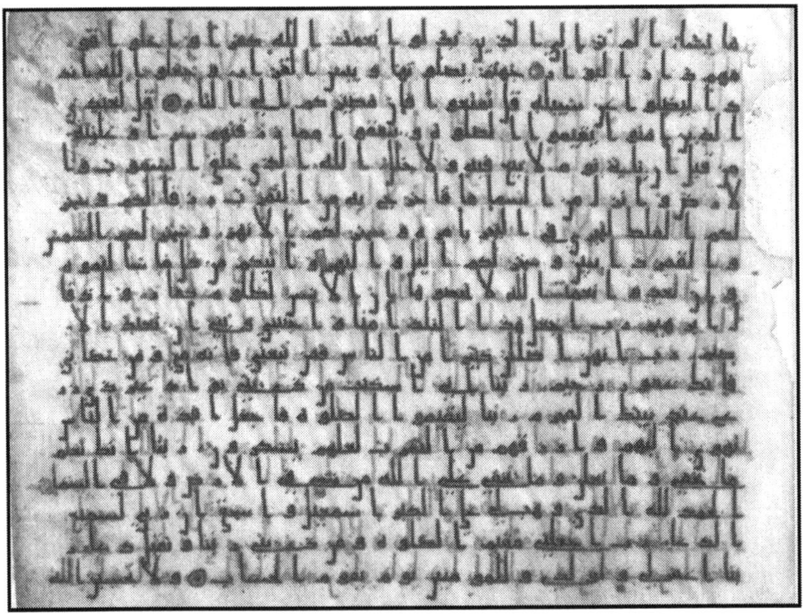

Figure 12. BNF 325a, fol. 4r, S. 14:27-41. Used with the permission of the BnF.

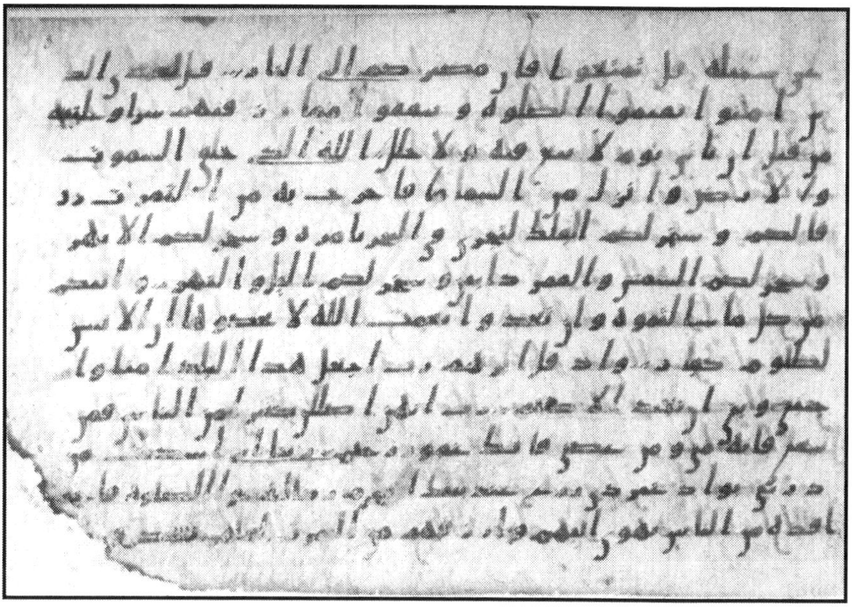

Figure 13. BNF 326a, fol. 3r, S. 14:30-37. Used with the permission of the BnF.

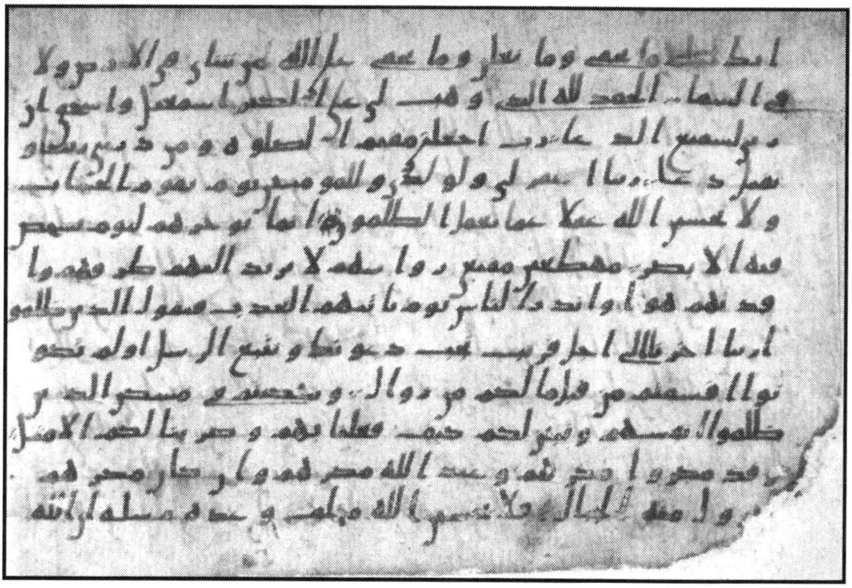

Figure 14. BNF 326a, fol. 3r, S. 14:37-43. Used with the permission of the BnF.

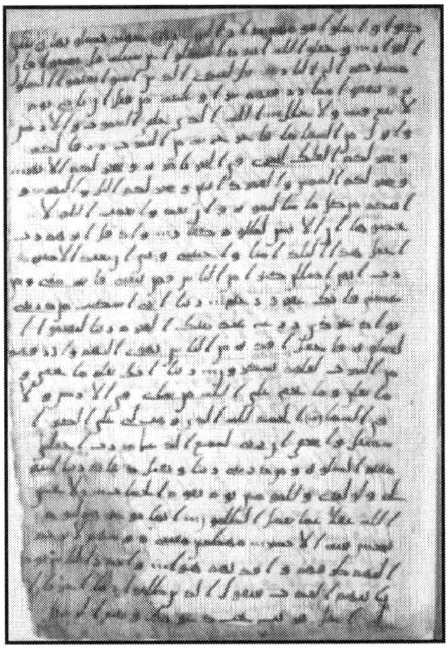

Figure 15. BNF 328a, fol. 53r, S. 14:28-44. Used with the permission of the BnF.

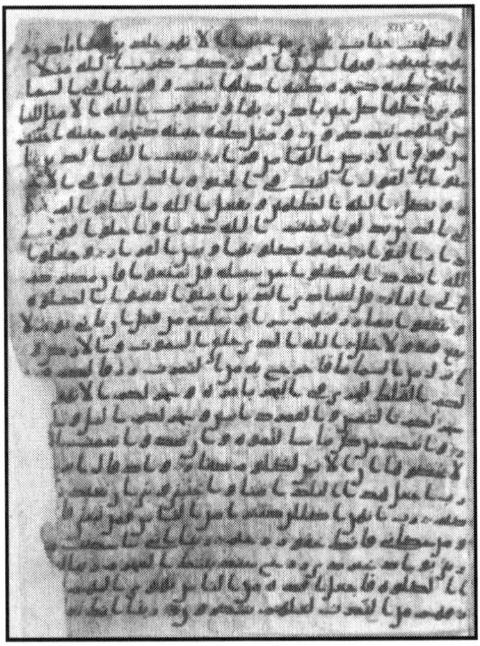

Figure 16. BNF 330a, fol. 3r, S. 14:30-37. Used with the permission of the BnF.

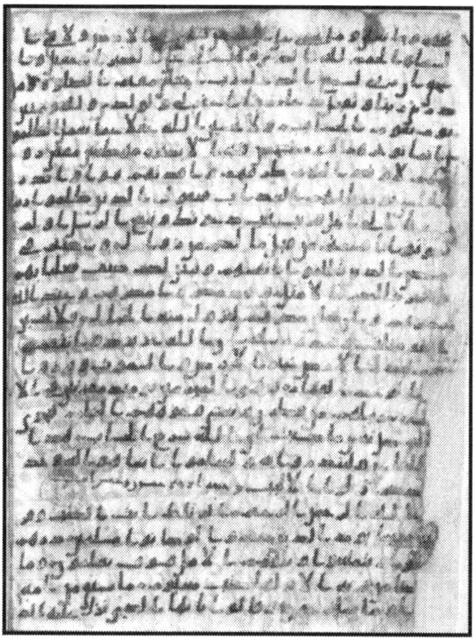

Figure 17. BNF 330a, fol. 3v, S. 14:37-43. Used with the permission of the BnF.

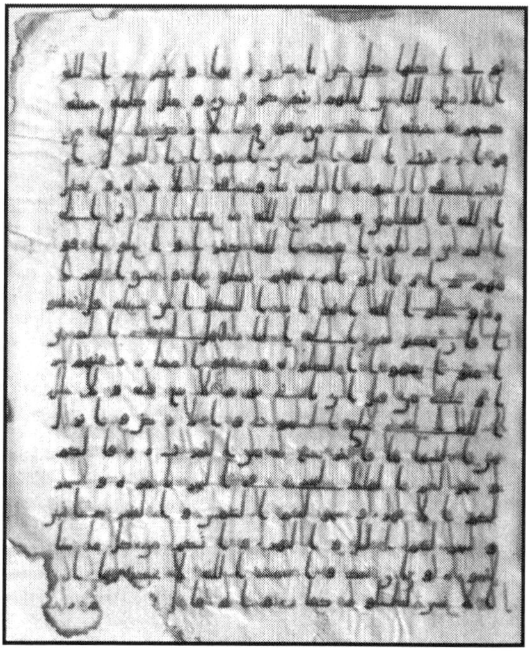

Figure 18. BNF 331, fol. 23r, S. 14:25-35. Used with the permission of the BnF.

Figure 19. BNF 331, fol. 23v, S. 14:35-44. Used with the permission of the BnF.

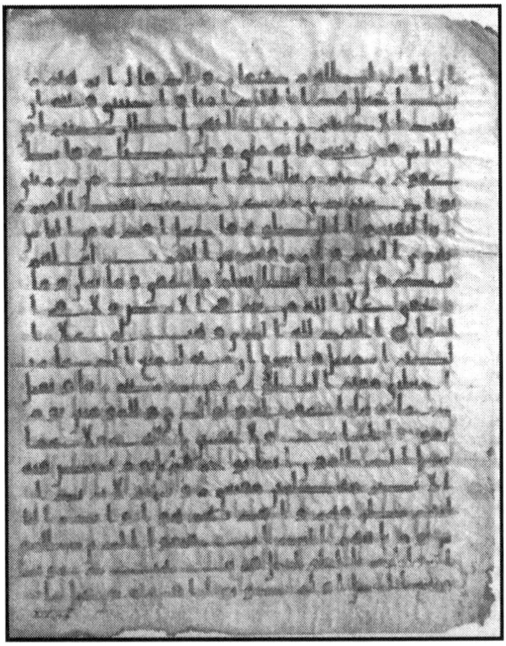

Figure 20. BNF 332, fol. 27v, S. 14:34-44. Used with the permission of the BnF.

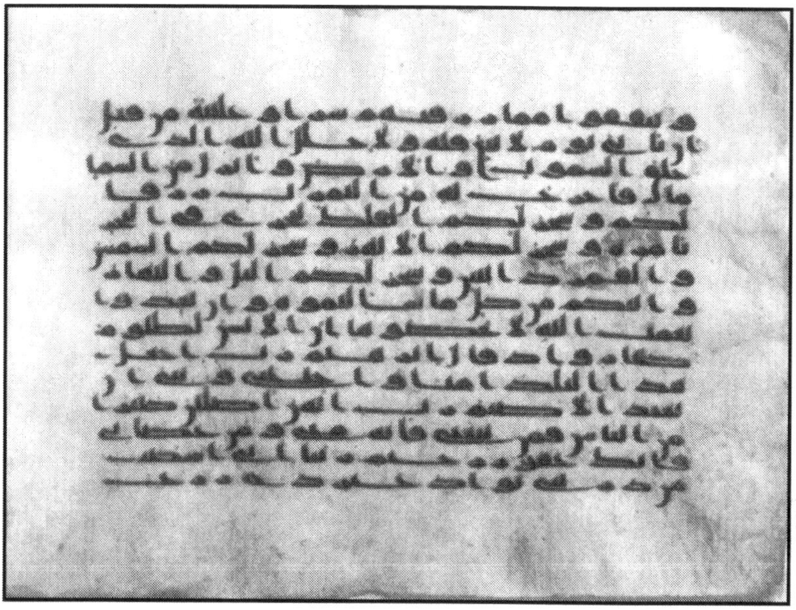

Figure 21. BNF 333c, fol. 41v 14:31-37. Used with the permission of the BnF.

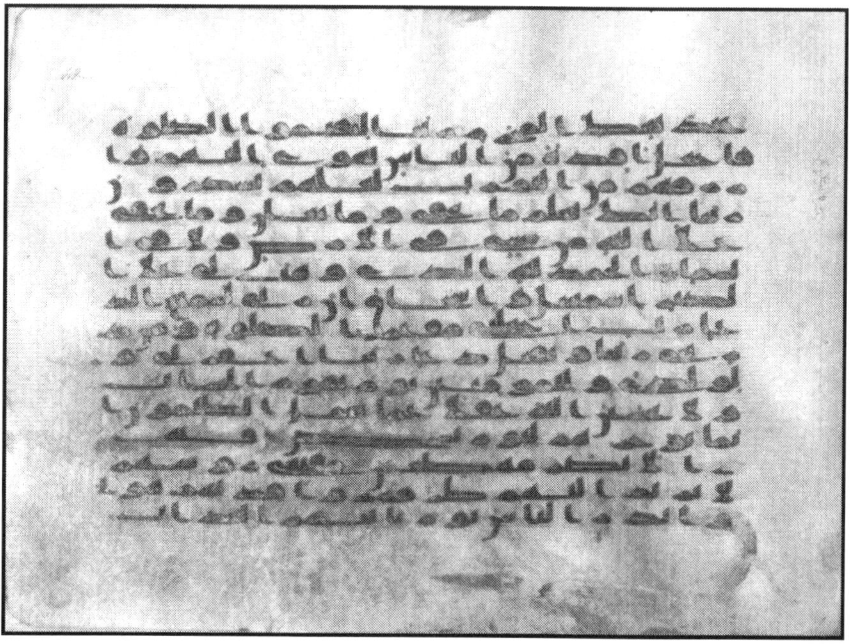

Figure 22. BNF 333c, fol. 42r, S. 14:37-44. Used with the permission of the BnF.

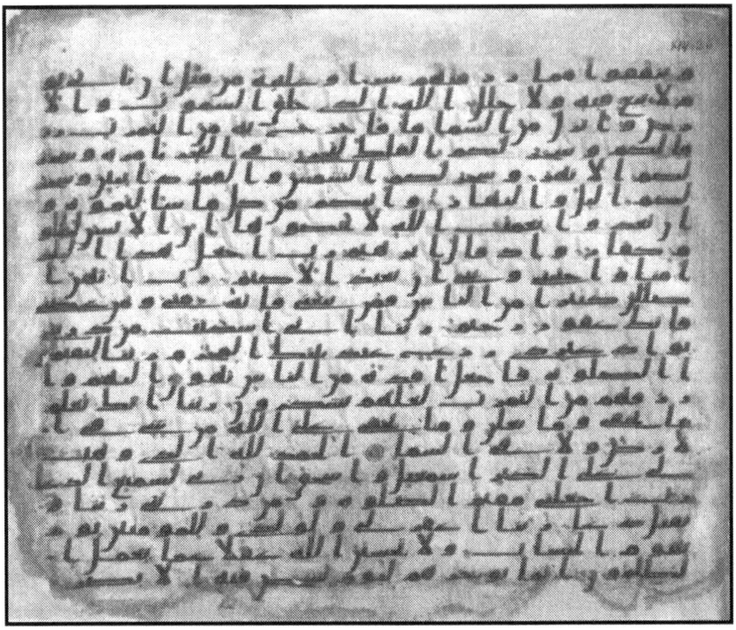

Figure 23. BNF 334c, fol. 34r, S. 14:31-43. Used with the permission of the BnF.

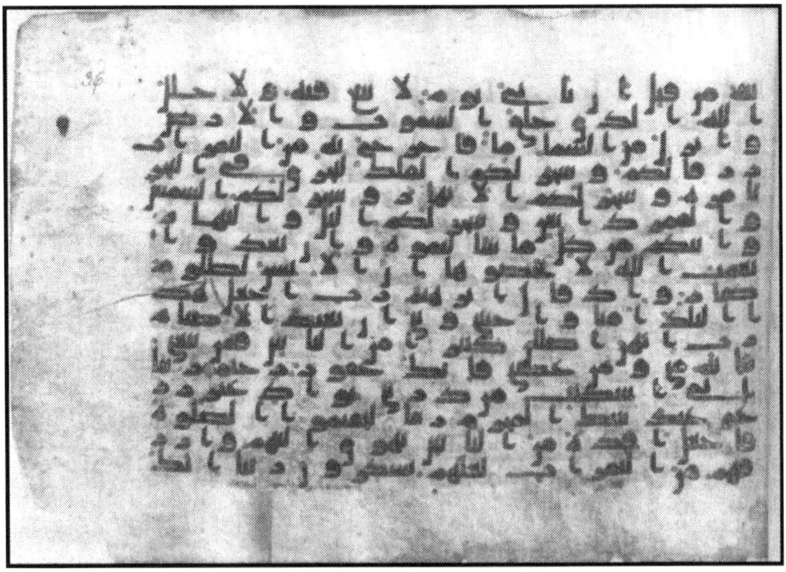

Figure 24. BNF 340c, fol. 36r, S. 14:31-38. Used with the permission of the BnF.

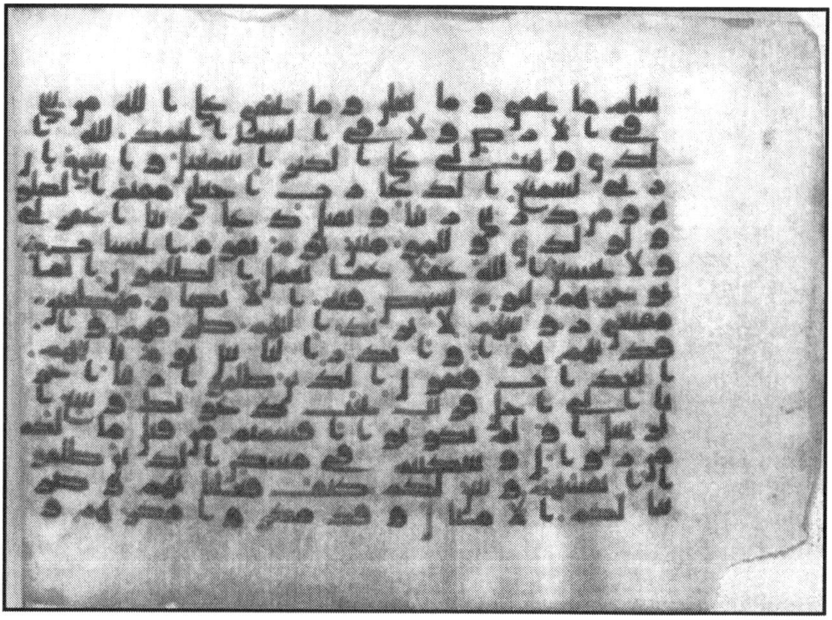

Figure 25. BNF 340c, fol. 36v, S. 14 38-46. Used with the permission of the BnF.

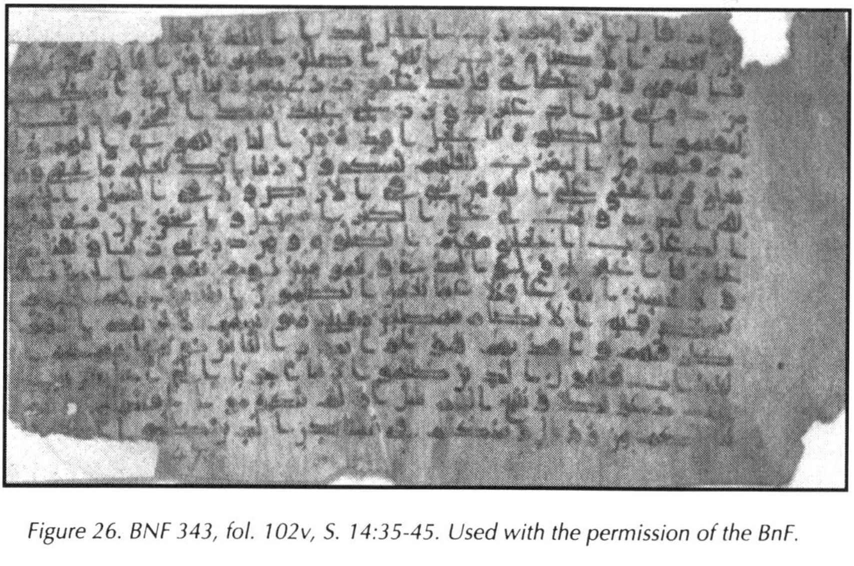

Figure 26. BNF 343, fol. 102v, S. 14:35-45. Used with the permission of the BnF.

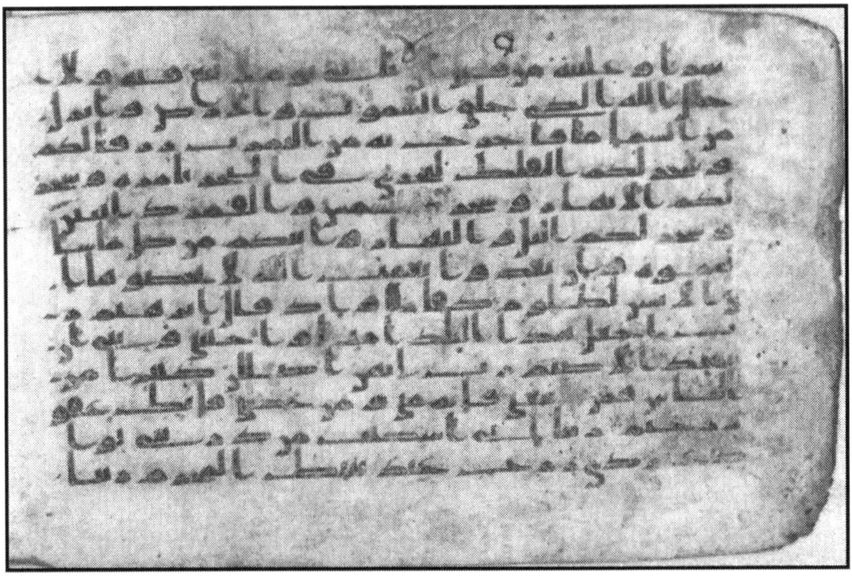

Figure 27. BNF 370a, fol. 2v, S. 14:31-37. Used with the permission of the BnF.

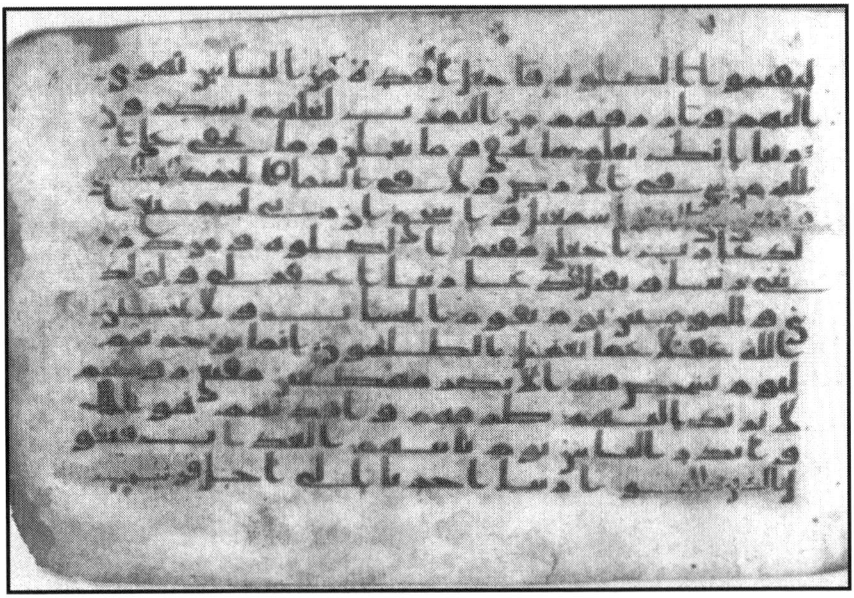

Figure 28. BNF 370a, fol. 3r, S. 14:37-44. Used with the permission of the BnF.

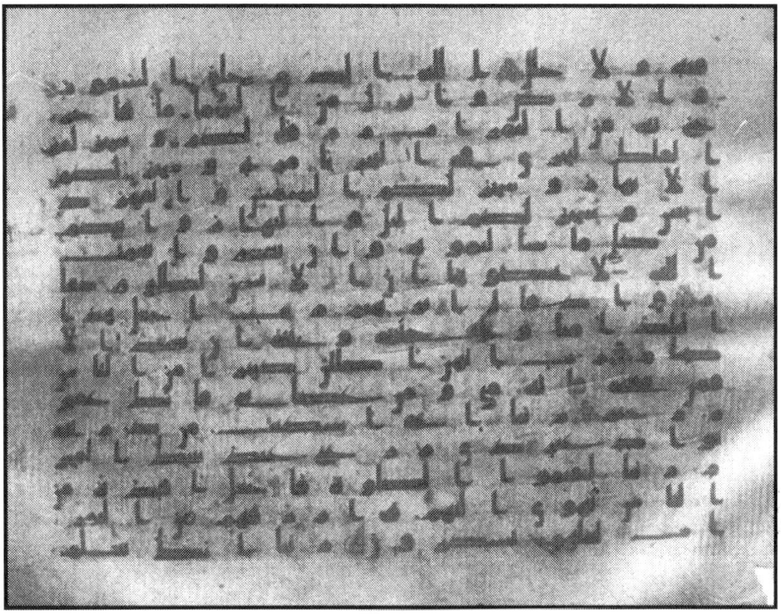

Figure 29. Meknes Manuscript, S. 14:31-38. Used with the permission of Corpus Coranicum.

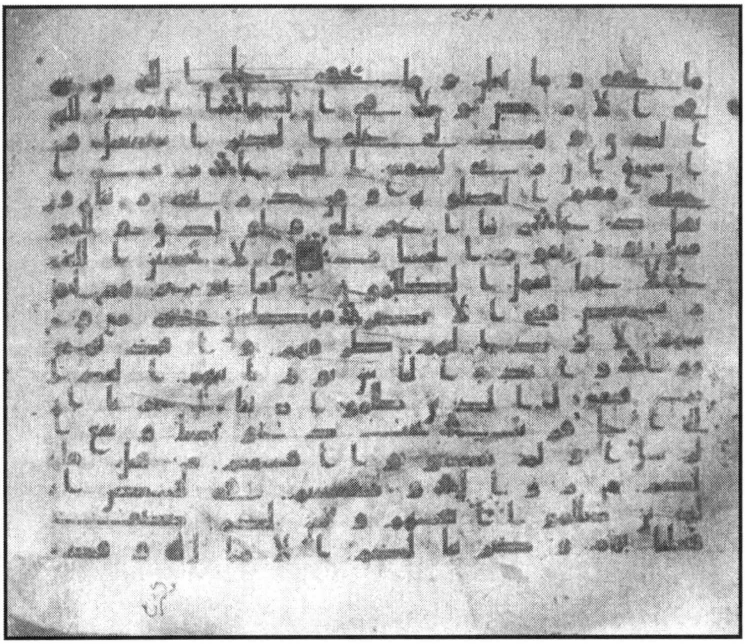

Figure 30. Meknes Manuscript, S. 14:38-45. Used with the permission of Corpus Coranicum.

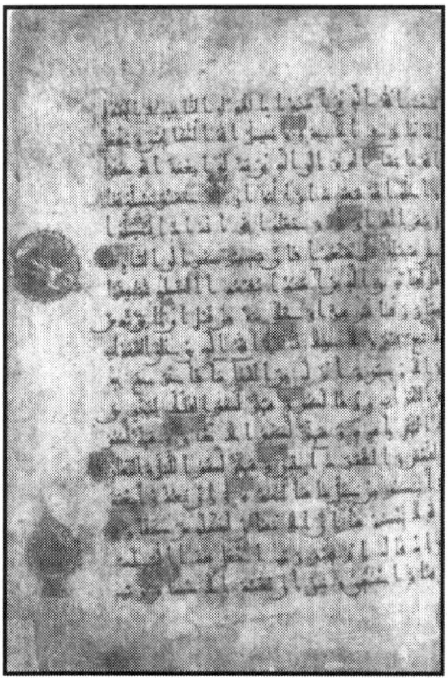

Figure 31. BL Or. 12884, fol. 142r, S. 14:27-36. © The British Library Board.

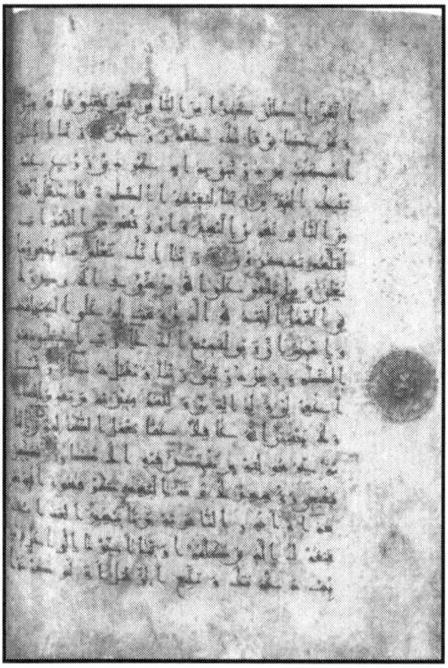

Figure 32. BL Or. 12884, fol. 142v, S. 14:36-43. © The British Library Board.

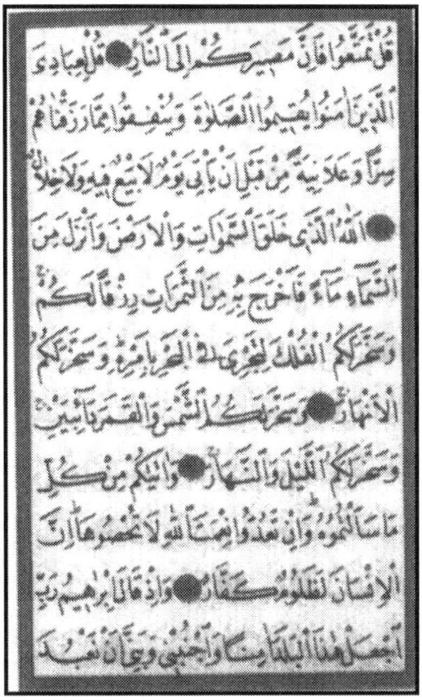

Figure 33. Mushaf Sharif, S. 14:31-36. © The British Library Board.

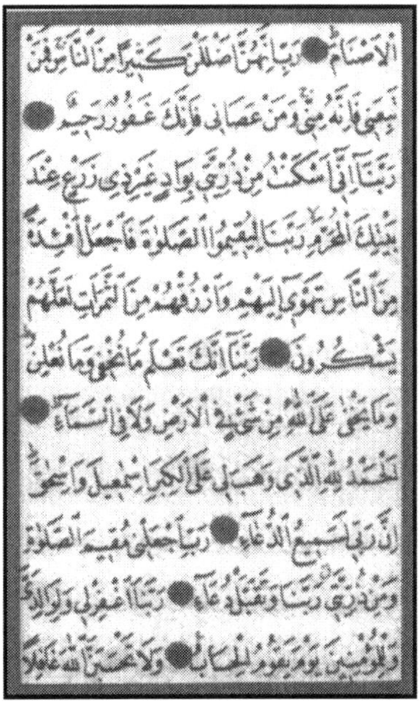

Figure 34. Mushaf Sharif, S. 14:36-43. © The British Library Board.

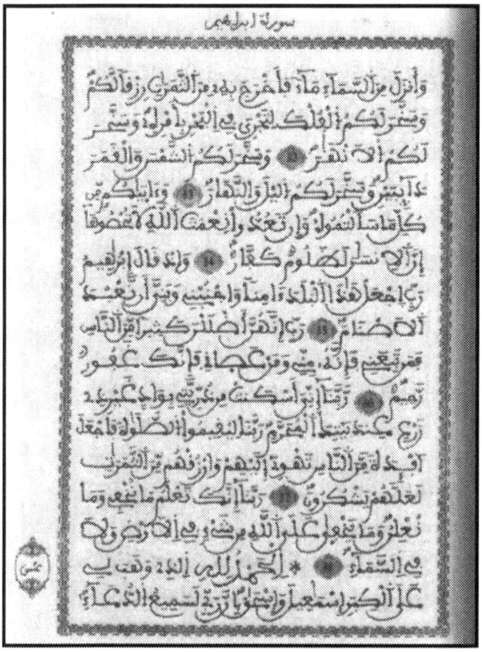

Figure 35. Warsh, p. 269, S. 14:31-39. Public Domain.

Figure 36. Warsh, p. 270, 14:40-49. Public Domain.

8

Physical Corrections to Manuscripts

While occurrences of different words in extant manuscripts are extremely rare, corrections and the overwriting of erased words and sections of text are very common.[1] Corrections were physically made to the texts of the Qur'ānic manuscripts surveyed. Historically, conventions developed to note corrections to the text. Wright notes the use of particular words and letters written either in the text or margins for noting variants, indistinct words, and emendations.[2] Gacek has made a survey of the kinds of corrections made in the general Arabic manuscript tradition.[3] Separate studies of the corrections made specifically in Qur'ān manuscripts, though, are rare.[4]

In her examination of palimpsest pages, Fedeli identifies three types of correction.[5] First, there are corrections "due to different variants with textual significance, be they canonical readings or pre-'Uthmānic (non canonical) variants." These are changes to the text to make it conform to what the scribe perceived to be a standard reading. Two interrelated issues which need to be tested are 1) if in the earliest period of extant manuscripts scribes were concerned with specific forms of the text, whether canonical or non-canonical, and 2) how much did they exercise individual judgment in the choice of variant readings. In other textual traditions scribes often exercised individual judgment in correcting what they thought was deficient style, grammar or even teaching in a manuscript from which they were copying.[6] One issue to be discerned is if the corrections in early Qur'ān manuscripts demonstrate the exercise of individual reasoning and choice on the part of the scribe, or if there were set patterns of text from the outset from within which the scribes made their intentional changes.

Second, Fedeli identifies corrections made to update the orthography of an old manuscript after a reform in orthography. This would include the later addition of diacritical marks on consonants, the later addition of vowel indicators like colored dots, and the later addition of letters like *alif* and *ḥamza*. These are corrections which made phonetic pronunciation more explicit and also limited choices of grammar and interpretation by more precisely fixing the degree of variability presented by a partially pointed consonantal text.

Third are changes to correct simple copyist mistakes. These are the mistakes scribes made through inattention, fatigue, and also in some later cases, a lack of understanding of Arabic. Corrections of all three types were observed in the manuscripts surveyed.

CORRECTIONS TO CONFORM THE TEXT TO A STANDARD READING

There were four instances of this first category, a change involving consonantal letters to conform the text to a standard reading:

1) At 14:35:2 in the Topkapi manuscript, the word هذا (*hādhā*) is written over another word, possibly *fā'* or *fāla*, without the underlying word having been completely erased.
2) At 14:35:3 in the Meknes manuscript a word was erased leaving the remnants of an initial *alif* or *lām*, and الا (*ālā*) of الاصنام (*al-āṣnām*) was inserted in a different hand causing the reading to conform to the present text.
3) At 14:39:1 in manuscript 01-20.x the space of three letters of text at the beginning of the verse was erased and new text in a slightly different hand was written making it conform to what is now considered to be the standard text, الحمد (*al-ḥamdu*). The initial *alif*, however, is still defaced, possibly from the ink not adhering well after the correction.
4) At 14:39:1–2 in manuscript BNF 370a, a phrase of text was erased and rewritten with what is now considered to be the standard text, الحمد لله الذى وهب لى على الكبر (*al-ḥamdu-lillahi al-dhīy wahaba līy 'alā al-kabīri*). The standard text is actually too long to fit in the space left by the defaced text. This was overcome by writing the new portion in a smaller hand to make it fit. Also, this rewritten text has not adhered well to the surface of the manuscript, and though enough is still visible to discern the form of text, most of the rewritten portion has come off the page. There are two other places on this manuscript page at S. 14:44 on the bottom line where this kind of correction has also been made. Also,

similar corrections are visible on other surviving pages of this particular manuscript.[7]

The variants described above are all examples of variants made deliberately to conform the text to a form the scribe considered to be correct and which matches the form of text which by the fourth Islamic century was considered to be standard or canonical. For these variants, elements of religious dogma and political concern were very possibly involved in that by the third Islamic century, the 'Uthmānic *rasm* was considered by most to be the Qur'ān text for liturgical use, theological belief, and legal reasoning. Modifying existing texts to read according to its standard form was thus an act to bring a greater degree of unity and conformity to the manuscripts surviving from an earlier era of the manuscript tradition. It is also worth mentioning that none of the marginal notations that Wright mentioned seeing could be observed on these manuscript pages. Their textual changes were evidently made before such conventions had become standard scribal practice.

There was, however, one instance where the correction of a consonantal letter was away from what came to be considered the standard reading to a non-standard and non-canonical reading. This occurs in the very early manuscript, BNF 328a. A prefixed *fā'* that was erased and in its place was written a *wāw*.

14:37:5 BNF 328a- واحعل, instead of فاحعل

Originally, the manuscript had the prefixed conjunction *fā'*- which is now considered the standard reading. Either the original scribe, or one using a similar kind of ink and script style, changed the reading to *wāw*. This variant was discussed in detail in Chapter 6, and was seen to affect the meaning of the text in its immediate context.

Also, though this particular variant is not recorded in the early Islamic literature concerning Qur'ān variants, this same kind of substitution of conjunctions has been recorded for other locations in the Qur'ān in other manuscripts. This phenomenon could be testimony to an unrecorded pattern of recitation at this point, or it could be testimony to a degree of fluidity of reading that was still in place at the time this manuscript was inscribed, where there were still minor elements of recitation and inscription of the text that were considered to be within the discretion of the scribe. Melchert suggests that in the first three Islamic centuries there was a degree of this kind of latitude from his examination of the relations of variants between the recitations of teachers and students as recorded in the collection *MQQ*.[8] Whereas Melchert's observations are particularly the case for the variable placement of diacritical marks on the *rasm*, this variant would be an instance of a minor change to that *rasm* itself.[9]

CORRECTIONS TO UPDATE THE ORTHOGRAPHY

There were six instances observed of the second kind of correction where the orthography was updated and/or clarified by the addition of a letter or diacritical marks. These particular clarifications are considered to be an updating of the text in that their addition marks a chronological development to make the text more phonetically explicit in order to limit the inherent variability of the unpointed consonantal text.

1) Topkapi 14:37:1: Consonantal diacritic variant: *nūn* for *tā'* in ذريتي (*dhurrīyatī*). This appears to be a heavier slash added by a later hand to make this explicitly read *dhurrīyanī*. This variant was discussed in detail in Chapter 5. This clarification of the diacritical mark denotes what would now be considered a non-standard way of pointing the text.
2) BNF 330a 14:38:1: Four diacritical marks are added to the word نخفي (*nukhfī*) to make each of its letters clearly understood, where the average use of diacritics in that part of the manuscript is only one or two per word. Also, the fourth diacritic is a dot after the *fā'* over the first part of the *yā'*, as if there were a *nūn* between the two, like a first person singular pronoun suffix. The stem for the *nūn* is not there, though, so it is probably an extra dot that was accidentally placed there. The addition of these dots clearly points the reader to read what has become the standard form of the word.
3) At 14:38:2 in the Meknes manuscript one diacritical mark appears to have been added later to make a letter clearly a *nūn* in نعلن (*nu'linu*), removing the possibility of it being read as a *tā' or yā'*, as in the next variant, which can both provide plausible alternative readings.
4) Topkapi 14:38:2: Consonantal diacritical variant. *Yā'* instead of *nūn* in نعلن (*nu'linu*), so that it reads يعلن (*yu'linu*). This clarification denotes what would now be considered a non-standard way of pointing the text. This variant is discussed in detail in Chapter 5.
5) At 14:40:1 in the Istanbul manuscript, an *alif* is added in the small space between two letters and it partially obscures the final letter *hā'*, of الصلوة (*al-ṣalawāt*). This is perhaps to make an understood pronunciation of the long "a" explicit, or it could be to make this part of the text conform to a new orthographical practice that required the addition of *alifs*. Such a practice is said to have been ordered by the Umayyad governor Ziyād

b. Abīhi (d. 684) when he ordered two thousand *alifs* to be added to the text of the Qur'ān.[10]

6) At 14:41:1 in the Istanbul manuscript, an *alif* is added in the small space between the second *wāw* and the *lām* in ولولدى (*waliwālidayya*). This is perhaps to make an understood pronunciation of the long "a" sound explicit, or it could be to make this part of the text conform to the new orthographical practice mentioned in 3). This added *alif* is notable for another reason. It makes the reading of this particular word match what is attributed to have been the reading in the version of Ibn Mas'ūd at this point in the text.[11]

Again, these variants could be testimony to unrecorded patterns of recitation, or they could be testimony to a degree of fluidity of reading that was still in place at the time this manuscript was inscribed where there were still minor elements of recitation and inscription of the text that were considered to be within the discretion of the scribe.

CORRECTING A COPYIST MISTAKE

There were five instances of this last category. The first was at 14:37:4 in manuscript BNF 333c where a *lām* was partially erased to make it a medial *yā'* in the word ليميموا. Originally, للميموا was written. Rezvan notes that this kind of correction can be found in the later Qur'ānic manuscript tradition as well. He documents many, including ones involving words and phrases, in Qur'ān manuscripts from the fifteenth to eighteenth centuries C.E.[12] However, his conclusion concerning these later manuscripts is that they were copyist errors transcribing the standard consonantal text, rather than legitimate alternative variant readings. It appeared to Rezvan that Arabic was not the native language of either the copyists or their proofreaders who were correcting their work. A scribe's poor Arabic, though, was probably not the situation for the much earlier examples surveyed for this study.

The second was at 14:37:5 in the Topkapi manuscript involving an erased tooth letter. An extra tooth letter was originally in فاجعل (*fāja'al)* between the final two consonants *'ayn* and *lām*. It was in the same style and form as other tooth letters in the main text and was erased, very possibly by the original scribe. It can be safely concluded to be a copyist mistake because no word forms which include the letter can be found which fit the context. There is also no reference to such a variant at this point in any of the Qur'ān variants collections.

The third was at 14:37:6 in the Topkapi manuscript. Again, this involves an erased tooth letter, this time between the two consonants *rā'* and *zā'* in وارزقهم

(*wārzuqhum*). It was in the same style and form as other tooth letters in the main text and was erased, very possibly by the original scribe. It can be safely concluded to be a copyist mistake because no word forms which include the letter can be found which fit the context. There is also no reference to such a variant at this point in any of the Qur'ān variants collections.

It is interesting to note the number and kinds of corrections made. Thirteen corrections were observed over seven verses of text in twenty manuscripts. If this proportion were extended to the rest of the Qur'ān it would confirm Fedeli's assertion that corrections in early Qur'āns are very common.[13]

Also, the majority (seven of thirteen) of corrections are to change the text toward what is traditionally considered to be the standard reading. This confirms what Fedeli observed in her study of palimpsests.[14] The original texts of the palimpsests were evidently too different to be corrected, so that they had to be completely erased and rewritten with the "standard" text. The manuscripts surveyed for this study conformed to that standard enough that evidently only small erasures and rewrites were necessary.

The manuscripts that contain more examples of different words are mainly palimpsests. The Mingana palimpsest has at least three occurrences of different words.[15] Fedeli observed at least seven in the Bonham palimpsest, two in the Fogg palimpsest, and one in a non-palimpsest manuscript in the Österreichische Nationalbibliothek.[16] E. Puin also observed differences in wording in both the *superior* and *inferior* texts of a palimpsest from the Ṣan'ā' manuscripts.[17] The significance of the rarity of this phenomenon in non-palimpsest manuscripts is also highlighted by the large number of reports of different words asserted to have been in the Companions' collections of the Qur'ān. With just a cursory glance through Jeffery's list of variants in the collection of Ibn Mas'ūd one will find many examples, starting with a synonym in the very first surah, 1:6, with ارشدنا instead of اهدنا for "path" in "Guide us in the straight path."[18] For S. 14, Jeffery records that Ibn Mas'ūd's codex reputedly had six different word variants.[19]

For the Qur'ān, only three of the thirteen corrections observed (23 percent) are to correct a copyist mistake. Seven of the thirteen (54 percent) intentionally conform the text in the manuscript to the consonantal form of the standard text. Three of these thirteen (23 percent) are also efforts to update the orthography, but to a new reading system of the text no longer considered to be standard or canonical.

There are few unintentional copyist mistakes corrected in the Qur'ān manuscripts surveyed. Three are corrected and eighteen are not corrected (14 percent). Though the sampling for these mistakes and corrections is small and any conclusions made from them are tentative, this perhaps indicates that as a tendency many copyist mistakes escape correction in these manuscripts.

Also, the overall number of corrections makes it possible that the great majority of the corrections in the Qur'āns were made with a dogmatic purpose in mind: to establish the standardized form of the consonantal text. That this was a process to reinforce a dogmatic position can be seen in the contrast between the ways the variants for conforming the text to another text were made. According to Islamic tradition, the standardization of the precise text of the Qur'ān in the seventh/first century had been a political as well as religious action. It was also a political and religious action in the tenth/fourth century with Ibn Mujāhid only choosing readings that would support particular Sunni orthodox political and theological positions.[20] In between these two dates, when alternative versions were still in use in competition with the 'Uthmānic version, it is known that pressure from the religious and legal establishment was applied to conform the text against competing text-forms. For instance, there was a decree by the prominent Medinese jurist Mālik ibn Anas (d. 795/179) that a ruler had the duty to prevent both the sale and recitation of the version attributed to Ibn Mas'ūd.[21] A scribe making such changes in Qur'āns was not acting in isolation to only clarify and correct a text with unintentional errors. He was also not just reinforcing what he as an individual scribe thought was a more correct reading. Instead, if the greater picture described by Islamic tradition is correct, the Qur'ān scribe was consciously participating in a broader ideological project to make the text conform to one

Table 8.1

Location	Manuscript	Change Made	Reason(s)	Later Scribe
14:35:2	Topkapi	*hāḍā* written over other letters	Conform text to standard reading	yes
14:35:3	Meknes	*ālā'* added	Conform text to standard reading	yes
14:37:1	Topkapi	Diacritics added	Designate a non-standard reading	yes
14:37:4	BN 333c	*lam* corrected to *yā'*	Correct copyist mistake	no
14:37:5	BN 328a	*Fā'* corrected to *wā'*	Designate a non-standard reading	no
14:37:6	Topkapi	Erased tooth letter	Correct a copyist mistake	no
14:38:1	BN 330a	Diacritics added	Conform text to standard reading	yes
14:38:2	Topkapi	Diacritics added	Designate a non-standard reading	yes
14:38:2	Meknes	Diacritics added	Conform text to standard reading	yes
14:39:1	01-20.x	*āl* added to make *āl-hamdu*	Correct a copyist mistake	yes
14:39:1-2	BN 370a	Major erasure	Conform text to standard reading	yes
14:40:1	Istanbul	*alif* added	Update orthography/Conform text to standard reading	yes
14:41:1	Istanbul	*alif* added	Update orthography/Conform text to standard reading	yes

precise standard consonantal reading. Powers examines an intriguing double correction in BNF 328a that perhaps demonstrates corrections for legal and theological reasons.[22]

The extensive scope of such a project becomes more apparent when the Qur'ānic palimpsests are brought into the picture. It may be legitimately suggested that the original texts of the palimpsests were too different from the standard to be corrected, so that they had to be completely erased and rewritten with the "standard" text. The manuscripts surveyed for this study conformed to that standard well enough that only small erasures and rewrites were necessary. The most severe example in these manuscripts was BNF 370a which had half of a line of text defaced. This section is too short to contain the full standard text so the full text was squeezed in. It was defaced so effectively that the original reading cannot be determined with certainty.

With the Qur'ānic manuscript tradition, that so many dogmatic corrections were observed in a limited random sampling is a significant testimony to the strength of the efforts made to standardize its text. This is perhaps a significant representative indication of the directions in which corrections were made.

NOTES

1. Alba Fedeli, "A.Perg.2: A Non-Palimpsest and the Corrections in Qur'ānic Manuscripts," *MO* 11:1:20–27, 22. Fedeli lists a sampling of corrections she has observed in various early manuscripts. This author has also observed corrections in numerous images on the UNESCO CD and in various images of Qur'ān manuscript pages in auction house catalogues. Rezvan helpfully catalogs the corrections made to the text of manuscript E 20 in Efim A. Rezvan, *The Qur'ān of 'Uthmān* (St. Petersburg: St. Petersburg Centre for Oriental Studies, 2004), 142–43, table 11. Déroche mentions specific corrections in the course of his discussion of variants in Codex Petropolitanus François Déroche, *La transmission écrite du Coran dans les débuts de l'islam: Le codex Parisino-petropolitanus* (Leiden: Brill, 2009), 105–8.

2. W. Wright, *A Grammar of the Arabic Language* (Cambridge: Cambridge University Press, 1986), 26.

3. Adam Gacek, "Taxonomy of Scribal Errors and Corrections in Arabic Manuscripts," in Adam Gacek, *Theoretical Approaches to the Transmission and Edition of Oriental Manuscripts* (Beirut: Ergon Verlag Würzburg, 2007), 217–35.

4. Gacek, "Taxonomy," 217. Fedeli has done two pioneering studies: Alba Fedeli, "Early Evidences of Variant Readings in Qur'ānic Manuscripts," in Karl Heinz-Ohlig and Gerd-R. Puin, eds., *Die dunklen Anfänge* (Berlin: Hans Schiler, 2005), 293–316, and Fedeli, "Non-Palimpsest." E. Puin also catalogs in detail corrections made to the *superior* and *inferior* scripts of a San'ā' palimpsest page in Elisabeth Puin, "Ein früher Koranpalimpsest aus San'ā' (DAM 01-27.1)," in Markus Groß and

Karl-Heinz-Ohlig, eds., *Schlaglichter* (Berlin: Hans Schiler, 2008), 461–93. Gacek provides an overview of practices in the wider Islamic manuscript tradition: Adam Gacek, "Technical Practices and Recommendations Recorded by Classical and Post-Classical Arabic Scholars Concerning the Copying and Correction of Manuscripts," *Actes du Colloque d'Istanbul*, Istanbul, Turkey, 1986, L'Institut Français d'Études Anatoliennes d'Istanbul la Bibliothèque Nationale de Paris, 51–59.

5. Fedeli, "Non-Palimpsest," 22. I have divided her second category into two distinct categories.

6. B. M. Metzger and Bart D. Ehrman, *The Text of the New Testament.* New York: Oxford University Press, 2005, 302–3 has a succinct statement of some of the individual choices scribes made in the New Testament tradition.

7. Paris BNF 370a, folios 1 v., 2 r. and v., 3 r. and v., 4 r., and 10 r. The portion exhaustively surveyed for this study is contained on folios 2 v. and 3 r.

8. Christopher Melchert, "The Relation of the Ten Readings to One Another," *JQS*, 10:2:73–87, 78–79.

9. Melchert, "Relation," 82.

10. Rezvan, *Qur'ān,* 68.

11. Arthur Jeffery, *Materials for the History of the Text of the Qur'ān* (Leiden: Brill, 1937), 52.

12. M. E. Rezvan, "Qur'ānic Fragments From the A. A. Polotsov Collection at the St. Petersburg Branch of the Institute of Oriental Studies," *MO* 7:2:20–35, citing 23–29.

13. Fedeli, "Non-Palimpsest," 22.

14. Fedeli, "Evidences," 313.

15. Alphonse Mingana and Agnes Smith Lewis, *Leaves From Three Ancient Qur'āns, Possibly Pre-'Uthmānic* (Cambridge: Cambridge University Press, 1914), xxxviii–xxxix, numbers 15, 17, and 20, as verified in Alba Fedeli, "Mingana and the Manuscript of Mrs. Agnes Smith Lewis, One Century Later," *MO* 11, 3, September 2005, 3–7, citing 7.

16. Fedeli, "Evidences," 300, 302, 305–6, 312, note 70, respectively.

17. Puin, "Koranpalimpsest," 462–63.

18. Jeffery, *Materials,* 25.

19. Jeffery, *Materials,* 51–52, records Ibn Mas'ūd as having different words in the text of Surah 14 in verses 6, 7, 8, 24, 32, and 46.

20. Yasser Tabbaa, "Canonicity and Control: The Sociopolitical Underpinnings of Ibn Muqla's Reform," *Ars Orientalis*, XXIX, 91–100.

21. Michael Cook, *The Koran: A Very Short Introduction* (Oxford: Oxford University Press, 2000), 119.

22. David S. Powers, *Muhammad Is Not the Father of Any of Your Men: The Making of the Last Prophet* (Philadelphia: University of Pennsylvania Press, 2009), 193.

III

EVALUATING THE TEXTUAL VARIANTS

> Write down my poetry, for the written word is more pleasing to me than memory. . . . A book does not forget, nor does it substitute one word for another.
>
> —Dhu'l Rumma[1]

> For how could you establish even the most obvious fact when there existed no record outside your own memory?
>
> —George Orwell[2]

This section presents an in-depth evaluation of the variants discussed earlier. So far, the variants have been discussed mainly as isolated individual units in their immediate context, according to the canons of the textual criticism method of reasoned eclecticism. This section will evaluate the variants in regard to some issues that are distinctive to the Qur'ānic manuscript and textual tradition.

First, the variants will be examined against the backdrop of the records of variants in early Islamic literature concerning the different reading systems and collections of the Qur'ān that were attributed to Muḥammad's companions. Though many consonantal variants are discussed in these records, they are perhaps more notable for the variants they record for the oral pronunciation of a unified consonantal text. As much as being a record of written variants once thought to have been in the tradition, they are extensive records of the oral transmission of the text which accompanied the written transmission. In recent years a plethora of materials has appeared from Arabic presses concerning this respect of the Qur'ān's transmission and reflects the historical mainstream of methods that Muslims have used when they have performed textual criticism on the text of the Qur'ān. These include reprints of classic medieval works of the Qur'ānic sciences, to ancient commentaries, to collections of recitation systems keyed to the text of the Qur'ān, a sort of critical text to the Qur'ān presenting the canonical variant readings.[3] For this study, the variants observed in the surveyed manuscripts will be compared to the variants recorded in the early authorities to have once been in the tradition. The major sources for this will be the compendiums by Jeffery, the *MQQ* and the *MQ*, and these will be supplemented from other available sources. This is not an exhaustive study of the available variant readings in the secondary Islamic literature, but it is representative of the kinds of variants recorded to have existed in the earliest Islamic centuries. This will comprise chapter 9, Variants in Islamic Literature.

With the analysis of the individual variants as they compare to the records in the secondary literature, comments will be made as to how the variants relate to the text forms presented in the Introduction. As a reminder, these were:

1. *Predecessor text-form*: the oral or written sources the author used.
2. *Autographic text-form*: the form the author wrote as it left his desk.
3. *Authoritative text-form*: a form of text that acquired a degree of local consensual authority.
4. *Canonical text-form*: a form of the text that acquired a degree of wide consensual authority.
5. *Interpretive text-form*: any later intentional reformulation for stylistic, practical or dogmatic reasons.

Some Islamic sources claim that there were only twelve differences between al-Ḥajjāj's and 'Uthmān's versions.[4] A more recent examination of the traditions concerning al-Ḥajjāj's version asserts that it could have been a much more thorough revision of the text.[5] Since this debate cannot be settled by a clear testimony from within the tradition, this book will treat al-Ḥajjāj's version as the earliest available Canonical text-form, but also with the understanding that it was directly related to a possible one by 'Uthmān.

The second chapter in this section, chapter 10, will consider the variants in regard to issues of intentionality. This concerns what can be surmised of the intentions of the scribes who actually recorded the textual variants in manuscripts. Reference to these aspects has already been made to a degree in the classification of the variants as Copyist Mistakes, Grammatical Variants, etc., and possibilities of intentionality have been mentioned in the individual analysis of the variants themselves. Chapter 10, Intentionality, will discuss the larger issues involved when one attributes intentionality to scribes as well as the particular issues the Qur'ān's textual history brings to this discussion from the various accounts of editions of the text recorded in historical records and the Qur'ān sciences literature.

Third, the variants will also be discussed in regard to the unique facet of the Qur'ān's textual tradition of its oral genesis and transmission, and the extensive written records that there came to be of this oral tradition. Chapter 11, Orality, will examine the oral dynamics of the transmission of the Qur'ān's text and the complex relation of this oral transmission to the written transmission of the text in manuscripts. Comments will be made as to what can be discerned concerning the oral transmission from what has been recorded in manuscripts.

These chapters will then lead on to the final section, where the strands will be pulled together with conclusions and a suggested overview of the history of the text of the Qur'ān.

NOTES

1. Dhu'l Rumma (d. C.E. 735), an early Arabic poet quoted in English in Alfred Guillaume, *The Traditions of Islam* (Oxford: Oxford University Press, 1924), 16, and in Arabic at www.fikrwanakd.aljabriabed.com/n37_12abdellaoui.htm.

2. George Orwell, *Nineteen Eighty-Four*, 1971 reprint edn. (Harmondsworth: Penguin, 1949), 32.

3. 'Ahmad 'Isā Al-Mu'sirāwī, *Al-Qirā'āt al-'Ashar* (Damascus: Dar al-Maarifah, 2007).

4. M. M. Al-Azami, *The History of the Qur'anic Text* (Leicester: UK Islamic Academy, 2003), 102.

5. Omar Hamdan, "The Second Masāhif Project: A Step Towards the Canonization of the Qur'anic Text," in Angelika Neuwirth, Nicolai Sinai, and Michael Marx, eds., *The Qur'ān in Context* (Leiden: Brill, 2010), 795–836.

9

Variants in Manuscripts Compared to Those in Islamic Records

The Islamic records of textual variants for the Qur'ān are remarkable for their sheer volume and scope in regard to the entire text of the Qur'ān. In addition to generating a genre of *qirā'āt* (recital systems) literature, they permeate the early and medieval commentaries and grammatical literature. In the earliest Islamic centuries, there seems to have been an understanding, at least among the scholars, that the Qur'ān they had received had come with a tremendous degree of internal variety.

Conversely, and anomalously in comparison with other bodies of literature,[1] the variants in the early Islamic literature are of greater number and a much broader span of types and sizes than is found in extant Qur'ān manuscripts. This section explores the question of how the variants observed in the manuscripts compare with what variants are said to have once existed in manuscripts and the accompanying oral tradition asserted in this early Islamic literature.

Bergsträsser noted that Qur'ān manuscripts have played no observable role in Islamic Qur'ān studies since the tenth /fourth century.[2] By that time, a sizeable body of literature had developed concerning textual variants in the Qur'ān. Also, variants could be found in other early literature like commentaries, grammatical works, and hadith. Jeffery found one significant early collection of textual variants which he published and supplemented with readings he had gleaned from other literature.[3] From his own study, he stated that the textual variants of substance that exist are to be found in the early Islamic literature but not in Qur'ān manuscripts.[4]

In these records, one sometimes finds two different spellings of a word attributed to the same ancient authority.[5] This is one feature that has led some scholars to believe that the literature presents a pious fiction made up of invented readings.[6] However, some of the variants are found in the manuscripts, though so far none of the major variants which contain substantial portions of text have been discovered. Jeffery mentioned in the preface to his collection his opinion that,[7]

> When we have assembled all the variants from these earlier Codices that can be gleaned from the works of the exegetes and philologers, we have only such readings as were useful for the purposes of *Tafsīr* (commentary) and were considered to be sufficiently near orthodoxy to be allowed to survive.

He evidently believed that they did at one time exist but had been purposefully suppressed.

The readings used for this book that were obtained from the collections of textual variants in addition to Jeffery's confirm part of his conclusion that the Islamic records do contain an authentic memory of readings once contained in the manuscript tradition. Though there may be inconsistencies in the recorded variants, they should not be dismissed as wholesale inventions. This is so even though the overall degree of their accuracy is impossible to precisely quantify because of the lack of sufficient primary source materials, and because of the general tendencies of the variants that fit with the variables allowed by a developing orthography.

This section will test this general picture of Qur'ānic variants on the basis of the variants found in the manuscripts examined compared to those recorded in the literature. The spectrum of manuscripts examined for this study provides some hope that other variants could be found, since some of the manuscripts used in this study were not available to Jeffery, Bergsträsser, or Pretzl, and these manuscripts are at least as old as those that were at their disposal.[8] What follows will not be an exhaustive survey of variants found in the secondary Islamic literature but will be a representative presentation of what can be found in the literature from the most important collections available compared to what was found in the surveyed manuscripts.

Islamic sources group Qur'ānic textual variants into categories that Western scholars have come to refer to as "canonical" and "uncanonical":[9]

> We now have, then, two classes of variants to the Qur'ān text, the canonical, consisting of the variants of the Seven canonized by Ibn Mujāhid, and with lesser degree of authority those of the Ten, and uncanonical . . . consisting of all other variants.

These Seven and Ten are currently referred to in the scholarly literature as "canonical" variants but in terms of the categories used in this study are more precisely later Interpretive text-forms of al-Ḥajjāj's consonantal text. The canonical Seven refers to the seven precise ways of reciting the consonantal Qur'ān text as published by Ibn Mujāḥid in 936/324. These are termed canonical because for the most part they remain within the textual boundaries set by the consonantal text attributed to 'Uthmān and they were deemed acceptable by a large group of Muslim authorities. At about that same time, these Seven were supplemented with three other versions which commanded general assent as well as the Seven.[10] Four additional ones also achieved acceptance, but not to quite the same degree as the Ten.[11] The uncanonical variants consist of all other known variants. These are variants from versions attributed to the Companions of Muḥammad as well as any other recitations systems. They are termed "uncanonical" because they are not recognized as being legitimate variants within the parameters set concerning the Ten.

The variants from the manuscripts surveyed will be compared to the variants in Islamic literature under three headings:

1. Canonical Variants from the Ten Readings
2. Uncanonical Variants from the Fourteen[12] and other collections
3. Shī'ite variants

The records of variants from the Islamic literature will first be discussed as to their possible relation to the Autographic text form and their relative place in the textual history of the Qur'ān. They will then be compared to the textual readings found in the manuscripts.[13]

The following readings are listed according to how their form relates to the manuscripts surveyed for this study. On the left, after the verse citation, the Arabic form of the word in question is given in the most prominent form in which it appears in the manuscripts. This might be with or without the diacritical marks and without *ḥamza* that it has later come to be read with. The readings on the right are given with a minimum of diacritical marks to distinguish the reading from the reading in the manuscripts and to show how it would have appeared in the early manuscripts. Mention will be made as to if the variant was found in the surveyed manuscripts or not.

CANONICAL VARIANTS WITHIN THE TEN READINGS

14:35:1 ابرهيم   ابراهام Ibn 'Āmir (7),[14] al-Muṭaw'ī (Nāfi', 7)[15]

Consonantal variant: *alif* in last syllable rather than *yā'*. Variants concerning the spelling of Ibrāhīm were discussed in detail in the section on variant spellings of names. However, it should be mentioned that this one canonical spelling variant of Ibrāhīm's name was not found in any of the manuscripts surveyed. It makes a particular pronunciation of his name explicit, one that is more in line with the pronunciation of Syrian Christians of the time.[16] Since it is not found in any of the earliest manuscripts surveyed, and since it makes explicit a pronunciation that is ambiguous in the earliest spellings observed, it is almost certainly a later form which cannot be considered to be what was in the Canonical text-form.

14:37:5 افده	افيده	Ibn 'Āmir (7), al-Ḥulwānī (Ibn 'Āmir, 7), Hishām (Ibn 'Āmir, 7),[17] Khalaf (10)[18]

Consonantal variant: added medial *yā'*, which does not change the meaning. The variant with the medial *yā'* was found in only BL Or. 12884. BL Or. 12884 represents a transitional stage in the *ḥamza*'s development in that it is not marked, as the later texts and current Arabic script are, with a small *'ayn* (ء) on the consonantal line, or as an even smaller *'ayn* above vowel seats (أ). Instead, it is marked occasionally with a thick "s" shape above vowels in medial or final position, and it is never found above or below an *alif* in initial position, or as a full consonant in initial position. In the passage 14:35-41, excluding the thirteen initial uses of *ḥamza*, it is marked in only five of the nine medial and final positions where it is found in the Cairo text. At this word in 14:37:5 there is a *ḥamza* marked above the *yā'* with the "s" symbol, but there is not a separate stem for it.

Overall, this appears to be a spelling variant to make a particular pronunciation explicit, and also represent a transitional orthographic form before uses of *ḥamza* were clearly codified. Its presence in the relatively late manuscript BL Or. 12884 and the reasons just mentioned reflect that this is not the earliest form of this word in the transmission of the text in manuscripts.

	افده	Ibn Kathīr (7)[19]

Consonantal variant: no *ḥamza* or its stem in the middle of the word. This variant involves no change in meaning. The form without the *yā'* or stem for *ḥamza* is however the normal form of the word found in sixteen of the manuscripts,[20] but it should be mentioned that these manuscripts were inscribed before *ḥamza* was a written consonant in manuscripts. This makes it impossible to determine if the manuscripts recorded this intended variant or not. The absence of *ḥamza* is understandable in that the convention for writing *ḥamza* was one introduced later into the Arabic Qur'ānic script. *Ḥamza* did not exist as a separate consonantal letter until the third Islamic century, and before that was only marked by *alif* if it began a word. [21] This is confirmed in that *ḥamza* on the consonantal line is only found in the later texts, the Cairo, the Sharīf, and the Warsh. Because of the prevalence of this form in the earliest manuscripts and it being the reading that best explains the origins of the other variants, it is probably the reading of the Canonical text-form.

14:37:5 تهوى	يهوى	Ja'far b. Muḥammad (Nāfi', 7), Ibn Mujāḥid (Ibn Kathīr , 7, or Abū 'Amr, 7) [22]

Diacritical mark variant: changes person from "you incline their hearts" to "they incline their hearts." This variant with the initial *yā'* was not observed in any of the manuscripts, though the form تهوى was purposefully indicated in some of the early manuscripts possibly to remove the ambiguity of the unpointed form.[23] This variant involves a change of person, the variant reading "he inclines," or the group "they" treated as a singular, instead of "you incline." Only one of the manuscripts that has the explicit standard reading "you incline" is of the earliest stratum of manuscripts, which tend to have no diacritical marks on the initial letter.[24] This would be a negative indication that the scribe was making sure the variant version, يهوى , and any other potential variant versions were not to be read at this point of the text. There is also a significant number of early manuscripts, though not of the earliest level, that have no diacritics here.[25]

Grammatically, either reading makes sense in this passage. The standard second person reading, "You incline to them," has Allah divinely moving the hearts of the people toward his progeny. The variant third person reading, "the people incline to them," has the people's response as a result of Allah's answering the prayer. It is difficult to decide which of these two interpretations of the unpointed text explains the origin of the other. Since the Canonical text-form was probably mostly unpointed, it is perhaps best to leave it ambiguous.

14:40:2 دعاء	دعاي	Ibn Kathīr (7), 'Āsim (7), Abū Ja'far (10), Qunbul (Ibn Kathīr, 7), Ibn Shanabūdh (Ibn Kathīr, 7)[26], Ḥamza (7), Abū 'Amr (7), Ḥafṣ [27](7), Ya'qūb (10)[28]

Consonantal variant: attached possessive pronoun suffix: 'my prayer'—it makes explicit an implicit vowel mark. Though this was not found in any of the manuscripts, one similar was found in 01-29.1: دعا (*du'ā*) with a *nūn* added in the space above the line immediately after the final *alif*. If this word was once part of the manuscript tradition, it was most likely a later development to improve the meaning of the text to make an understood meaning more explicit. It is also interesting that one of the readers that used this variant was Ḥafṣ. This disagrees with the form of the text currently attributed to him used as the standard form of text in this study.

UNCANONICAL VARIANTS FROM THE FOURTEEN[29] AND OTHER COLLECTIONS

14:35:1 ابرهيم ابرهام Abū Mūsā al-Ash'arī, Ibn az-Zubayr[30]
ابراهيم ، ابرهم an-Nawawī [31]

Consonantal variants: these variations all affect the pronunciation of Ibrāhīm's name. The second version attributed to an-Nawawī was found in Istanbul, BL Or. 2165, BNF 326a, and 328a. Variants of this name are discussed at more length in the names section. However, it should be noted that the forms ابرهام and ابراهيم do not match what was actually found in the manuscripts. Only the form ابرهم matches what is found in some of the manuscripts, and it is a form found only in some of the very earliest manuscripts: Istanbul, BL Or. 2165, BNF 328a, and 326a. That an uncanonical form is found in manuscripts as a regular feature provides evidence that when the judgment between canonical and uncanonical was being made, manuscripts of the Qur'ān were not closely studied, or used as an authority for deciding the issue.

These variant spellings make sense as attempts to make explicit particular pronunciations that are among several allowed by a defective script. Since two of the three reported forms are not found in the manuscripts, they are also evidence that the oral tradition was not sufficiently controlled to preserve only one pronunciation, but that the ambiguity inherent in the unpointed script was a departure point for alternative pronunciations. Also, two forms of Ibrāhīm's name were found in the earliest manuscripts, ابرهيم and ابرهم , so both should be considered to have been part of the Canonical text-form. There was flexibility on this point of detail.

14:35:2 اجعل اجعلنى al-A'mash (14), Ḥasan al-Baṣrī (14)

Consonantal variant: attached direct object pronoun suffix: "make safe for me." This was not found in any of the surveyed manuscripts. It makes explicit what is already implied in Ibrāhīm's prayer, "Make *for me* this place a place of security." Perhaps it is an exegetically inspired variant to heighten the sense of insecurity of the place to which Ibrāhīm was bringing Ismā'īl and Hagar. According to Islamic tradition it was a desolate place without water before the miraculous discovery of the Zamzam spring.[32] Since it was not in any of the manuscripts, and since it can be viewed as exegetically inspired, it was probably not the form in the Canonical text-form.

14:37:1 انى اسكنت | انك اسكنت Ubayy b. Ka'b[33]

Consonantal variant: different attached pronoun suffix: "I have made dwell" is changed to "Truly, You have made dwell." This was not found in any of the manuscripts. Since it is attributed to one of the companions of Muḥammad, Ubayy ibn Kā'b, it deserves extra consideration. This variant shifts the emphasis of responsibility from Ibrāhīm to Allah for Ibrāhīm's action for settling some of his family in "this place." It strengthens the conception of Allah's divine plan of establishing Ibrāhīm's progeny in Mecca. If the reading of the text originally attributed the action to Allah, it is hard to imagine why it would then have been changed to place the emphasis on Ibrāhīm's action. However, if the reading originally stressed Ibrāhīm's responsibility, then it is conceivable that a change would later be made to stress Allah's divine plan in this action. This variant, then, seems to be an exegetically inspired variant, rather than a legitimate contender for the reading of the Canonical text-form.

14:37:5 افىده	افاده	Ubayy b. Ka'b, Ibn Mijlaz[34], Anonymous[35]
	افده	'Isā b. 'Amr[36]
	افودة	Anonymous[37]

Consonantal variant/Word variant: the *alif* instead of *ḥamza* changes this to a different word: "hearts" to "group." The variant with *alif* attributed to Ubayy b. Ka'b and Ibn Mijlaz was observed in 01-28.1 and 01-29.1. The variant attributed to 'Isā b. 'Amr was also attributed to the Canonical reciter Ibn Kathīr, and was the basic form found in twelve of the manuscripts.[38] However, since these manuscripts were inscribed before *ḥamza* was used as a written consonant in manuscripts, it is impossible to determine if this was the intended variant or not. Also, Puin asserts that the presence of the full *alif* in this word in manuscripts 01-28.1 and 01-29.1 presents a very early convention in orthography before *alif* and *yā'* and their uses in relation to *ḥamza* were fully distinguished and codified.[39] As such, the variants in these two manuscripts represent orthographic forms that represent an early inherent flexibility in pronunciation which preceded in time the formal distinction of recitations into canonical and uncanonical. The last variant attributed to an anonymous source listed above was not observed in any of the manuscripts.

Since the earliest manuscripts contain a form that can be interpreted with either choice, this form, when found in a manuscript, could represent a later change to make the text conform to an understood interpretation of the word. Because of the witness of the earliest manuscripts, and the way the reading افاده makes the meaning explicit, it is almost certainly a later reading and not part of the Canonical text-form. However, since it is found in two of the earliest manuscripts surveyed, there is a small chance it is the more original reading and the one without *alif* represents a dogmatic omission, but in view of the inherent ambiguities of Arabic in this early period, this writer thinks adding in the *alif* was more likely to be an intentional addition.

The second variant, افده , was also in the canonical variants. It is the form found in most of the early manuscripts. It is a form that can accommodate either of the main readings, "hearts" or "group," as they would have been written in the earliest orthography. Because of the prevalence of this form in the earliest manuscripts and it being the reading that best explains the origins of the other variants, it is probably the reading of the Canonical text-form.

The third variant, افودة , was not observed in the selected verses in any of the manuscripts surveyed. If it appeared in early manuscripts, it would be representative of the flexible use of the long vowels before their phonetic values were fully standardized. It is difficult to imagine a reason for a scribe to introduce this reading after the values were set. As such, it would be a form that could conceivably precede the Canonical text-form, or indicate a flexible level of spelling within the Canonical text-form.

14:37:5 تهوى يهوى al-Yamānī, 'A'isha, Masālama b. 'Abdāllah[40]

Diacritical mark variant: changes person from "you incline their hearts" to "the people incline their hearts." This was not observed in any of the manuscripts. This variant was also found in the canonical listings of variants. Seven of the older manuscripts do designate the consonant *tā'*.[41] The others would allow for either reading. As mentioned earlier, the Canonical text-form at this location was probably unpointed and allowed for the ambiguity that inspired or allowed both forms.

14:39:1 وهب لى وهبنى Ibn Muḥayṣin (14)[42]

Word variant: instead of preposition with attached pronoun, the pronoun is attached directly to the noun and the preposition "to" is omitted. This was not observed in any of the manuscripts. Since it is found in the Fourteen

Readings, it must have attained a fair degree of recognition. Grammatically, the two forms represent two ways of saying the same thing: "He gave to me," one through the use of a pronoun attached to a preposition, the other through the method of attaching a pronoun suffix directly to the verb to create an indirect object. The variant is the simpler of the two methods, and it is difficult to determine which might have given rise to the other. Also, both sound very similar in recitation and it would be easy to mistake one for the other aurally. Since the manuscript tradition is so unanimous on the version using the preposition, and since there is no dogmatic or stylistic reason why one should be preferred to the other, the standard reading should be viewed as that of the Canonical text-form.

14:41:1 ولوٰلدى ولولدى Yaḥyā b. Ya'mar, az-Zuhrī, Ibrāhīm an-Nakha'ī, Ja'far Muḥammad b. 'Alī, Sa'īd b. Jubayr[43], Ibn Mas'ūd[44]

Consonantal variant: the dagger *alif* represents the pronunciation of a full *alif* while recognizing that a full *alif* may not have been present in the earliest consonantal text. With the *alif,* the word means "and to my parents." Without the *alif* the word means "and to my children," or it could mean "parents" if the *alif* is understood to be pronounced though it is not present. The omission permits a degree of ambiguity in the choice of reading of this word. The form without *alif* was found in seventeen of the manuscripts surveyed.[45]

ولوالدى Sa'īd b. Jubair[46], Ibn Mas'ūd[47], Yahya b. Ya'mar[48]

Consonantal variant: the full *alif* is written in this form, making the word explicitly "parents." This form was observed in five manuscripts.[49]

The disagreement at the heart of these two variants is what is meant by the word if Ibrāhīm is praying for the forgiveness of himself and his parents, or for himself and his children or descendants. It is also important to note that both forms are attributed to the close companion of Muḥammad, Ibn Mas'ūd, indicating either a mistaken attribution or an invented attribution.

The reading ولوالدى makes the understood pronunciation of the word meaning "parents" explicit in the orthography. Since it is observed in two of the earliest manuscripts surveyed, Istanbul and 01-29.1, it has a strong claim to being the reading of the Canonical text-form. More of the early manuscripts had the form without *alif,* having been written before the convention of dagger *alifs* was introduced, which if pronounced without the *alif* meant "children" or "descendants." This was the case in six early manuscripts: Topkapi, BL Or. 2165, BNF 328a, 01-28.1, 01-20.x, and the Samarkand Kufic Codex.

Dogmatic reasons arose within Islam's first three centuries for distinguishing the two readings. If it refers to parents (with *alif*), then this verse provides the initial impetus for later Qur'ānic verses that present Ibrāhīm's personal struggle over his parents' eternal destiny, and Allah's decision that one should not pray for the forgiveness of confirmed idolators. If it refers to children (without *alif*), then it is at least a reference to the immediate context from verse 39 concerning Ismā'īl and Isḥāq, and possibly further to other descendants of Abraham who were monotheists. This would have a bearing on views of the extent of Ibrāhīm's prophetic knowledge and could provide a proof text for later Muslims seeking to include others under Ibrāhīm's prophetic mantle.

It is not an easy issue to resolve. From a text-critical point of view, the form without *alif* is the simplest, and best explains the origins of the others as attempts to alleviate the inherent ambiguity of the early script. Also, the meaning "children" has the appeal of fitting the context most closely with the near reference to Ibrāhīm's sons. This is all complicated, however, in that there is very early testimony to the form with *alif*, which would make the meaning of "parents" explicit. Overall, the version of the word without alif is probably the form of the Canonical text-form, since it represents a level of orthographic ambiguity known to exist at this time, and provides a basis for why some might wish to add in the alif to clarify the text.

ولابوي Ubayy b. Ka'b[50]

Word variant: this different word means "father." This was not found in any of the manuscripts. This variant is of special interest in that a ninth/third century authority on non-canonical variants, Ibn Ḥālawaīh, said this was in the original copy of the Qur'ān.[51] Unfortunately, he gave no further explanation. A dogmatic reason for this reading can be found in that within the Qur'ān itself there is a development in how Ibrāhīm's relationship with his idolatrous parents is presented. 14:41 is the only passage within the Qur'ān that refers to Ibrāhīm praying for both his parents' forgiveness. The other verses present him praying concerning just his father, before the later verses were given that he was not to pray for his forgiveness.[52] Perhaps we have in this reading an attempt to make the Qur'ān passages consistent on the matter and have them all relate to just Ibrāhīm's father. Unfortunately, because there is such little reference to actual manuscripts in early Islamic literature concerning variant readings, and because there is strong evidence that even by Ibn Ḥālawaīh's time any original manuscripts 'Uthmān may have sent out were probably destroyed,[53] it is difficult to take Ibn Ḥālawaīh's testimony as more than an inaccurate belief common to his time.

ولذريتي Anonymous[54], Some unnamed codices[55]

Word variant: this different word means "descendants." It was not found in any of the manuscripts. This variant makes explicit a particular interpretation of ولولدى, "children," that includes later generations. This reading was not found in any surveyed manuscript, and is only referred to in the secondary sources without any specific attribution to a Qur'ān reader or Companion of Muḥammad. If this had been the original reading, there would have been no reason to change it. However, it can be explained as an intentional variant to strengthen a particular interpretation of this verse so that it would include Muḥammad's descendants. It can therefore be safely regarded as not of the initial canonical text-form.

SHI'ITE VARIANTS

Shi'ite variants are a particular subcategory of uncanonical variants in their relation to the Qur'ān. They are variants asserted by some Shi'ite writers that they were once part of the Qur'ān but were changed or deleted for political and dogmatic reasons. There is a sizable literature on the existence, legitimacy, and importance of these variants.[56] The earliest Shi'ite scholars asserted that 'Uthmān had falsified the text of the Qur'ān, though later and current scholarship mainly upholds the authenticity of this text.[57] This study will not directly seek to uphold or disprove 'Uthmān's alleged falsification. Instead, it will present the variants reported in various lists and compare them to what has been found in the manuscripts surveyed. The main sources used are the major variant collections by Jeffery, *MQQ*, and *MQ*, Jeffery's collection of the readings of Zayd b. 'Alī,[58] a website devoted to comparing Shi'ite and Sunnī variants,[59] various articles,[60] and a significant newly available source, the *Kitāb al-qirā'āt of Aḥmad b. Muḥammad al-Sayyārī*.[61]

14:37:5 افىده افاده Zayd b. 'Alī[62]

Consonantal variant/Word variant: the *alif* instead of *ḥamza* changes this to a different word: "hearts" is changed to "group." As mentioned in the section concerning uncanonical variants, this form was observed in two of the earliest manuscripts surveyed, 01-28.1 and 01-29.1. It makes the word explicit that "group" is what is intended at this point, and not "hearts." It could also be indicative of an early use of *alif* for *ḥamza* that was later interpreted to be a different word. Because of the flexible orthographic conventions in the earliest period, and the way the reading افاده makes the meaning more explicit, reading it as 'group' is probably a later reading and not part of the Canonical text-form.

14:38:3 من شى   شان شى   al-Sayyārī[63]

Word variant: replacement of the preposition *min*, "of a thing" (e.g., "nothing"), with the adjective *shāy'*, "dishonorable thing." This variant is not attested in the manuscripts surveyed. It was also not listed among the canonical and uncanonical variants. If it were original, there seems to be no apparent reason why the text would have been changed away from it. However, changing the unspecific من شى ("of a thing," e.g., "nothing") to the specific شان شى ("a dishonorable thing") heightens the sense that Allah knows even the worst things that people conceal. A dogmatic reason could also be asserted in that it is only found in Shi'ite sources, and a common theme regarding the force of alleged Shi'ite variants is that they restored the honor and position of 'Alī and his family that had been taken by their enemies. Perhaps inserting this word strengthened the Shi'ite polemic that Allah was watching and would judge the dishonorable deeds done to 'Alī and all of the Shi'ites. Since this variant is so poorly attested in the literature and not at all in manuscripts, and since its existence can be explained as an exegetical and possible dogmatic strengthening of the text, it is almost certainly not the Canonical text-form.

14:41:1 ولو لدى   ولولدى   al-Ḥasan b. 'Alī,[64] Zayd b. 'Alī [65]

This is listed in both the canonical and uncanonical variants lists, but in Shi'ite sources it is attributed specifically to Ḥasan, son of 'Alī. With what is said concerning it in the prior sections, here may be added that the Shi'ite sources consistently present this reading as the authentic one, and use it as part of their justification for the prominence of 'Alī and his family. For textual and contextual reasons, this reading has excellent support for being in the Canonical text-form and possibly of an earlier Authoritative text-form from 'Alī's collection, though one cannot be certain. The dogmatic interpretations that can be adduced have no effect on the question of its originality, other than to add the fact that Shi'ites from early times have held this view of the reading of the text, perhaps back to 'Alī himself through his son Ḥasan.

The al-Burhan website notes that Shi'ites tend to favor the spelling without the *alif* meaning "children" or "sons" and interpret it various ways from Ismā'īl and Isḥāq to including the entire family of 'Alī together with them.[66] All of these variants agree with the accusation 'Alī is reported to have made to 'Abdallāh b. 'Amr b. al-'Āṣ concerning the extent of 'Uthmān's editing work on the Qur'ān being limited to the falsification of just letters and words, not phrases and portions.[67] But this cannot be asserted definitively since these variants are also found in Sunni sources and serve no clear dogmatic purpose. Also, they are all variants that are easily due to the ambiguities found in the earliest Arabic script found in Qur'ān manuscripts. They are all credible ways of reading an ambiguous script.

GENERAL OBSERVATIONS CONCERNING VARIANTS IN ISLAMIC LITERATURE

In view of the variants that have been listed, when one compares the kinds of variants present in these three categories of variants, Canonical, Uncanonical, and Shi'ite, some important observations emerge. First, the Canonical variants had many fewer variants in total than the Uncanonical ones, and had the ones that affected meaning the least. Two of the five listed Canonical variants were found in the manuscripts. One was an orthographic improvement found in later manuscript BL Or. 12884 and the other was one of three variants concerning the name of Ibrāhīm. Perhaps this was to be expected, in that being canonical there had already been selection according to a definite criterion for conforming to the 'Uthmānic *rasm*. That selection, however, was not one that did away completely with disagreement and variety in the process of supporting the Canonical text-form attributed to 'Uthmān.

Among the Canonical variants listed in the literature, there were three instances of a consonantal variant and one diacritical mark variant. The diacritical mark variant did affect meaning, as did one of the consonantal variants. The change of meaning involved a change of person with a verb and an added pronominal suffix that made an implied meaning explicit. The Canonical variants actually found in the manuscripts only involved small differences to the consonantal line of text that did not affect the meaning. They presented a smaller degree of variety in form and effect than those listed in the literature as having at one time existed.

All of these Canonical variants would have affected the sound of the recitation of these verses as well. These differences would have been noticeable to the listener or reciter. In a liturgical setting, the use of these various readings could have caused confusion, even though the basic meaning of the story was kept intact.

As one would expect from the title, the Uncanonical variants had many more variants affecting meaning and recitation when compared with the Canonical ones. Including the Shi'ite variants in this category, seventeen variants were listed in the literature, seven of which were found in the manuscripts. Among the ones listed in the literature were sixteen consonantal variants, one diacritical mark variant, and eleven word variants. Eleven of these affected the meaning of the verses in which they are located. This is a significant increase on the degree of variability compared with the listed canonical variants. It must be said, though, that the degree of variability is still relatively small. None of the Uncanonical variants changes the meaning in a drastic way away from the basic story line. It is still the same story, but with some small differences in detail.

All of these Uncanonical variants would have affected the sound of the recitation of these verses as well, and the degree of variability is increased in like manner to that of meaning. These differences would have been much more noticeable to the listener or reciter than with the Canonical variants. In a liturgical setting, the use of these various readings would probably have caused confusion, even though the basic meaning of the story was kept intact.

The Shi'ite variants were mainly a subset of the Uncanonical category, sharing many of the same readings. There were three consonantal variants and three word variants. All six of these affected the meaning of the verses in which they are located. None of them, however, changes the meaning in a drastic way away from the basic story line. Only two of them change the meaning in a way that can be used to support Shi'ite dogma, but it is not necessary to interpret these words in that way, and some Sunni scholars share these readings. Also, all of the Shi'ite variants would have affected the sound of the recitation of these verses, on a level comparable to that of the other Uncanonical variants.

A noticeable omission from all of these types of variants recorded in Islamic Qur'ān literature are ones that consist of larger portions of text from a multiple word phrase to a block of verses. There are records of these larger kinds of variants existing in the Qur'ān prior to 'Uthmān's initial standardization, but none of them are recorded in the records of the Canonical, Uncanonical, or Shi'ite variants for S. 14:35-41. If the records of these larger kinds of variants contain an authentic memory of what the Qur'ān once contained, then they are an additional measure by which the efficiency of efforts to conform the text of the Qur'ān to a standard consonantal text can be judged.

Examples of these larger variants can be found in regard to the reported collections of Muḥammad's companions. Ibn Mas'ūd is said to have had three fewer surahs in his collection, omitting what are now considered to be surahs 1, 113, and 114. Ubayy b. Ka'b's collection included these three surahs plus two additional ones consisting of short prayers.[68] Jones records a variety of records from the hadith that record forgotten surahs of substantial length.[69] There are claims that Surah 9 was once three or four times as long as it is in the present Qur'ān, which would have given it an additional 258–387 verses.[70] The Christian writer John of Damascus writing in the 730s/112–122, the mid-Umayyad period, mentioned the titles of surahs as separate writings, and included one called 'The Camel of God' together with 'the Women' (S. 4), 'the Table' (S. 5), and 'the Cow' (S. 2).[71] A Syriac Christian text, also thought to be from this time, mentions 'the Cow' as a book separate from the Qur'ān.[72] There are also other sources that list omitted or missing portions.[73] If these accounts are true, when they are viewed in light of the form of the text in the earliest available Qur'ān manuscripts, they testify to a very extensive standardization project for the text of the Qur'ān, and an equally extensive program to have extant manuscripts conform to that text. They also testify to a degree of fluidity of readings persisting into the mid- to late Umayyad period. If true they would testify that a canonical version was not firmly in place, even after the time of al-Ḥajjāj, though it is possible one existed and was still competing with other text-forms for priority.

Also, concerning the Companions' collections, among the variants listed in the literature were five attributed to Companions: two to Ibn Mas'ūd and three to Ubayy b. Ka'b. The two attributed to Ibn Mas'ūd were contradictory and were both found in manuscripts. One of the three attributed to Ubayy b. Ka'b was found in a manuscript. These also were relatively minor consonantal variants. If the Companions' collections at one time contained the full variety attributed to them in the literature, it appears that the more significant ones were edited out by the time of the earliest available manuscripts.

A second observation concerns the phenomenon that there were also many variants in the manuscripts that were not mentioned in the variants literature, though they were usually of a similar scope and significance. There were proper name variants not listed, diacritical mark variants not listed, *rasm* variants not listed, orthographic variants not listed, and the portions containing corrections were not listed. The variants found in the manuscripts were of similar types as those recorded for this section of text, but there were more found in the manuscripts than were recorded in the literature, and there were ones in the literature not found in the manuscripts. This confirms the observation also made concerning the palimpsests that in the earliest period at least, there was a greater degree flexibility of reading than what later became the case.[74] Also, it demonstrates that the records of variants may not have been made by a close examination of actual manuscripts, though they do record the main types of variants that are found in them.

CONCLUSIONS CONCERNING VARIANTS IN ISLAMIC LITERATURE

Many more textual variants are listed in the Islamic literature than are found in the manuscript tradition. This was mentioned earlier as a factor demonstrating the degree of external control exerted on the text of the Qur'ān in the manuscript tradition. Many of the sources that list these variants precede the standardization which followed Ibn Mujāhid's work. If the variants listed in these works were extant in manuscripts of the second and third Islamic centuries, then the complete absence of such manuscripts today can be best explained as evidence of a tremendous suppression of manuscript material and the consequent neglect of text forms that were proscribed.

That the consonantal form of the Canonical text-form attributed to 'Uthmān contains authentic material dating back to Muḥammad does not seem to be in doubt. What is in doubt is the precise content and organization of the material, and how this material was originally pronounced and its meaning understood, since both the Autographic text-forms and the Authoritative text-forms are missing. It is impossible to quantify how much material has been lost through the various programs to standardize and improve the text. Also, the meaning of any text can be drastically altered in the editing process by the selective inclusion and omission of words, phrases, and portions. How much the meaning of the text of the Qur'ān was changed by this editing before the era of the earliest manuscripts available today is impossible to quantify one way or the other.

Perhaps the single most significant observation that comes out of comparing variants in Islamic literature to those found in the early manuscripts is that there are many more listed in the literature than found in the manuscripts. The manuscripts show a very high degree of uniformity with a complete absence of word variants that were described in the Islamic literature. The spelling variants that were observed in the manuscripts were also much less variable than those described in the literature.

Often, the variants seemed to have arisen out of various legitimate ways of interpreting the ambiguous defective script of the early Arabic. Sometimes, though, memory of different words was asserted that differed from the consonantal skeleton of the current text. If these did exist in manuscripts at one time, their absence now attests to the efficiency of efforts to suppress them and to regularize the basic consonantal line to a very precise text-form. Also, evidence was found of dogmatically inspired alterations to the text.

That the literature contains some fabrication has been demonstrated.[75] That the literature contains variants that are present in some manuscripts and especially palimpsests has also been demonstrated by others.[76] That the manuscripts used in this study and the palimpsests contain variants on a wider scale than is described in the literature is also demonstrated.[77] The variants in the palimpsests and other manuscripts that are not mentioned in the literature, however, are not radically different from what are found in the literature, merely more of the same kind. There may be more word variants and some phrase variants, but they present the same basic kinds of texts in regard to themes, form, and general content.

For the Qur'ān manuscripts used in this survey, there is an almost complete lack of both word variants and a complete lack of larger phrase-length variants. The only examples of word and phrase length variants in extant manuscripts known to this writer in the wider scope of the Qur'ān are those collected from various sources by Alphonse Mingana,[78] ones in articles by Noja and Fedeli,[79] ones in an article by E. Puin,[80] two manuscript pages pictured in an appendix of a doctoral thesis,[81] versions mentioned in early Christian apologetic writers,[82] and the larger phenomenon of variant surah orders observed in the Ṣan'ā' manuscripts.[83] None of these sources, however, presents word or phrase variants for S. 14:35-41.

While containing an authentic memory of the kinds of variants found in the Canonical text-form, the variants listed so extensively in the Islamic literature are at best an incomplete record of the variants that the manuscript tradition once contained, and perhaps they are also a selective list with records of the larger and more significant variants having been suppressed along with variant text-forms. Looking at the variants in the manuscripts against the backdrop of the Islamic records points to an early editing process on the text that was intensive and extensive, intensive in its application to the precise consonantal text of the Qur'ān, and extensive in its application geographically and numerically to the textual tradition of the Qur'ān as it spread with the conquests.

NOTES

1. Keith E. Small, *Mapping a New Country: Textual Criticism and Qur'an Manuscripts* (Brunel: London School of Theology, 2008).
2. Theodor Noldeke, Friedrich Schwally, G. Bergsträsser, and O. Pretzl, *Geschichte des Qorāns* (Hildesheim: Georg Olms Verlag, 2005), 3:249.
3. Arthur Jeffery, *Materials for the History of the Text of the Qur'ān* (Leiden: Brill, 1937).
4. Jeffery, *Materials*, 2.
5. See 14:41:1 in the section on Uncanonical Variants where contradictory variants are attributed to Ibn Mas'ūd, both ولولدى and ولوالدى .
6. A. Fischer, "Grammatisch schweirige Schwur- und Beschwörungsformeln des Klassichen Arabisch," *Der Islam* 28:1–105, 5, footnote 4.
7. Jeffery, *Materials,* 10.
8. The manuscripts they did not have access to are the San'ā' manuscripts 01-20.x, 01-28.1, and 01-29.1. Also, it is possible they did not have access to the Istanbul manuscript.

9. Arthur Jeffery, "Progress in the Study of the Qur'an Text," *MW*, 25:1, 4–16, here 10.

10. Labib as-Said, *The Recited Koran* (Princeton, NJ: Darwin Press, 1975), 54; C. Melchert and A. Afsaruddin, "Reciters of the Qur'ān," in *EQ* 4:391, citing Nöldeke, *GQ* 3, 225. Also see Christopher Melchert, "Ibn Mujahid and the Establishment of Seven Qur'anic Readings," *Studia Islamica* 91: 5–22 and Christopher Melchert, "The Relation of the Ten Readings to One Another," *JQS* 10, 2: 73–87.

11. Ahmad Von Denffer, *'Ulūm al-Qur'ān* (Leicester: The Islamic Foundation, 1994), 117–18.

12. The Fourteen referred to here are often called, "the four Past the Ten." They are four reading systems that are often cited as having almost the same degree of authority as the Ten canonical systems.

13. Here are the Ten readers in order. The Seven are the first seven in the list: 1. Nāfi' (Medina, d. 785/169), 2. Ibn Kathīr (Mecca, d.737/119), 3. Abū 'Amr (Basra, d. 770/154), 4. Ibn 'Āmir (Damascus, d. 736/118), 5. 'Āṣim (Kufa, d. 745/128), 6. Ḥamza (Kufa, d. 772/156), 7. al-Kisā'ī (Kufa, d. 804/189), 8. Abū Ja'far (Medina, d. 747/130), 9. Ya'qūb al-Ḥadramī (Basra, d. 820/205), 10. Khalaf (Kufa, d. 843/229). Details of the Ten and its eighty sub-readings are taken from as-Said, *Koran,* 127–30, and Watt and Bell, *Introduction*, 49–50.

14. Abd al-'Āl Sālim Makram and Ahmad Muktār 'Umar, *Mu'jam al-Qirā'āt al-Qurānīyah, Ma'a Maqaddimah fī Qirā'āt wa Ashhar al-Qurrā'* (Cairo, Egypt: 'Ālam al-Kitab, 1997), 2:514. This is also reported to be the reading of three *riwāyas* of Ibn 'Āmir's reading: al- Ṣūrī's, Ibn Dhakwān's and Hishām's. Also, al-Bannā', *Ithāf fudalā' al-bashar fī'l-qirā'āt al-arba' 'ashr* (Beirut: Dar al-Kotob al-Ilmiyah, 2001), 343, records it of Ibn 'Āmir. Also listed in the *MQ*, 494.

15. Makram and 'Umar, *MQQ,* 2:514.

16. J. Horovitz, "Jewish Proper Names and Derivatives in the Koran," *Hebrew Union College Annual* 2 (1925): 146–227, citing 160.

17. Makram and 'Umar, *MQQ,* 2:515; al-Bannā', *Ithāf,* 343 also cites Hishām.

18. Shams al-dīn Muhammad bin Khalīd al Qabāqanī, *'Īsanāh al-Rumūz wa Maftāh al-Kunūz* (Amman, Jordan: Amar House, 2003), 475.

19. G. Bergsträsser, *Ibn Hālawaih's Sammlung Nichtkanonischer Koranlesarten* (Leipzig: BEI F.A. Brockhaus, 1934), 69.

20. Istanbul, Topkapi, 01-20.x, BL Or. 2165, BNF 325a, 326a, 328a, 330a, 331, 332, 333c, 334c, 340c, 343c, 370a, Meknes.

21. Gruendler, "*Script*," *EQ*, 1:140.

22. Bergsträsser, *Ibn Hālawaih,* 69.

23. تهوی was found in manuscripts: 01-28.1, BNF 325a, 330a, 331, 334c, Meknes, BL Or. 12884. 01-28.1 is the one of the earliest strata of manuscripts.

24. The manuscripts without diacritics here are: 01-29.1, 01-20.x, BL Or. 2165, BNF 328a, and BNF 326a.

25. These manuscripts are: BN 332, 333c, 340c, 343, and 370a.

26. Makram and 'Umar, *MQQ,* 2:515.

27. Ibn Mujāḥid, *Kitāb al-Sab'ah fi al Qirā'āt* (Cairo: Dar al-Mu'ārif, No date), 323. He added these three to the list.

28. Ibn Mihrān, *al-Mabsūt fī'l-qirā'āt al-'ashr* (Damascus: Matyū'āt Majma' al-Lu'at al-'Arbayyat bi Damashiq, No date), 258. He added this one to the list.
29. The four readers that make up the four past the ten are: Ḥasan al-Basṛī, Ibn Muhasịn, Yahyā al-Yazīdī, and al-A'mash.
30. Jeffery, *Materials,* 211.
31. Arthur Jeffery, *Foreign Vocabulary of the Qur'an* (Baroda: Oriental Institute, 1938), 45.
32. Ibn Kathir, *Stories of the Prophets* (Riyadh, Saudi Arabia: Darusslam), 148.
33. Jeffery, *Vocabulary,* 140.
34. Jeffery, *Materials,* 140.
35. Makram and 'Umar, *MQQ,* 2:515.
36. Bergsträsser, *Ibn Hālawaih,* 69.
37. Makram and 'Umar, *MQQ,* 2:515.
38. Istanbul, Topkapi, 01-20.x, BL Or. 2165, BNF 325a, 326a, 328a, 330a, 331, 332, 333c, 334c, 340c, 343c, 370a, Meknes.
39. Gerd-R. Puin, "Vowel Letters and Ortho-epic Writing in the Qur'an," in Gerd-R. Puin, *TBA* (Saarbrücken: 2010), 32.
40. Bergsträsser, *Ibn Hālawaih,* 69.
41. These are 01-28.1, BNF 325a, 330a, 331, 334c, Meknes, and Or. 12884.
42. Makram and 'Umar, *MQQ,* 2:516.
43. G. Bergsträsser, *Nichtkanonische Koranlesarten im Muhtasab des ibn Ginni* (Munich: Sizungsberichte der Bayerischen Akad. D, Wiss., 1933), 44. These are also listed in Makram and 'Umar, *MQQ*, 517.
44. Jeffery, *Materials,* 52.
45. Topkapi, 01-28.1, 01-20.x, BL Or. 2165, SamK, BNF 325a, 326a, 328a, 330a, 331, 332, 333c, 334c, 340c, Meknes, 370a, and Warsh.
46. Bergsträsser, *Ginni*, 44.
47. Jeffery, *Materials,* 52.
48. Bergsträsser, *Ibn Hālawaih,* 69.
49. Istanbul, 01-29.1, BNF 343c, BL Or. 12884, and the Muṣḥaf Sharīf.
50. Makram and 'Umar, *MQQ,* 2:517. Also in Jeffery, *Materials,* 140. Ibn Ḥālawaih said this word was in the master copy of the Qur'an, "al-'Imām," Bergsträsser, *Ibn Hālawaih,* 69.
51. Makram and 'Umar, *MQQ,* 2:517; Jeffery, *Materials,* 140; Bergsträsser, *Ibn Hālawaih,* 69.
52. These are S. 2:118-124; 9:114; 19:47; 26:86; 60:4.
53. Noldeke, Schwally, Bergsträsser, and Pretzl, *GdQ*, 3:6-8.
54. Makram and 'Umar, *MQQ,* 2:517.
55. Jeffery, *Materials,* 340. Ibn Ḥālawaīh says "in some of the codices" Bergsträsser, *Ibn Hālawaih,* 69.
56. A good overview and bibliography are found in Meir M. Bar-Asher's article, "Shī'ism and the Qur'ān," in Jane Dammen McAuliffe, *EQ* (Leiden: Brill, 2001–2004), 4:593–604.
57. Bar-Asher, "Shi'ism," *EQ*, 4:593–95.

58. Arthur Jeffery, "The Qur'an Readings of Zaid B. 'Ali," *Rivista Degli Studi Orientalia* XVI (1936): 40.

59. www.alburhan.com, accessed 28 December 2007.

60. M. M. Bar-Asher, "Variant Readings and Additions of the Imami-Si'a to the Qur'an," *Israel Oriental Studies* 13: 39–74; Todd Lawson, "Note for the Study of a 'Shī'ī Qur'ān," *JSS* 36, 2 (Autumn 1991): 279–95; Muhammad Ismail Marcinkowski, "Some Reflections on Alleged Twelver Shī'ite Attitudes Toward the Integrity of the Qur'ān," *Muslim World* 97:137–53.

61. Etan Kohlberg and Mohammad Ali Amir-Moezzi, *Revelation and Falsification: The Kitāb al-qirā'āt of Ahmad b. Muhammad al-Sayyārī* (Leiden: Brill, 2009).

62. Jeffery, "The Qur'an Readings of Zaid B. 'Ali," 265.

63. www.alburhan.com/book_articles.aspx?num=1328, page 12 of 19, 459.

64. Jeffery, *Materials,* 140.

65. Jeffery, "The Qur'an Readings of Zaid B. 'Ali," 265. Jeffery mentions that this recitation system was used "especially among the Ahl al-Bait," the family of 'Alī.

66. www.alburhan.com/book_articles.aspx?num=1328, page 12 of 19, 450–57.

67. Bar-Asher, "Shī'ism," *EQ,* 4:593.

68. W. M. Watt and R. Bell, *Bell's Introduction to the Qur'ān* (Edinburgh: Edinburgh University Press, 1970), 46.

69. A. Jones, "The Qur'ān - II," in A. Jones, *Arabic Literature to the End of the Umayyad Period* (Cambridge: Cambridge University Press, 1983), 238–39. One he mentions had 150 verses.

70. Hossein Modarressi, "Early Debates on the Integrity of the Qur'an," *Studia Islamica,* 77:5–39, 12.

71. Robert Hoyland, *Seeing Islam as Others Saw It* (Princeton, NJ: The Darwin Press, 1997), 487.

72. Hoyland, *Islam,* 471.

73. Claude Gilliot, "Un Verset Manquant du Coran ou Réputè Tel," in Marie Thérèse Urvoy, ed., *En Hommage au Père Jacques Jomier, O.P.* (Paris: CERF, 2002), 73–100; Arthur Jeffery, "Abū 'Ubaid on the Verses Missing From the Qur'an," *MW,* 28:61–65; Modaressi, "Debates"; Noldeke, Schwally, Bergsträsser, and Pretzl, *GdQ,* I:234–64.

74. Alba Fedeli, "Early Evidences of Variant Readings in Qur'ānic Manuscripts," in Karl-Heinz Ohlig and Gerd-R. Puin, eds., *Die dunklen Anfänge* (Berlin: Hans Schiler, 2005), 293–316, 304–5.

75. Andrew Rippin, "Qur'an 21:95: 'A ban is upon any town,'" *JSS* XXIV:43–53; Andrew Rippin, "Qur'ān 7.40: 'Until the camel passes through the eye of the needle,'" *Arabica* XXVII:107–13; Andrew Rippin, "Ibn Abbas's al-Lughat fi'l-Qur'an," *BSOAS,* 44:15–25.

76. See Small, *Mapping.* Also, for examples of larger variants see Alba Fedeli, "Early Evidences of Variant Readings in Qur'ānic Manuscripts," in Karl Heinz Ohlig and Gerd-R. Puin, eds., *Die dunklen Anfänge* (Berlin: Hans Schiler, 2005), 293–316.

77. Fedeli, "Evidences."

78. Alphonse Mingana and Agnes Smith Lewis, *Leaves From Three Ancient Qur'āns, Possibly Pre-'Uthmānic* (Cambridge: Cambridge University Press, 1914);

Alphonse Mingana, *An Ancient Syriac Translation of the Kur'ān Exhibiting New Verses and Variants* (Manchester: The University Press, 1925).

79. Fedeli, "Evidences," and Sergio Noja Noseda, "La Mia Visita a Sanaa e il Corano Palinsesto," *Instituto Lombardo Rendiconti* 137 (2003):1:43–60.

80. Elisabeth Puin, "Ein früher Koranpalimpsest aus San'ā' (DAM 01-27.1)," in Markus Groß and Karl Heinz Ohlig, eds., *Schlaglichter* (Berlin: Hans Schiler, 2008), 461–93.

81. Adrian Alan Brockett, *Studies in Two Transmissions of the Qur'ān*. PhD thesis, University of St. Andrews, Department of Arabic Studies, 1984.

82. Sidney H. Griffith, *Disputing with Islam in Syriac: The Case of the Monk of Bêt Ḫālê*. Washington D.C.: 2005, unpublished paper.

83. Gerd-R. Puin, "Observations on Early Qur'an Manuscripts in San'ā'," in Stefan Wild, ed., *The Qur'an as Text* (Leiden: Brill, 1996), 107–11, 110–11, and the UNESCO CD-ROM, *The San'ā' Manuscripts*, manuscript 35, Showcase 12, presents an irregular order which does coincide with that attributed to Ibn Mas'ūd in Bayard Dodge, *The Fihrist of Ibn al-Nadīm* (Chicago: Kazi Publications, 1970), 53–61.

10

Intentionality and Non-intentionality with Variants

One must not imagine the transmission of texts as a static process of precise copying of a text from one copy to another. Changes occur in the transmission history of a work by accident and also by the careful, intentional action of scribes. With sacred texts this can become a controversial subject because of dogmatic investment in particular forms of the text. However, intentional change to the text occurs for a variety of reasons, and these changes provide an essential part in tracing the history of the development of the respective text. One scholar provides this helpful observation:[1]

> versions are united not through similar mechanical mistakes and common passages, but by certain ideas, stylistic principles, etc. Every version of a literary monument is not a mechanical stage of its life, not the result of common mistakes transferred from the arch-type into its copies . . . but the result of conscious and deliberate activities of one of the scribes.

Though copyist mistakes do get passed on in a manuscript tradition, the intentional changes are the ones that have a more enduring effect and which shape further defined versions of the text. This observation can be applied to the intentional variants observed in the manuscripts used in this study.

While analyzing the variants a major consideration was to decide what measure of choice the scribe actively employed in writing the text as it came to be in that particular manuscript. Scholars have noted many reasons why such choices are made within a textual tradition. Hobbs sets out a simple set of four categories from the perspective of Classics and New Testament studies: orthographic improvements, harmonizations, explanatory changes, and doctrinal correction.[2] All of these kinds were usually made without an intention to substantially change the meaning of the text away from its original basic meaning. Ehrman, after an intensive study concerning intentional changes to the early New Testament texts states:[3]

> In fact, however, there is scarce need to posit any kind of ulterior motive for this kind of scribal activity. It is enough to recognize that when scribes modified their texts, they did so in light of what they already believed their Scriptures taught.

This is also true in great measure for the Qur'ānic manuscript tradition with the placement of diacritical consonantal marks that made a particular grammatical form explicit. The scribe was likely clarifying what he thought the unpointed text taught. It is also true of other orthographic improvements such as the addition of *alifs* and the standardization of the values of the long vowels *alif*, *yā'*, and *wāw*. It is true of the application of systems of colored dots to designate reading systems, and it applies to the development of fully pointed Arabic which presents every phonetic value precisely. These changes to the text were made with an intention to clarify what it was believed by many these texts meant. These kinds of changes would apply to any informal process of standardization of a text where scribes were working within the normal development of orthography and a language over centuries.

With the Qur'ān, however, we also have an additional force at work providing a platform for scribes to intentionally change the text. Early on in the Qur'ān's transmission history Islamic sources present a very conscious desire to establish a fixed text and one which was authorized by the highest political and religious authority. Such an action would require the normal categories of intentional variants to be augmented with an additional category to conform the text to a perceived standard text-form. This adds a factor of formal standardization to the transmission of an ancient text that is already subject to many less formal and informal scribal actions with the possible net result of a more unified textual tradition than with traditions without this extra element. In this study, corrections give the clearest window into this more formal phenomenon, though it is augmented by some of the orthographic improvements, and these against a background of the wider scope of variants found in some of the Qur'ānic palimpsests.

Also, just the effect of un-intentioned and well-intentioned textual changes, apart from more formal efforts, can be cumulative and significant. They can obscure the original form and meaning of the text. Ehrman, concerning well-intentioned changes, adds a significant observation:[4]

> This is exactly what the scribes did: they occasionally altered the words of the text by putting them "in other words." To this extent, they were textual interpreters. At the same time, by physically altering the words, they did something quite different from other exegetes, and this difference is by no means to be minimized. Whereas all readers change a text when they construe it in their minds, the scribes actually changed the text on the page. As a result, they created a new text, a new concatenation of words over which future interpreters would dispute, no longer having access to the words of the original text, the words produced by the author.

This effect occurs with general informal transmission dynamics, and the effect is heightened when dogmatic and political intentions enter transmission history through the efforts of religious and political authorities.

That the Qur'ānic manuscript tradition remained largely unpointed and unvoweled for centuries shows the reluctance scribes showed toward altering a particular form of the text. Their conservatism in this allowed the maintenance of one form of text and as this text gained official and widespread acceptance over other forms of the text, it made it more difficult to recover prior and competing forms of the text. Corrections and palimpsests possibly provide a small window into these other forms of the text.

The maintenance of a largely unpointed and unvoweled consonantal text did not, however, fully prevent new forms of the text. It allowed various recitations within the limited variability allowed by the phonetically incomplete orthography. The introduction of consonantal diacritical points limited this variability further while also allowing the creation of new forms of the text. These new forms, once adopted, would restrict and even deny access to earlier forms of the text. Established as interpretive text forms, they could also become new authoritative and then canonical text forms. When multiple manuscripts with slightly variant texts are available for examination, this phenomenon can be traced with a possible greater degree of success in recovering the earlier text-forms. When a lack of variant texts is available through the accidents of history and transmission, and when a version of the text becomes fixed and becomes the main one in use through active suppression and legal proscription of variation, then the possibilities of recovering the earlier text-forms diminish significantly. Hobbs provides a helpful comparison between textual criticism in the Classics and with the New Testament:[5]

> A problem in various types of textual criticism is posed by the extent to which we have materials. In beginning with classical textual criticism, I quickly learned that the big problem was that we have so little material; because of this, methods develop rather differently in classics than they do in the case of a sacred text in the West, where writing and copying became a major activity in the monasteries

for nearly a millennium. For the New Testament, the fact that you have *so* much material poses problems, but in most of the classics you have so little material that it is often difficult to reconstruct the history of the text.

The Qur'ān's situation is more similar to the classics, in that one form of the text predominates from an early period that represents the majority of extant manuscripts. Fedeli observes that Islamic records speak openly of various forms of the basic text of the Qur'ān that were in use during the first three Islamic centuries.[6] A greater variety is spoken of than can actually be observed in the manuscripts. This disparity could well be the result of efforts to suppress variant texts, as well as being testimony to the fact that these variant texts went out of use and suffered the ignominy of neglect. A brief survey of the unintentional and intentional variants observed would be useful to further illumine these issues.

UNINTENTIONAL VARIANTS

Qur'ānic scholars recognize that unintentional variants are a normal part of their respective manuscript tradition. Al-Azami recognizes that in the Qur'ānic tradition there are "scribal blunders resulting from fatigue."[7] Gacek catalogues many types of unintentional errors found in the wider Arabic manuscript tradition as well as the ways they were corrected.[8] He also makes the assertion that most of the variants in the wider Arabic manuscript tradition are unintentional scribal errors.[9]

Unintentional variants were observed throughout the surveyed manuscripts. They were usually easily identifiable, comprising a letter, a combination of letters, or an omission that did not make sense in the immediate context. A few of the manuscripts had corrections of such mistakes by later scribes. Occasionally, an omission needed more careful evaluation to discern if it was intentional or unintentional. Also, occasionally, when a correction was involved, it was necessary to evaluate whether or not the correction was rectifying a copyist mistake or conforming the text to a standard form. These kinds of variants had no appreciable effect on the form of the Canonical text of the selected passage, though a misplaced diacritical mark or letter could occasionally have an effect on the meaning of the text.

Twenty-one unintentional variants were observed in the Qur'ān manuscripts surveyed. The unintentional variants made up only six percent of the total textual variants. When one adds to these the intentional variants due to different orthographic conventions, especially in relation to dagger *alifs* and spelling differences in proper names, the overall figure for variants climbs into the hundreds.[10] If the ones due to varying orthographic conventions where the meaning was not affected are omitted, only seventeen remain (5 percent) that affect the meaning. The significant issues these figures and observations bring out are, first, that the variants concerning orthographic conventions were by far the greatest number of variants in the Qur'ān manuscripts. This reflects the dynamic situation of the Qur'ān's orthography in the first three Islamic centuries. Second, these can also be testimony to the effectiveness of the efforts to regularize the text in the early Islamic centuries when the emphasis of unifying the text of the Qur'ān was greater than the conviction to preserve or allow variant readings.

INTENTIONAL VARIANTS

It has been demonstrated that the Qur'ān manuscripts surveyed contained a variety of intentional variants and that the majority of variants had a demonstrable element of intention. The major category was the improvement of the orthography, which included standardizing and supplementing the use of *alifs*, adding diacritical marks to distinguish consonants, adding colored dots to indicate placement and pronunciation of short vowels and *ḥamza*, and then to implement a complete system of vocalization to indicate precise pronunciation of all consonants and vowels. Smaller categories were variants that were apparently done for grammatical improvements and to support a dogmatic position on an issue. These can be viewed as exegetical variants, introduced to clarify or establish the meaning of a text.

One more category was variants introduced to conform the text to a particular form of the text established by political and religious authority. Together, these kinds of variants greatly illumine the textual history of the Qur'ān, illustrating the steps that were taken to make a script a fully sufficient vehicle to convey precise meaning and pronunciation.

To Clarify a Particular Reading: Standard or Otherwise

Intentional variants were observed in the application of consonantal diacritical marks. The application of diacritical marks in BNF 334c at 14:37:6 could have been intentional to make the general word "fruit" the more specific word "dates." At 14:41:2 in 01-29.1 diacritical marks changing the person increased the intimacy of the invocation of Ibrāhīm to Allah.

Unclear Purpose

There were two intentional additions to the text that have an unclear purpose. At 14:35:3 in the Meknes manuscript, the letters لا were added for no easily discernible purpose. Also, at 14:40:2 in 01-29.1 a *nūn* was added to the end of a word for no clear purpose.

To Update the Orthography

The single greatest kind of variant for updating the orthography was the variants related to the incorporation of dagger *alifs* and the implementation of *alifs* which later came to be represented by dagger *alifs*. The intention for these was to clarify in the orthography what the text was already thought to mean. Since the net effect of any changes to meaning they brought is very small, they will not be discussed in detail. However, it should be noted that such additions and clarifications, once adopted into the wider manuscript tradition, did obscure earlier and more ambiguous forms of the text.

Five additional occurrences were observed where the orthography has been intentionally updated, at 14:38:1 in BNF 330a; 14:38:2 on the Meknes manuscript; 14:40:1 and 14:41:1 in the Istanbul manuscript. The first two involved the intentional addition of diacritical marks to make an ambiguous word especially clear. There may have been many more of these with the potential of many of the diacritical marks in the manuscripts being added later in their history. The two involving the Istanbul manuscript were the additions of full *alifs* to the text. This could have been to make an understood pronunciation explicit, or they could have been added in response to an edict to add *alifs* into the text, as has been suggested for another manuscript, St. Petersburg E 20, where this kind of addition can be found.[11] One could also include the introduction of *ḥamza* seen in BL Or. 12884.

Dogmatic/Exegetical

One of the most important, and also the most controversial sources of intentional variants are those made to cause the text to agree with or support a theological and/or political doctrine. Hobbs makes the following helpful observation:[12]

> People who are quite sure that a work is canonical, but are also sure that the theology that they have been taught is true, are certain that the text could not say anything that disagrees with their theology; therefore, the text in front of them must be wrong if it says something contradictory to their theology. This motivation is very powerful, but another works against it: the notion of a fixed text. In the case of the Hebrew text, this occurred when the Masoretic text was established; people count the letters and prescribe all kinds of ways to guarantee that no changes will occur.

The Qur'ān's textual history also has this tension between the desire to have the text read a certain way to support particular dogmas and to have a fixed text which does not vary through the transmission process. Rippin examined variants discussed in the early exegetical tradition of Islam and found ones that were tendentious, the variant word forms having been created from the ambiguous orthography to support a clear lexical or dogmatic argument.[13] Two of the variants observed in the manuscripts could be this type: the possible introduction of *alif* into افاده (S. 14:37:5) so that it could be interpreted as the word "group," and the introduction of *alif* in ولوالدى (S. 14:41:1) to make it mean explicitly "parents." These variants have been used in Shi'ite exegesis to support dogmatic claims for the family of 'Alī. These were discussed in detail in the last chapter.

CORRECTIONS AND PALIMPSESTS

One form of correction provides a larger example of a dogmatic/exegetical type of variant. This is when a portion of text is erased or crossed out and replaced with text in a way that shows a particular identifiable form of the text is being fixed or established. This is more than correcting a copyist mistake in an isolated manuscript. It is the conformation of a particular manuscript to a standard which is held to apply across the textual tradition. David Powers notes many small corrections and particularly, the correction of an important word in an early manuscript which conforms that word to what is now considered to be the standard consonantal text.[14] Powers demonstrates the effect even such a small correction can have for justifying a particular position in Islamic inheritance law. Examining corrections for these kinds of effects is a relatively unexplored area of Qur'ān manuscript studies.

The manuscript used in this study, BNF 370a, had a portion containing a few words that were erased and rewritten with what is now considered to be the standard form of the text. Unfortunately, the underlying corrected portion of text was so effectively defaced it cannot be reconstructed. However, what can be discerned is that whatever the original text was, it was a shorter form than what it was replaced with. Two other such corrections can be observed on the same page of text, though they occur in S. 14:44, outside of the portion exhaustively examined for this study. These were also smaller corrections exhibiting this concern for conforming a variant reading to the standard form of text. Two such corrections were observed in other manuscripts, each involving three letters of text (14:35:3 in the Meknes manuscript and 14:39:1 in 01-20.x).

If palimpsests had been available with S. 14:35-41 to represent the earliest period when the least amount of control on the text was exerted, it is very possible that the numbers of Qur'ān variants would increase in number, variety, and significance. This disparity being observed between palimpsest and non-palimpsest manuscripts is perhaps further evidence of an extensive project to standardize and unify the text of the Qur'ān in its early years, and to a firm conviction to continue limiting variation in the centuries since.

One of the phrases Fedeli notes as omitted in the Bonhams palimpsest was three short words from S. 5:42, *fa-'in jā'ūka* (فان جاءوك) , "And if they come to you."[15] The other is in the Fogg palimpsest from S. 2:217, *'an dīnikum*, (عن دينكم) "from your faith."[16] The omission of these phrases does affect the meaning of the text. Fedeli argues that this last one is possibly an indication of the construction of the Qur'ānic text confirming the justification that fighting in the holy month of *Rajab* was then permitted to Muslims.[17] As such, this particular omission could have been intentional for political and religious reasons. Further discussion of intentional variants will be reserved for that section later in this chapter.

CONCLUSIONS

Perhaps the greatest underlying issue related to intentionality in the Qur'ān manuscripts is that a unified official consonantal text was maintained and strengthened in these manuscripts. All of the surveyed manuscripts seem to date from a time after the basic consonantal text was established. Since there was not a uniform system of diacritical mark placement in use, and since there was opposition in some places to the addition of diacritical marks at all, the diacritical marks that are found were intentionally placed to make the ambiguous features of the text more explicit. One confirmation that there was no complete system in place was the observation on the different placement of the same kinds of diacritical marks between BL Or. 2165 and BNF 328a. Some of this placement seems to reflect early orthographic conventions that are not necessarily there to make the text easier to read. E. Puin notes that this is especially the case with final or independent *nūns*, which are often given dots even though these forms cannot be mistaken for another letter.[18] This issue still requires further research in order to make definitive statements, but it can perhaps be stated as a general principle that since the vast majority of the diacritical marks found in these manuscripts at least partly match what is held to be the standard text, they demonstrate intentionality of placement to make the text conform to a standard reading.

The scribes who penned the Qur'ānic intentional variants, however, while exhibiting an attitude of staying true to the basic storyline and while making the text more internally consistent, had the added overriding conviction that the text ought to conform to a precise form of the consonantal text. This attitude is seen in the corrections made in the manuscripts surveyed and when the entire shape of the text is compared to the kind of texts observed in the extant Qur'ānic palimpsests. The palimpsests seem to be the only extant manuscripts that possibly point to a form of text before an initial strong standardization. In all of the early manuscripts, also, there is a discernible attitude of limited freedom in the placing of diacritical marks while the consonantal *rasm* remained unchanged. This period of freedom, however, largely disappeared with the appearance of the fully vocalized texts in the tenth century.

Perhaps the greatest underlying issue related to intentionality is that a unified Canonical text-form was maintained in these manuscripts. The assumption of a fixed standard text in the first four centuries of Qur'ān scholarship is so assumed that it is often not even mentioned. There is the reference to the *Imam* in Sībawayhi,[19] and the ever present backdrop of comparison to a standard that variants are held against in the grammars, commentaries, and Qur'ān sciences books. It is an assumed ideal standard which all efforts are viewed against.

NOTES

1. D. S. Likhachev, *Tekstologiia. Na materiale russkoĭ literatury* 10–18 vekov (*Textology. On Materials of the Russian literature of the 10th–18th centuries*) (Moscow, Leningrad, 1962), 23, quoted in O. F. Akimushkin, "Textological Studies and the 'Critical Text' Problem," *MO* 1, 2:22–28, 24.

2. Edward Hobbs, "Prologue: An Introduction to Methods of Textual Criticism," in Wendy Doniger O'Flaherty, *The Critical Study of Sacred Texts* (Berkeley: Berkeley Religious Studies Series, 1979), 1–27, 5–7.

3. Bart D. Ehrman, *The Orthodox Corruption of Scripture* (Oxford: Oxford University Press, 1993), 279.

4. Ehrman, *Corruption,* 280.

5. Hobbs, "Sacred," 2.

6. Alba Fedeli, "Early Evidences of Variant Readings in Qur'ānic Manuscripts," in Karl Heinz-Ohlig and Gerd-R. Puin, eds., *Die dunklen Anfänge* (Berlin: Hans Schiler, 2005), 293–316, 315.

7. M. M. Al-Azami, *The History of the Qur'anic Text* (Leicester: UK Islamic Academy, 2003), 151.

8. Adam Gacek, "Taxonomy of Scribal Errors and Corrections in Arabic Manuscripts," Adam Gacek, *Theoretical Approaches to the Transmission and Edition of Oriental Manuscripts* (Beirut: Ergon Verlag Würzburg, 2007), 217–35, 219, 222–25.

9. Gacek, "Taxonomy," 219.

10. One count sets it at at least 410. See Keith E. Small, *Mapping a New Country: Textual Criticism and Qur'an Manuscripts* (Brunel, London School of Theology, 2008), 203.

11. Efim A. Rezvan, *The Qur'ān of 'Uthmān* (St. Petersburg: St. Petersburg Centre for Oriental Studies, 2004), 66.

12. Hobbs, "Sacred," 7.

13. Andrew Rippin, *The Qur'an and its Interpretative Tradition* (Burlington: Ashgate, 2001), xiv.

14. David S. Powers, *Muhammad Is Not the Father of Any of Your Men: The Making of the Last Prophet* (Philadelphia: University of Pennsylvania Press, 2009), 155–96. The word is كلالة (kalāla) which is the remaining form after two corrections at this point of the text in S. 4:12b.

15. Fedeli, "Evidences," 300.

16. Fedeli, "Evidences," 314.

17. Fedeli, "Evidences," 314; Alba Fedeli, "The Interdiction of Fighting in the Holy Month: The Struggle for the Abolition of an Early Tradition in the Scriptio Inferior of a Qur'ānic Palimpsest," Actes des congrès: Le Judaïsme en Arabie, des origines a l'aube de 'Islam, Jerusalem, 2006.

18. Elisabeth Puin, "Ein früher Koranpalimpsest aus San'ā' (DAM 01-27.1)," in Markus Groß and Karl Heinz-Ohlig, eds., *Schlaglichter* (Berlin: Hans Schiler, 2008), 461–93, 468.

19. Adrian Alan Brockett, "Qur'an Readings in Kitab Sibawayhi," *University of St. Andrews School of Abbasid Studies: Occasional Papers of the School of Abbasid Studies*, 2:129–206.

11

Oral and Written Textual Transmission

An important feature that must be taken into account in any examination of the textual tradition of the Qur'ān is its genesis and early transmission in a culture featuring predominantly oral literary conventions. Donner summarizes the traditional Islamic view of the complementary roles of oral and written transmission dynamics:[1]

> In sum, the traditional Muslim view of the Qur'ān's origins as a written text takes it as axiomatic (1) that the Qur'ān text we have today is a direct descendent of a single original text that first coalesced in the time of the prophet, and (2) that the accuracy of the transmission of this text was ensured by a living tradition of oral recitation going back uninterruptedly to the many companions of the prophet who first heard him utter it.

This mixture of oral and written transmissions raises a number of issues when examining the earliest extant manuscripts and the transmission of the text in Islam's first three centuries. For instance, that the Qur'ān coalesced in a largely oral milieu is perhaps part of the explanation why written texts from its earliest period do not survive. They were not considered at the time as important as the memorized and recited versions. Also, though, since the earliest available manuscripts date to within a century of Muḥammad's death, written preservation came to be valued relatively quickly. Within the 600s, the relationships of oral and written transmission were evidently shifting to more of a reliance on the written in that the Arabic used was already a written idiom with an established, though still flexible orthography.[2] Déroche notes that this early reliance on writing reflects a suspicion of an inherent degree of inaccuracy in oral tradition.[3] The written tradition, however, was not without its problems since early Arabic script contained an inherent level of ambiguity, and oral tradition came to occupy a supplementary role transmitting details that could not be expressed by the limited orthography.

Madigan ably demonstrates that the original form of the Qur'ān was oral, and that for much of these early centuries the written version was much less important in practice and in thought than the oral. He asserts that the full written text of the Qur'ān played quite a limited role in the early decades of Islam, since all of the text was not recited in worship or used for establishing a Muslim way of life.[4] Concerning the process of recording the earliest versions of the Qur'ān with an incomplete script, he says there is[5]

> the possibility that the scattered revelations were collected and transcribed early; the transcripts were preserved, but only parts of the oral tradition survived intact, since very little of the Qur'ān was required for worship and only a small amount offered any practical guidance in developing a characteristically Muslim style of life. At some later time, the integrity of the oral tradition would have been restored based upon the transcripts, even with their flaws.

Also, the traditions concerning 'Uthmān collating the text give as his main reason the conflict caused by soldiers reciting the Qur'ān in different ways, and his solution was to unify the written text rather than send reciters to unify an oral transmission of an existing standard written text.[6]

Madigan also demonstrates the difficulty of asserting that Muḥammad had it in mind to produce a written scripture and that early Muslims do not seem to have particularly wanted one. He asserts that Muḥammad never intended a written form for the Qur'ān:[7]

> To fulfil [sic] such a function, even an incomplete oral tradition would have been adequate. Indeed it still is, in practise, adequate. Wilfred Cantwell Smith maintains that "Muslims, from the beginning until now are that group of people that has coalesced around the Qur'ān." There is a sense in which this is true, but the evidence indicates that they "coalesced" around it while it was still incomplete, still oral, still in process. They committed themselves to belief in a God who had initiated a direct communication with them, and who had thereby established a continuing relationship with them. They gathered around the recitations as the pledge of God's relationship of guidance with them rather than as a clearly defined and already closed textual corpus.

If the environment was so dominated by oral literature conventions and a recited oral Qur'ān, then according to Madigan's argument, it would be wrong to look for a complete written form of the Qur'ān from this period. It would be improper to expect the product of a written literary milieu from an oral one, like expecting a carefully composed literary work like the individual books or letters in the New Testament, or the classic literatures from Rome, Persia, or Byzantium from late near eastern antiquity. With this in mind, it is possible that the collection stories which emphasize written precision contain a degree of authentic memory of an early need for unity on the recitation of the Qur'ān and the standardization of some form of written text to be an anchor for an oral tradition. While containing this memory, they would also be reading back on that early period a viewpoint of orthographic precision crafted in a later era after the initial conquests when the Qur'ān had become a written literary product and Islamic society had itself made the transition from an oral literary milieu to a written one. This anachronistic reading back would explain the discrepancies between the hadith collection stories that Burton has presented.[8] Another example of an anachronistic Islamic look back at this period, one depicting an inappropriate standard of proficiency in written literature, comes from the medieval polymath Ibn Khaldūn (d. 1406/809):[9]

> Arabic writing at the beginning of Islam was, therefore, not of the best quality nor of the greatest accuracy and excellence. It was not (even) of medium quality, because the Arabs possessed the savage desert attitude and were not familiar with the crafts.
>
> One may compare what happened to the orthography of the Qur'ān on account of this situation. The men around Muḥammad wrote the Qur'ān in their own script, which was not of a firmly established, good quality. Most of the letters were in contradiction to the orthography required by persons versed in the craft of writing. The Qur'ānic script of [the men around Muḥammad] was then imitated by the men of the second generation, because of the blessing inherent in the use of an orthography that had been used by the men around Muḥammad, who were the best human beings after [Muḥammad himself] and who had received his revelation from the book and word of God.

Though there might be some truth in this as to the lack of training of Muḥammad's companions, the earliest scripts found in the Qur'ān manuscripts are of the same quality and level of development as the Arabic used in business and administrative papyri.[10] It was of a normal quality for the secular standard of the time.

An earlier Islamic scholar, Qāḍī Abū Bakr al-Bāqillānī (d. 1012/403), also inadvertently made this kind of mistake in that he claimed that within Muḥammad's lifetime, the complete arrangement of the text of the Qur'ān was fixed, including the precise vowels and consonantal readings of the text.[11] In view of the extant manuscript evidence, this appears to be anachronistic, in that the precise vowels and readings could not have been preserved in the script of the seventh century, and the oral transmissions of whatever texts were being recited were so varied they were causing strife threatening civil war. Roxburgh observes similar retrospective claims attributing the invention and application of vocalization marks to named figures and dates from within Islam's first century, well before such features appear in manuscripts.[12]

Only a standardization of the basic consonantal text could have provided an anchor for a more unified oral version. But the script used for this standardization, while establishing a basic consonantal parameter for oral recitation, was one which was not precise enough to prevent the development of various further consonantal bases, and also various oral versions. These had to await further improvements to the orthography.

Concerning the earliest attainable text, what these factors demonstrate is that a defective consonantal line of text, as is found in the earliest manuscripts used in this study, was the vehicle used for a collated and edited version of the Qur'ān which then became canonized through a possible combination of political action and consensual agreement. While this text stands within close proximity to the era of the first generation of Muslims, perhaps only a couple of generations away, it cannot represent the earliest forms of the Qur'ān if multiple and/or partial versions were being used before and after Muḥammad's death. It can be reasonably said to contain authentic portions of those forms of the text, but portions that had been collated and edited after being reduced to writing.

QUR'ĀNIC ORAL TRADITION: ITS RELATIONSHIP TO THE WRITTEN TRADITION

The Qur'ān was given in an oral setting which started to shift to one which relied on written literary conventions. At the time of Muḥammad's death, this shift had been initiated but was not complete, having possibly started in the Medinan period.[13] After his death, various collections of these materials circulated in written and oral form. None of these collections was strictly uniform, but they apparently contained the same kind of material in the basic written and oral literary forms we find present in the current Qur'ān. Within the first Islamic century, from the evidence of the surveyed manuscripts, a major program was undertaken to unify the basic consonantal form and content of the text.

The coexistence of oral and written literary cultures continued, though the oral became more and more restricted and tied to the memorization of set texts, and the set texts were restricted to the revised and unified corpus of written material, which was recorded in an ambiguous script. The ambiguities of the script, together with the continuing conviction of the necessity of oral recitation, and with a somewhat flexible attitude toward the precision of readings, allowed variable versions of reciting the set texts to coexist and multiply. Some of the material originally proscribed for the purposes of political unity continued to be recited and in the flexible situation even gather a following. Jeffery notes that at least fifty systems for reciting the Qur'ān were still known after the canonization of the Ten in the tenth/fourth century.[14]

In other genres of early Islamic literature, the reliability or unreliability of the written records of oral tradition are governed by the use of *asānīd (isnād, sg.)*, chains of names or oral transmitters attached to the report of the historical event, legal ruling, or instruction from Muḥammad or a companion. There is considerable debate in Western scholarship as to whether or not these are a helpful tool or an irrelevant and possibly fabricated attachment.[15] Motzki has demonstrated that when *isnād* and *matn* criticisms are judiciously combined, they can have a helpful use in tracing the forms of text of particular hadith and of establishing more extensive timelines for their transmission.[16] However, when it comes to the Qur'ān, it is in an entirely different category from hadith literature. Neither the actual portions of the text of the Qur'ān, nor the precise form they are in, nor their precise orthography are supported by these chains of names of oral transmitters.[17] Instead, a more general form of the recitation of the entire text is said to be supported by the *isnād*. Also, the development of precise *asānīd* for Qur'ān recitations followed after their development for hadith studies. There developed a greater concern for more detailed *asānīd* in the tenth century, while before that it was a much less rigorously applied criterion for criticism of Qur'ānic recitation systems.[18]

The stories of the collection of the Qur'ān do have *asānīd* attached, and complete systems of recitation will have the pedigrees of the reciters from past generations, but the exact contents of these systems and the precise form of the text are not documented by them. Al-Azami claims that such documentation was not needed because of the ubiquitous use of the Qur'ān in the lives of Muslims in that early era since it was a vital element in all prayers. This is an overstatement, in that only a small proportion of the complete text of the Qur'ān was needed for prayers and daily devotional needs.[19] Also, he claims there were professional reciters who had certificates listing their pedigrees as to which line of reciters they stood in going back to Muḥammad.[20] This may have been the situation after a couple of centuries with the consolidation of the empire and the development of Qur'ān recitation into its own sub-discipline of Qur'ānic studies, but from the picture already developed from manuscripts and the dynamics of oral transmission, it is difficult to envision that such a comprehensive and detailed system of oral and written transmission could have been set up from the outset. Pretzl gives an important observation concerning how these chains of reciters were viewed in the time of Ibn Mujāḥid (924/323):[21]

> Now it has become considerably clearer that the books on the unified canonical readings are not the outcome of surviving oral traditions, but conversely the oral tradition of later times is very heavily dependent on the sketchy literary tradition. . . . It is extremely characteristic that Ibn Mujāhid of all people . . . , in order to solve the dispute which already existed in his time, argued with quotations from literary sources and did not refer back to an oral tradition. If such a tradition was known to anyone, then it must be to him, the founder of the unified canonical reading.

Instead of a well developed, standardized, and regulated system of professional reciters, it appears that there was a very unregulated system with many oral transmissions of the text that matched the variety of ways with which the unpointed Qur'ān text of that era could be read and pronounced. Welch notes that the situation at one point became so confused with the development of new ways of reading the text that it became impossible to recover with confidence even the "original" 'Uthmānic text.[22] Though it was held as a theoretical possibility, it was commonly accepted by Qur'ān scholars of all groups that numerous competing reading systems were a fact of life. Melchert recounts Ibn Mujāḥid's reply when asked why he had not chosen just one reading. He said, "We need to engage ourselves in memorizing what our imams have gone over more than we need to choose a variant for those after us to recite."[23]

The initial forms of the text were ambiguous to a degree that no one oral tradition was able to control. Instead, oral recitations were limited to the unified consonantal text defined by scholarly decision, consensus, and government encouragement to ten versions in the tenth/fourth century. These approved oral transmissions were each able to be precisely recorded and transmitted in the written tradition by the improvements that had by then been made to Arabic orthography, though these also continued to develop further oral versions based on the ten. In time, eighty interrelated though distinct oral transmissions of the ten recitation systems came to have an authoritative status.[24]

When Ibn Mujāḥid set out the seven recitation systems he believed were best, he did not rely solely on oral tradition to establish which had the best claim to reach back to Muḥammad's practice. Instead, he relied more on criteria which in his time seemed best suited for eliminating improper versions. The fifty-plus versions he was sifting through were presumably based on 1) the 'Uthmānic consonantal text, 2) versions attributed to the Companions that were still in use, and 3) possibly other versions with a different consonantal structure.[25] In the midst of this complicated situation, Ibn Mujāḥid settled on seven versions that could be traced back by named reciter (not written records of the pronunciation) to the eighth/second century.[26] Note these were not traced back to one version given by Muḥammad[27] or even a particular version given to a Companion. The Qur'ān resulting from Ibn Mujāḥid's actions was in effect a compromise measure between an "exact text" and a "generalized variant."[28] Melchert observes of Ibn Mujāḥid's work that he never asserted that his chosen seven readings were pure, integral, unchanged readings passed on from the earliest times. Rather, the major Qur'ān readers he cites used systems which they created by synthesizing the readings of multiple earlier readers.[29] It was a scheme that could find the support of a large portion of the population and the government, while not reaching for the impossible task of requiring unity on one form of the text. It also brought the written text of the Qur'ān into as close agreement with the dogma of one eternal Qur'ān as was possible by the situation presented with the plethora of variant reading systems, the developments needed with Arabic orthography, and religio/political considerations at this volatile time when the debate was raging between the Mu'tazilites and the Orthodox.[30] Ibn Muqla's reforms with the Arabic script also provided a suitable and timely vehicle for recording precise pronunciations of the Qur'ānic text.

This brief historical overview of the relationship between the written and oral transmissions of the Qur'ān implies that the oral transmissions, while retaining some degree of independence of transmission, also became inescapably tied to written versions of the text, and to the reforms in the precision of the orthography of the written manuscript tradition. When the text of the Qur'ān changed through limiting consonantal variants or improving the orthography, these gave a departure point for new versions of the oral transmission of the text.

To further clarify the issues involved in relating the oral tradition of the Qur'ān to the written one, here are some basic issues that demonstrate the dependence of the oral on a written form of the text:

1. Variants in the manuscripts concerning the spelling of proper names, grammatical variants from inserted or omitted long vowels, and grammatical variants due to diacritics, originally allowed a plurality of possible readings, and orthographic changes were necessary to limit the options for pronunciation and meaning.[31]
2. Madigan and Bellamy highlight various early orthographic peculiarities that the oral tradition could not control, from the decision to pronounce an ending with *imālah*,[32] to correcting scribal errors in the 'Uthmānic text.[33]

3. The oral traditions seem to have been encouraged or suppressed in accordance with whatever form of the text was then the recognized or permitted standard. Muḥammad left a variable situation with multiple forms of the Qur'ān being recited. The 'Uthmānic *rasm* was developed and introduced to limit this situation, though there was continued use of some of the Companions' collections. Because of the defective script and the multiple versions in use, these versions spawned at least fifty different ways of reciting the Qur'ān by the fourth/tenth century. Ibn Mujāhid's action could only limit this to seven based on a largely unified consonantal text, and three more were later found which met the same criteria. Then from these ten, eighty further versions have come to be recognized, eight for each of the ten.[34] The ten may have been a refining measure to stop the excesses of forty-plus wrong recitations, but then they themselves developed into eighty precise recitations, all of which had not been committed to writing prior to 936/324.
4. Pretzl's observation that even Ibn Mujāhid depended on literary tradition for determining the proper oral transmissions was augmented by the further observation that the *Qirā'āt* literature itself developed in sophistication and detail as the written and oral versions themselves evolved into more complicated and precise systems.[35] Dutton implicitly confirms this by relying on written records of consonantal variants in BNF 328a and BL Or. 2165 to identify them with particular reading traditions.[36] With these early partially pointed manuscripts, only written variants can serve as a guide for determining to which oral transmission they might be related.
5. It has been demonstrated by others that textual variants were at times invented for exegetical reasons, and this also confirms this general situation in that the orthography permitted ambiguity which some were minded to use to their advantage.[37] The oral and written transmissions were not strong enough in the early period to completely prevent this phenomenon.
6. The degree of uniformity of the *rasm* of these manuscripts is perhaps another indication of the high priority put on preservation of the written text, even if it was written in a phonetically defective orthography and open to various interpretations. The history of the development of the script is then one of innovations to correct the degree of ambiguity that could lead to alternative interpretations. The introduction of *ḥamza*, for instance, and the standardization of usage of *alif* and *yā'*, the corrections observed in manuscripts, the standardization of the spellings of proper names, the addition of other readers' helps that have become the full vocalization system—all of these are innovations to lessen the degree of interpretive variability.

The written and the oral versions of the text are often thought of as being separate, parallel, and also mutually supportive of the other.[38] However, this parallel view does not adequately explain the growth in the variety of the oral and written versions of the Qur'ān in Islam's first three centuries, and it does not seem to have been the kind of mindset scholars of the time were using when they constructed their own reading systems by synthesizing others. Whatever oral traditions were in place were not strong enough to prevent variants in meaning and pronunciation, both of which must be avoided if there is to be a precisely unified recitation of scripture.

MUḤAMMAD AND MULTIPLE VERSIONS?

Bellamy helpfully summarizes the situation if one has in mind that Muḥammad brought a single version of the material that later came to be viewed as the Qur'ān:

> One cannot argue that the prophet used one variant one day and the other the next. Nor can one maintain that there is a firm oral tradition that guarantees the reading of the unambiguous words but breaks down when more than one reading is possible. It seems clear that the earliest readers got their readings from the *written* text of the Uthmanic recension, and since Arabic was their native language, they read the unambiguous parts correctly, and where the text was ambiguous, they exercised their knowledge of the language and came up with what pleased each of them the most.[39]

If one views the genesis of the Qur'ān as occurring in mainly an oral milieu, however, multiple performance variants of the basic material are probable, and this could partially account for the kinds of textual variants and differences that are described in the secondary sources. This does, however, cast later Muslim reflections back to this period as anachronistic descriptions expecting a greater degree of precision and written development than was possible in the early period. This view also agrees with later literary conventions as Arabic language and Islamic culture became more bound by written literary conventions. Later generations, trying to make sense of the inherent ambiguity of the early script, and also of the variety of readings they had received through their tradition, found ways to limit the variety through orthographic improvements, evaluating the lines of oral transmission they had received historically and dogmatically, and so imposed an order on a chaotic situation to the best of their knowledge, method, and belief.

The oral and the written transmissions of the Qur'ān were interrelated from the start, but in the final analysis, the oral has consistently followed the lead of the written, as in an intricate and evolving dance trying to balance oral and written literary conventions. And as the written tradition increased in precision and sophistication, and decreased in flexibility, so too did the oral tradition. After the initial standardization of the written text, the oral traditions evolved from what the ambiguities in the Arabic script at each stage of its development would permit. Whether any of the oral versions of the earliest pedigrees do go back to Muḥammad is impossible to document because of the lack of precise written records of those recitations. Bellamy says of the *qirā'āt*:[40]

> They are important to us here because they prove that there was no oral tradition stemming directly from the prophet strong enough to overcome all the uncertainties inherent in the writing system.

Margoliouth, reflecting on the apparent situation that Ibn Mujāḥid was not drawing his conclusions on a single tradition of Qur'ān reading going directly back to Muḥammad (but rather several), made this insightful comment about this process of the standardization of the seven readings:[41]

> We should have expected the Various Readings to be based on Tradition; the commentators rather assume that they are based on consideration of the evidence. . . . They were not, then, reproducing what they had learned from teachers, but doing their best to decipher a text.

Traditional Islamic views of the readings do not take these issues sufficiently into consideration. They tend to view the seven or ten readings as being reliable tradition in some way going back to Muḥammad. Some contemporary Muslim scholars believe that the seven readings are authentic presentations of pronunciations of the Qur'ān from the seventh/ first century, even going back to Muḥammad himself. Al-Azami states unequivocally, "where more than one authoritative reading existed, the source of this multiplicity was traceable to the Prophet."[42] But he is not viewing the multiplicity of versions allowed in an oral milieu. Rather, he is anachronistically asserting various versions containing a degree of precision only possible in a more developed later written literary milieu. Melchert has demonstrated that the concern for precision and the ability to maintain precise imitation of recitation developed over Islam's first three centuries, and this appears to be the kind of situation paralleled by the orthographic development seen in the manuscript tradition.[43]

Also, Al-Azami is referring to the memorized pedigrees of the Qur'ān reciters, not to *isnads* attached to and guaranteeing specific portions of text. There was not a parallel written guarantee that the details of the recitation went back to Muḥammad, only a more general form.

In choosing seven readings, Ibn Mujāḥid chose seven versions that were attributed to second/eighth century Qur'ān reciters and claimed their readings had divine authority.[44] Though Ibn Mujāḥid did not quote a hadith in support of his choice of seven, there was at that time a well known hadith which asserted that the Qur'ān was revealed in seven ways,[45]

> Allah's Messenger (peace be upon him) said, "Gabriel recited the Qur'an to me in one way. Then I requested him (to read it in another way), and continued asking him to recite it in other ways, and he recited it in several ways till he ultimately recited it in seven different ways."

Ibn Mujāḥid never identified his seven readings with these "ways" but their explanation has gotten caught up in debates within Islamic scholarship as to exactly of what the "seven different ways" or "modes" (*aḥruf*) consist. Von Denffer, a current Islamic scholar who is very familiar with Western scholarship, acknowledges that historically there have been at least thirty-five different interpretations of this word *aḥruf*, anything from the Companions' collections being the different modes, to different dialects, to different ways of pronouncing the same basic consonantal text, or to the current text somehow within itself containing the seven modes.[46] Von Denffer is careful to say that the "seven readings" chosen by Ibn Mujāḥid are not the same as the seven modes attributed to Muḥammad. But he never clearly defines his own view of the seven readings. Instead, he states his agreement with another scholar's confusing and self-contradictory statement that any reading/recitation system that is in accordance with Arabic grammar, has an approved pedigree of reciters, and is in accordance with the consonantal text attributed to 'Uthmān, is a correct reading somehow belonging to the seven modes, even if it is one of the Ten or beyond.[47] Nelson, a researcher into Qur'ān recitation systems and practices, states,[48]

> Whatever the precise definition of *aḥruf*, all of the *ḥadīth* on the subject indicate the following principles: all variants are of equal status in terms of their truth and rightness and all variation is the word of God as revealed to Muḥammad, with no human intervention involved . . . the relationship of the canonical variant readings, the *qirā'āt*, to the *aḥruf* is also the subject of much discussion in Islamic works, and there are differing opinions. However, most scholars agree that the seven *aḥruf* do not refer to the seven canonical readings, although they are the basis for them.

Welch states that this method of selecting rival systems and declaring them equally authoritative was used in other areas of Islamic life to avoid irresolvable disputes and likens it to the four Sunnī schools of jurisprudence.[49] The following description is a more consistent answer than many explanations of the seven modes: since exact knowledge of the original recitation of the earliest edited version of the Qur'ān had been lost among the many versions that had arisen from the flexibility and ambiguity of the orthography of the Qur'ān, Ibn Mujāhid chose what in his time were the readings that had the greatest chance of being viewed as authoritative and authentic. It was a pragmatic decision based on the best results the scholarship of that era could obtain. As Rezvan observed, it was a compromise between "the exact text" which could not by then be recovered, even of the earliest edited version, and a "generalized variant" that allowed some latitude of variation, and which would meet with broad acceptance from a variety of groups in his situation.[50]

CONCLUSION

That an oral tradition of the recital of the Qur'ān exists from the earliest period of the text is not contested. What is contested among scholars, both Islamic and Western, is how complete and strong this tradition was to preserve a precise pronunciation of the text as it was received. The manuscript evidence best supports a view that though it was a necessary feature accompanying the written text, an oral tradition of the precise pronunciation of the text was never strong enough or developed enough to unify the earliest Muslim community on a single standard recitation of the text. The mechanics and systems were not in place to establish and maintain a strong enough oral tradition to provide an undisputedly precise oral pronunciation of the ambiguous consonantal text of the Qur'ān. The textual mechanics were not in place in that there were multiple Authoritative text-forms after Muḥammad's death which would have each required a separate strong oral tradition. Otherwise, a written recension, like the one attributed to 'Uthmān, would not have been needed. The time frame for when this standardization took place was in Islam's first century, and it was possibly a two-stage standardization of the consonantal text, with those two steps occurring toward the middle and end of the first Islamic century. The attributions of an edition to Al-Ḥajjāj, the presence of corrections and alternative texts in the palimpsests, and the existence of manuscripts with variant surah orders, all support this scenario.

Second, there seems to have been in this period an attitude of flexibility of oral pronunciation that matched the flexibility of the written text. With the standardization of the Canonical text-form and the suppression of the Authoritative text-forms, the oral traditions for those text-forms would have also been suppressed or conformed to the new standard. Also, though this early standardization of the consonantal text did provide a basis of unity that still exists in Islam, it was not precise enough to prevent the development of rival recitation systems, even of its own consonantal text, nor did it completely displace the use of different recitation systems based on other forms of the consonantal text attributed to other companions of Muḥammad, which can be viewed as competing Authoritative text-forms. The most comprehensive explanation for the complexity of the records of textual variants and the Companions' collections is that a historical situation of competing recitals and written versions of the Qur'ān did in fact exist. This is seen in the existence and extent of the *Qirā'āt* literature with the systems of the Seven, the Ten, and the Fourteen reading systems, the various historical records concerning the existence and content of the Companions' collections, and the records of other portions that were known to have existed in the earliest period. If these variants were real, then the oral tradition was not strong enough to keep them completely in check.

Then, after the Canonical consonantal text-form was in place, there was a degree of flexibility allowed concerning its precise pointing and pronunciation that grew to the multiplicity of systems that were being practiced two hundred and fifty years later when Ibn Mujāḥid found it necessary to try to limit them to seven. Some of these fifty-plus systems were possibly tied to Authoritative text-forms that preceded the Canonical one, but most of them seem to have been based on different ways of applying diacritical and vocalization marks to the Canonical consonantal text-form. The manuscripts from this period would have allowed this degree of flexibility, and the systems of colored dots for vocalizations confirm that more systems than the seven or ten were being practiced. Melchert makes an observation that in the era before Ibn Mujāḥid there was growth in the reliance on and precision of the oral transmission. This confirms these conclusions reached from observing the development of orthography in the manuscripts.[51]

As the oral tradition became more precise it advanced the need for a more precise Arabic script, and at the same time the more precise Arabic script enabled the oral tradition to be recorded and maintained with greater precision. A strong, unified oral tradition was not preserved from the seventh/first century. A strong, more unified tradition came about in the third Islamic century having grown out of a more flexible tradition as measures were taken to limit orthographic variability.

Arguments that this entire edifice is a pious fabrication,[52] though, are unlikely, in that there are manuscripts that preserve discernible features of distinctive readings of the Qur'ān.[53] Also, there is a conspicuous lack of evidence of the survival of one form of recitation with a strong written and oral pedigree traced directly back to Muḥammad, which, if it ever existed, would have commanded a high degree of use and allegiance. Though political and religious motives may have provided sufficient reasons for people to abuse a system and create recitations that served their sectarian purposes, these are not sufficient reasons to cause the creation of the entire edifice of the reading systems in the first place. More sufficient reasons are at hand, with the defective character of the Arabic script and the transition from an oral literary environment to one that operated according to the conventions of written literature.

Though the colored dot systems do give an indication that some of these recitation systems may have existed from very early times, they do not present the short vowels with enough precision, they do not contain consonantal diacritical marks with enough precision, and they record other systems of pronunciation that are different from what later came to be regarded as the Seven and the Ten. Before the tenth/fourth century, the text was simply not in a state containing the degree of precision required to record and transmit one precise reading system, much less numerous systems. The chains of names of transmitters of these systems are also not enough of a guarantee of the precise pronunciation of these systems. The growth represented by the development of the eight eventual versions of each of the Ten recitation systems occurred when the script was developed enough to contain and preserve a precise recitation of the text. If there was this amount of flexibility and growth with such a system in place, there could have been no guarantee strong enough to prevent similar growth of reading systems before such a system was invented.

F. E. Peters makes an important observation with a comparison from the Jewish Masoretic tradition:[54]

> In Islam, the emphasis was and is quite different. The preservation and transmission of the Qur'an has been overwhelmingly oral in nature, and so experts in the Book have been reciters (*qurra*) rather than scribes (*kuttab*). Thus there have been no Masoretes jealously guarding a textual tradition and, in the process, noting the slightest variants. Among the Jews the effort was to preserve a properly written text, whereas the Muslims have been more concerned with a properly remembered text. . . . But absent a masoretic tradition among Muslims, the variants on the Quranic text—as there certainly must have been with the early defective Arabic writing system that scarcely distinguished some consonants, much less vowels—have largely disappeared, and those that have survived are largely inconsequential to the text.

There grew to be an Islamic masoretic tradition, but it was not there in Islam's beginning period.

This conclusion is confirmed by the relatively insignificant variants left in the great majority of manuscripts in the Qur'ānic manuscript tradition. Only the palimpsests have anything approaching the kinds of textual variants found in other ancient textual traditions. Though an extensive oral tradition has been claimed for the Qur'ān, and there is excellent evidence for its existence, it was never strong enough to guard one precise form of pronunciation of the text, and the oral traditions that have existed have always been tied to particular versions of the written text, particularly after orthographic improvements were added to the consonantal text to make it more precise syntactically and phonetically.

These factors all confirm the conclusion of Donner, that while there was an oral tradition very early on, it was not a secure or complete tradition that went back to the Prophet for the entire text.[55] They also confirm Rippin's conclusion that [56]

> the current accepted text might be viewed as the product of reflection upon a primitive written text and not upon the parallel transmission of an oral text as the Muslim tradition has suggested . . . it appears that there was a stage at which the written text of the Qur'ān was analyzed and determined as to its meaning and pronunciation on the basis of a skeleton consonantal text with no reference to a living oral tradition.

Once this analysis was done, however, or while it was being done, an oral tradition quickly grew to supplement and serve the written text. This oral tradition became an integral part of further textual transmission, and while contributing its own problems and complications to the transmission of the Qur'ān's text, it preserved and transmitted many of the cultural and religious values arising out of the original orality of the Qur'ān's genesis and initial reception and transmission. Though no longer a body of strictly oral literature, the Qur'ān as a written book came to have an intrinsic form and use which was inextricably bound with oral recitation and an aural experience of the text.

NOTES

1. Fred M. Donner, "Quranic *Furqān*," *JSS* 52, 2:279–300, 295.
2. Chaim Rabin, "The Beginnings of Classical Arabic," in Ibn Warraq, ed., *What the Koran Really Says* (Amherst, NY: Prometheus Books, 2002), 211–27, 218.
3. François Déroche, "Written Transmission," in Andrew Rippin, ed., *The Blackwell Companion to the Qur'ān* (London: Blackwell Publishing, 2006), 172–86, 172.
4. Daniel A. Madigan, *The Qur'ān's Self-Image* (Oxford: Princeton University Press, 2001), 51–52.
5. Madigan, *Self-Image,* 52.
6. al-Bukhārī, "WinHadith v. 1.5," 6.510 "Hudhayfah ibn al-Yaman came to Uthman at the time when the people of Sham and the people of Iraq were waging war to conquer Armenia and Azerbaijan. Hudhayfah was afraid of their (the people of Sham and Iraq) differences in the recitation of the Qur'ān, so he said to Uthman, 'O chief

of the believers! Save this nation before they differ about the Book as Jews and the Christians did before.'"

7. Madigan, *Self-Image,* 52.

8. John Burton, *The Collection of the Qur'ān* (Cambridge: Cambridge University Press, 1977).

9. Ibn Khaldūn, *The Muqaddimah* (New York: Bollingen Foundation, 1967), 2:382.

10. Adolf Grohmann, "The Problem of Dating Early Qur'āns," *Der Islam* 33:213–31, 221–22.

11. Madigan, *Self-Image,* 47.

12. David J. Roxburgh, *Writing the Word of God: Calligraphy and the Qur'an* (Houston: Museum of Fine Arts, 2007), 14.

13. Angelika Neuwirth, "Structural, Linguistic, and Literary Features," in Angelika Neuwirth, *The Cambridge Companion to the Qur'ān* (Cambridge: Cambridge University Press, 2006), 97–113, citing 101.

14. Arthur Jeffery, *Materials for the History of the Text of the Qur'ān* (Leiden: Brill, 1937), 2, note 3.

15. An excellent overview of these arguments is presented in Herbert Berg, *The Development of Exegesis in Early Islam* (Richmond, Surrey: Curzon, 2000).

16. Harald Motzki, "The Collection of the Qur'an, A Reconsideration of Western Views in Light of Recent Methodological Developments," *Der Islam* 78: 1–34.

17. M. M. Al-Azami, *The History of the Qur'anic Text* (Leicester: UK Islamic Academy, 2003), 192.

18. Christopher Melchert, "Ibn Mujahid and the Establishment of Seven Qur'anic Readings," *Studia Islamica* 91:5–22, 11.

19. Madigan, *Self-Image,* 52.

20. Al-Azami, *History,* 192.

21. Otto Pretzl, "Die Fortfuehrung des Apparatus Criticus zum Koran," *Sitzungsberichte der Bayerischen Akademie der Wissenshaften* 5:3–13, 8–9.

22. Alford T. Welch, "al-Kur'ān," *EI2* (Leiden: Brill, 1960), 400–29, 408.

23. Melchert, "Seven," 18, citing Al-Dhahabī, Tārīkh al-islām 24 (A.H. 321-330): 146.

24. Labib as-Said, *The Recited Koran* (Princeton, NJ: Darwin Press, 1975), 127–30.

25. It is worthwhile repeating that Jeffery collected records from this era of fifteen primary companions' collections, thirteen secondary collections, and numerous secondary codices not traced to a companion, and mentioned a lost source that reputedly had records of forty extra readers in addition to the Ten. Jeffery, *Materials,* v–vi, 2.

26. Their lineage to the eighth/second century was traced by their pedigree of named reciters, not written confirmation of the precise contents of the text.

27. Claude Gilliot, "Creation of a Fixed Text," in Jane Dammen McAuliffe, *Cambridge Companion of the Qur'ān* (Cambridge: Cambridge University Press, 2006), 41–58, citing 50–51; Efim A. Rezvan, "The Qur'ān: between *Textus Receptus* and Critical Edition," in Efim A. Rezvan, *Les problemes poses par l'edition critique des texts anciens et medievaux: Volume en collaboration internationale Institut d'Etudes Medievals* (Paris: 1992, 291–310), 294.

28. Efim A. Rezvan, "Mingana Folios: When and Why," *MO* 11, 4, 2.
29. Melchert, "Seven," 14, citing Ibn Mujāḥid, *Kitāb al-Sab'ah fi al Qirā'āt* (Cairo: Dar al-Mu'ārif), 62, 78.
30. Yasser Tabbaa, "The Transformation of Arabic Writing: Part I, Qur'ānic Calligraphy," *Ars Orientalis* 21:119–48.
31. Andrew Rippin, *The Qur'an and its Interpretative Tradition* (Burlington: Ashgate, 2001), xv.
32. James A. Bellamy, "Textual Criticism of the Koran," *JOAS* 121:1:1–62, note 3.
33. James A. Bellamy, "Some Proposed Emendations to the Text of the Koran," *JAOS*, 113:562–73, and Madigan, *Self-Image,* 42–43.
34. as-Said, *Koran.*
35. Pretzl, "Fortfuehrung," 9.
36. Yasin Dutton, "An Early *Mushaf* According to the Reading of Ibn 'Āmir," *JQS* III, 1:71–90, Yasin Dutton, "Some Notes on the British Library's 'Oldest Qur'an Manuscript' (Or. 2165)," *JQS* VI, 1:43–71.
37. See, for instance, Andrew Rippin, "Qur'an 21:95: 'A ban is upon any town,'" *JSS* XXIV:43–53, and Andrew Rippin, "Qur'ān 7.40: 'Until the camel passes through the eye of the needle,'" *Arabica* XXVII: 107–13.
38. Adrian Alan Brockett, "The Value of the Hafs and Warsh Transmissions for the Textual History of the Qur'an," in Andrew Rippin, ed., *Approaches to the History of the Interpretation of the Qur'an* (Oxford: Clarendon, 1988), 31–45, citing 44–45.
39. Bellamy, "Criticism," 2.
40. Bellamy, "Emendations," 563.
41. David S. Margoliouth, "Textual Variations in the Koran," *MW* 15:334–44, 340.
42. Al-Azami, *History,* 153.
43. Christopher Melchert, "The Relation of the Ten Readings to One Another," *JQS* 10, 2:73–87.
44. Welch, "Kur'ān," 408.
45. al-Bukhārī, "WinHadith," 6.513.
46. Ahmad Von Denffer, *'Ulūm al-Qur'ān* (Leicester: The Islamic Foundation, 1994), 113–15, citing Ṣuyūtī, *'Itqan,* I:45.
47. Denffer, *'Ulūm,* 119.
48. Kristina Nelson, *The Art of Reciting the Qur'an* (Austin: University of Texas Press, 1985), 201.
49. Welch, "Kur'ān," 409.
50. Rezvan, "Mingana," 2.
51. C. Melchert, "Relation of the Ten Readings to One Another," Oxford: Christopher Melchert, 2007. Lecture given at SOAS, University of London conference: The Qur'an: Text, Interpretation & Translation, 7–9 November 2007. Copy obtained from author.
52. A. Fischer, "Grammatisch schweirige Schwur- und Beschwörungsformeln des Klassichen Arabisch," *Der Islam* 28:1–105.
53. Dutton, "Mushaf," Dutton, "Notes," Intisar A. Rabb, "Non-Canonical Readings of the Qur'an: Recognition and Authenticity (the Himsī Reading)," *JQS* VIII, 2:84–127.

54. F. E. Peters, *The Monotheists* (Oxford: Princeton University Press, 2003), 33.
55. Donner, "*Furqān*," 296.
56. Rippin, *Qur'an,* x.

IV

CONCLUSIONS

To be a textual critic requires aptitude for thinking and willingness to think; and though it also requires other things, those things are supplements and cannot be substituted. Knowledge is good, method is good, but one thing beyond all others is necessary; and that is to have a head, not a pumpkin, on your shoulders, and brains, not pudding, in your head.

—A. E. Housman[1]

NOTE

1. A. E. Housman, "The Application of Thought to Textual Criticism," *Proceedings of the Classical Association*, xviii, August 1921, 84.

12

Concluding Reflections

Evaluating textual variants is often not a straightforward proposition. This research has examined a wide spectrum of textual variants and sifted them carefully to determine their significance for the transmission of the text of the Qur'ān. In this last chapter we will present a survey of the textual history of the Qur'ān informed by this research, revisit some of the key issues raised in the course of the research, and present some implications that follow for Qur'ān studies. The survey will take the form of a summary account of the textual history of the Qur'ān divided into six periods, with descriptive comments for each period.

In the Introduction to this book, a basic question was raised as to if and how a critical text of the Qur'ān could be constructed. This would involve the application of methods of textual criticism that have been developed in other literary disciplines over the last two centuries. The basic goals of this kind of textual criticism as applied to ancient manuscripts have been generally defined as 1) to recover the original text, and 2) to trace the historical development of the text. This book is an exercise in the application of textual criticism to early Qur'ān manuscripts to pursue these two goals.

For considering these goals with precision, a scheme was borrowed and adapted from New Testament studies for describing different levels of textual development in a written literary tradition. This scheme was as follows:

1. *Predecessor text-form*: the oral or written sources the author used.
2. *Autographic text-form*: the form the author wrote as it left his desk.

3. *Authoritative text-form*: a form of text that acquired a degree of local consensual authority.
4. *Canonical text-form*: a form of the text that acquired a degree of wide consensual authority.
5. *Interpretive text-form*: any later intentional reformulation for stylistic, practical, or dogmatic reasons.

To summarize how the application of these categories in this book informs the history of the text of the Qur'ān, a survey of the history of the text will be presented in six chronological periods. The first two categories above are discussed in Period One. The other three are used in periods Two through Six. A chart of these periods featuring particular textual features for each period will follow at the end of this section.

A HISTORY OF THE QUR'ĀN'S DEVELOPMENT INFORMED BY MANUSCRIPT STUDIES

Period One: Muḥammad's Prophetic Career (610–632)

The Qur'ān text was produced in a culture that, while there were forms of writing adequate for business and administrative functions,[1] religious and cultural literatures were kept according to mainly oral conventions. There was evidently in the seventh century CE still a culture where poetic and religious oral literatures were being created and performed, literatures not necessarily tied to written texts but related flexibly to bodies of oral stories and some written texts circulating in Arabia in those times.[2] The Qur'ān texts were written in a script conveying imprecise grammatical and syntactical meaning and phonetics, functioning more as an aid to memory in reciting already known texts than as a vehicle for recording and preserving written literature.[3] This is the period containing the very beginnings of the Qur'ān's existence during the lifetime of Muḥammad. It consists of what Muḥammad claimed to receive as revelations, and whatever oral or written materials came to be used as authoritative religious texts.

There is a lively scholarly debate as to the relative importance of the oral and written in the transmission of religious knowledge, as well as what form an "original" text of the Qur'ān could have taken. Donner helpfully discusses these issues and distinguishes between a closed text which was one marked by a defined content and an open text which may have been a somewhat defined core of material supplemented by flexible additions or omissions.[4] Some scholars hypothesize that there was an established Christian Arabic literature.[5] However, there is more consensus that there was not an established Arabic written religious literature, and that the actual writing down of material believed to be revelations seems to have been of secondary importance to the oral in that it was done on a variety of materials, and apparently not kept in a systematic manner. Arabic grammar was not codified until the eighth century, and the Qur'ān is commonly regarded as the first real work of written literature in Arabic which propelled the codification of Arabic grammar, as well as improvements to Arabic orthography.[6] Though it is universally held that there was a strong oral tradition from the outset because of the oral literary culture, it was not thorough enough to establish a precise vocalization of the written text, nor to completely contain variation to the written text. Schoeler has correctly observed that because of this situation, it is impossible to know how the Qur'ān was read during the lifetime of Muḥammad.[7] Unfortunately, there are difficulties recovering the forms of the text in use during this period because none of the original materials have survived. Also because of the nature of the efforts after Muḥammad's death to establish a uniform text, access to any such materials was prevented by their destruction and neglect.

Though Qur'ānic material was used under Muḥammad's authority within his lifetime, there does not seem to have been one written form of the text in use in his lifetime. Instead, individuals used collections of Qur'ānic material they were able to obtain for themselves. Because of this situation, if one uses Epp's categories, one can suggest a blending between the Predecessor text-forms and Autographic text-forms for this earliest period. The Autographic material used within Muḥammad's lifetime preceded authoritative versions. There was an authoritative body of material, but varying collections of it seemed to have been in use within Muḥammad's lifetime. This situation continued after his death, and it was in the years immediately following his death that defined authoritative bodies of Qur'ān material came into use. In this sense, the Qur'ān could be said to have multiple original texts, each with both distinct and overlapping content in relation to the others. Rezvan states succinctly,[8]

> Since we know that from the beginning there were several versions of the text related to different traditions of transmission, we should not reduce all of them to one: strictly speaking, from the time of the Prophet there was no one stemma of the Qur'ān text.

The most important sources needed which are not possible to obtain are primary source materials from the earliest periods of the collection of the Qur'ān from within the lifetime of Muḥammad and what was collected in writing after his death. Even if these kinds of materials were available, one should not speak of recovering the one original text of the Qur'ān, but instead original texts of the Qur'ān, or recovering some of the loose body of original material delivered from Muḥammad to his companions in its original forms. For the Qur'ān the earliest stage of text available for reconstruction is an early edited Canonical text-form from Period Three listed below.

Period Two: The Companions' Collections (632/10–653/30)

The text-forms of Qur'ānic material from the period between Muḥammad's death and the initial standardization of the consonantal text cannot be recovered because of the destruction and suppression of variant material. The best that can be done to recover material from this period is to evaluate the variants that exist in the literature as best one can, and to examine the *scriptio inferiors* of any qualifying palimpsests that come to light. This, however, leaves one with the situation that the earliest recoverable text is a revised version of perhaps the initial standardization of the consonantal text.

Both Muslim and Western scholars acknowledge that the order of surahs in the Qur'ān was not fixed by the time of Muḥammad's death, though there is disagreement as to the degree of variety. There were different orders found among the Companions' collections.[9] Puin believes on the basis of the manuscripts found in Yemen that there may very well have been a greater variety of surah order than is recorded in Islamic sources.[10] Two eighth-century Christian apologetic works mention surahs as literary works distinct from the Qur'ān.[11]

The earliest extant Qur'ān manuscripts appear to already be in an edited text form, which according to Islamic tradition was done to establish one form of the text against the rival versions in the Companions' collections. An earlier less edited version is possibly what is represented in the *scriptio inferior* of the Qur'ānic palimpsests, or they could be the remains of an unrecorded alternative Companion's version, or perhaps 'Uthman's version with the superior text being al-Ḥajjāj's. The greatest exceptions to the form of text found in the great majority of extant manuscripts is the form found in the *scriptio inferior* of the few extant palimpsests, and the few manuscripts that have non-standard surah orders.

According to Islamic tradition, the collections belonging to Muḥammad's companions were the earliest versions to be used in an official capacity, in that they were already in use in metropolitan centers of the empire when 'Uthmān sent out his edition to replace them. Jeffery gathered records of fifteen primary codices of Qur'ānic material belonging to companions and thirteen secondary or derivative ones, together with further records of codices attributed to unnamed companions of Muḥammad.[12] These could all be termed Authoritative text-forms. These codices have not been found in manuscript form and their content can only be approximated from the extant historical records of their contents.[13]

Period Three: 'Uthmān and Al-Ḥajjāj (653/30–705/86)

'Uthmān's reputed version can be considered the first Canonical text-form following after authoritative Companions text-forms (including his own), and the Autographic text forms from within Muḥammad's lifetime. Some have attempted to assert it was a direct version of an autographic text entrusted to Ḥafṣa by Muḥammad. Even if this was so, Ḥafṣa's was only one of a variety of apparently equally authoritative texts in use at this time. Also, if Ḥafṣa's version had the authority of coming directly from Muḥammad, then it seems that it would have been used as it was and there would have been no reason for 'Uthmān to take further editing action.

The action of destroying the other versions, prohibiting their further use, and promulgating one unified text-form implies that the other versions that needed to be destroyed were of sufficient authority to command the allegiance of significant groups of people. The resistance given to this order by Ibn Mas'ūd, Companion, keeper and reciter of one of the rival versions, is also evidence that he and his circle believed his was of greater authority than 'Uthmān's.[14] 'Uthmān's version became through Caliphal authority the first Canonical text-form, and it was very possibly replaced by an Interpretive text-form (al-Ḥajjāj's) which itself became a new Canonical text-form of the consonantal text.

Al-Ḥajjāj's version was produced in the early eighth/late first century to refine and improve the consonantal base of the initial edition. Diacritical marks are asserted to have been added as a major feature of this edition[15] but there is not a noticeable increase in their use nor standardization of their use in the manuscripts from this period. Both the initial and this second edition are reported to have been produced against a backdrop of the texts that varied from these being destroyed. The lack of manuscripts demonstrating a variant text in line with what was reported to exist seems to be confirmation of the efficiency of the suppression and destruction of these texts. There is also the possibility that these two editions were in fact one effort that in later Islamic tradition became divided and attributed to two different people in order to give it a more authoritative pedigree. If there was a distinct second edition by Al-Ḥajjāj, it was an Interpretive text-form of the Canonical text-form, which in turn became a new Canonical text-form. This would also be the earliest recoverable text-form with the current state of manuscript evidence.

This Canonical text-form in its earliest extant representatives is also already in a strongly edited form apparently designed for liturgical use. It contains rhyme schemes, verse markers, and is found in surah form which is a form more suited for recitation than for reading as literature or consulting as an organized collection of sayings or stories. Getting back to their autographic, less organized prior forms is extremely difficult because of the destruction of the earliest recorded forms of Qur'ānic material, and one must depend on the tentative results of the application of form and source criticism.

The edition attributed to 'Uthmān or its revision by al-Ḥajjāj, if they are two distinct versions, seem to be the more appropriate goals for the application of textual criticism. An important limitation of this version, however, would be that a consonantal text with full application of dots to distinguish consonants cannot be obtained since the earliest manuscripts themselves are so inconsistently dotted. In Western scholarship, three major views have emerged among critical scholars as to the date of this early recension:

Early Codification

There are those who hold mainly to the traditional Islamic view (with adjustments for oral tradition elements and refinement of the complete text of the Qur'ān) that 'Uthmān established a committee that established a uniform consonantal text. These would see al-Ḥajjāj's version as a relatively minor revision of 'Uthmān's. This view requires one to give preference to the testimony of Islamic tradition over the evidence found in manuscripts.

Later Codification

This is the view that the codification process happened later, as a gradual process or one predominantly under al-Ḥajjāj. This view would see the Qur'ān text assuming its current shape outside of the era of 'Uthmān but still within the Umayyad caliphate. If one gives precedence to manuscript evidence over tradition, this is currently the best supported view.

Late Codification

This is the view of the Revisionists that the codification did not reach its final shape until late Abbasid times. Though this view is true if the goal is a precise and full vocalization of the text, from manuscript evidence it appears that the consonantal line and content were stabilized in Umayyad times, though it could possibly have extended into early Abbasid times if Christian historical sources are included and given full weight and the variant surah orders observed in the Ṣan'ā' manuscripts testify to this degree of fluidity. All views agree that distinctly Qur'ānic material was present in the seventh century.

They disagree on what kind of a form this material was in by c. 700/81 and how well defined this material was as a body of written scripture.

Period Four: Editing and Development of Orthography (705/86–936/324)

Oral literature dynamics were for early Arabic culture the more foundational for the transmission of religious and cultural knowledge. The Qur'ān itself, followed by the Islamic conquests, started a transformation of its culture which within two centuries saw written literature ascendant in Islamic domains. The text of the Qur'ān had to be improved and its inherent oral flexibility stabilized. These things were achieved through almost Herculean efforts at editing and the devising of systems that could express with economy and precision all of the phonetic and semantic information necessary for the Qur'ān to be a complete piece of written literature and a source for religious law, theology, and devotion.

The next major edition of the Qur'ān came about in the third Islamic century at the time of Ibn Mujāḥid (d. 936/324). This edition, though united on a basic consonantal text, allowed flexibility in precise vocalization to the extent that seven versions were granted an authoritative status. This status was extended to three further versions, with another four also gaining a high degree of recognition.

These sources, however, are not available, and not even in later copies, such as a ninth century Qur'ān claiming to be of the reading of Ibn Mas'ūd or Ubayy b. Ka'b. This lack is interesting in itself in that there are historical records claiming that such versions were extant and being recited until the fourth/eleventh century.[16] Al-Kindī, a Christian official in the Abbasid court of Al-Ma'mūn mentioned the versions of Ibn Mas'ūd and Ubayy b. Ka'b in 830/215. This testimony from a Christian is especially interesting because it is from an outsider to Islam and it confirms what Muslims from the same general era also wrote. Ibn Nadīm, in his work *The Fihrist (c.* 377/987*)*, mentions the existence in his time of many manuscript copies of Ibn Mas'ūd's version, one of Ubayy b. Ka'b's, and one attributed to 'Ali.[17] Fedeli and Welch both mention the theoretical possibility of such Qur'āns existing until at least 934/322 when Ibn Mujāḥid published seven standardized ways of reciting the consonantal text attributed to 'Uthmān.[18] Von Denffer acknowledges that at this time many ways of reciting the text were being practiced including the reading systems of Ibn Mas'ūd and Ubayy b. Ka'b.[19] From this testimony, it is significant to note that there are no known copies of these Qur'āns extant amidst the many extant early Qur'ān manuscripts.

In this crucial period, the manuscript evidence demonstrates a great deal of experimentation in developing a more complete orthography for the Qur'ān text. To the bare consonantal text various colored dots were added to signify various systems of pronunciation. The academic study of these systems is still in a state of infancy, partly because of the complexity of the study, and also because there is very little documentation in Islamic sources as to the precise development of these systems. To make this even more complicated, Melchert observes that variation was also permitted according to the reader's personal understanding of grammar.[20]

What can be said, though, is that it was a period when a large degree of flexibility in the pronunciation of the Qur'ān's text was allowed. Much of the variety of systems seems to be tied to geography as well, that different centers of learning in the Islamic world had different ways of pronouncing the text.[21] One scholar has mentioned that at least fifty systems were in use by the early 900s.[22] He also noted that by 936/324 a consensus was being reached as to what constituted a correct way of pronouncing the text as opposed to an incorrect way:[23]

> any suggested reading was scrutinized to see whether it could be derived from the accepted consonantal text, whether it was defensible linguistically as being in accordance with the normal rules of Arabic language, and whether it gave a meaning that fitted the generally accepted interpretation of the text.

Examining these criteria carefully, it becomes clear that certain knowledge of the ways the text had been recited in the seventh century had been lost, and that the Islamic scholars were trying to limit the competing systems by attempting to decipher and define the text that they had received.[24]

Instead of the model used for Greek and Latin Classics, the Bible, and other ancient Western literature, Qur'ānic textual criticism as practiced within Islam has been an effort to standardize the text to a pre-conceived form, and to turn a piece of originally oral literature into a form of written literature while retaining a measure of its orality. Instead of seeking to recover or restore its original Autographic text-forms or even its earliest Authoritative text-forms, what has been sought instead has been to create from the flexible consonantal orthography a form that satisfied as many of the dogmatic and practical liturgical conditions as possible. It is a revisionist exercise that in becoming established as the authoritative and traditional text has led to the irreparable loss of the most original forms of its early text. Another way to say this is that the primary task in Qur'ānic textual criticism, as practiced historically in Islam has been instead to justify one form of the text against many others. And the efforts to establish and justify one text from among a group of collections of material, both oral and written, has resulted in the irreparable loss of the earliest authoritative forms of the text.

Period Five: Consolidation of the Ten Readings (936/324–1924/1342)

The ten main ones, however, have become Canonical text-forms in their own right, and have since undergone further development in that there are eighty recognized versions of the ten recitation systems authorized in the 900s/300s. All of these eighty are Interpretive text-forms of the second Canonical text-form. None of them represents the Authoritative text-forms or Autographic text-forms that preceded the first Canonical text-form.

The further development of eighty *riwāyas* of the ten approved readings of the 'Uthmānic text demonstrates that even Ibn Mujāḥid's effort did not control the growth of variant versions, and only the practical expedient of an almost universally printed copy in the last century is approaching success in completely unifying the text of the Qur'ān. This multiplication of readings is often a bit difficult for a Western student to fathom, but they are due to the heavy emphasis still placed on oral transmission and recitation of the Qur'ān text among Muslims. As-Said mentions this as he describes the process of the Ten readings becoming twenty and then further on to eighty:[25]

> Each of the more eminent disciples of the original master, that is to say, of the original "transmitter" of a Reading, in turn established a school composed of his own circle of disciples, and the process repeated itself. Within this school, a number of versions emerged associated with his most eminent disciples and containing select variants from his own corpus. . . . By this time the extent of the varieties within each version was rather limited, since the variants taught by the original master had been absorbed into the numerous versions that emerged in succeeding generations. A slight degree of variation was still possible, however, having to do primarily with intonation and diction rather than voweling or inflection.

This statement of as-Said's conflicts with the understanding of many people that there is just one Qur'ān. It also presents many challenges to critical scholarship to document these lines of transmission. Are they present in actual manuscripts? Some consonantal features of the ones that are more explicitly described in Islamic sources have been documented, though such features are not enough to document an entire recitation system.[26] Also, the documentary evidence available permits the reconstruction of the outline and details of some of the Fourteen reading systems and the eighty transmissions of the Ten. What it does not allow is the reconstruction of any of the Companion's Codices or of any precise vocalization of the Qur'ān from the period before 936/324.

Period Six: Primacy of the Ḥafṣ text (1924/1342–Now)

One development that has limited further proliferation of reading systems and even discouraged the use of the ones that are authorized was the printing of the Qur'ān in 1342/1924. This printed copy was one completed under the patronage of King Fu'ād I of Egypt (r. 1917–1936).[27] This text has become a "standard version"[28] in that it has come to be widely printed throughout the Muslim world. With minor editing improvements it is the Arabic text found in most Qur'āns one finds in the West as well. This text is said to be the transmission of Ḥafṣ of the reading of ʿĀṣim, the fifth of the seven authorized readings. An important thing to note about this text is that it was not taken from actual manuscripts of the Qur'ān, but was reconstructed from the written records of oral tradition of what this reading originally consisted.[29] Bergsträsser observed: [30]

> Sources for this consonantal text are obviously not handwritten Qur'an manuscripts but literature about it. It is therefore a reconstruction, the result of rewriting the usual consonantal text in the old style according to the (medieval Qur'ānic sciences) literature.

The material in the parentheses is mine to make the quotation clearer. They took the basic Qur'ān text that had been in use by the Ottomans and rewrote it in what their tradition told them the ancient 'Uthmānic orthography was like, and then to this they added the full set of diacritical marks and readers' aids. This was done under the authorization of the Egyptian government of King Fu'ad I to assert Egyptian Islamic leadership in the wake of the fall of the Ottoman Empire after World War One.[31] Bergsträsser also notes concerning the Muslim attitude to rely on the tradition rather than on actual manuscripts:[32]

> In fact, even the Koran manuscripts themselves have played no further role in Muslim Koran studies since the 4th century A.H.

There are other versions in print, but they have not achieved the same degree of proliferation and acceptance.[33]

Technically, the eighty recitation systems are still valid, but in practice they are being usurped by the printed text. One man's attempt to record twenty of the eighty (with the hope of eventually doing the full eighty) failed for both practical reasons and official opposition to the project. In the end, he was only able to record the Ḥafṣ recitation.[34]

It should also be noted that only these readings now enjoy any kind of "canonical" status. The readings that were proscribed in 936 included the readings attributed to the closest companions of Muḥammad. Though the 1924 Cairo text is a useful text because of the near-universal acceptance it now enjoys, it is only one of the eighty accepted readings.

Table 12.1

PERIOD 1	1 Body of Material	Muḥammad	610

Oral milieu predominantly, Oral performance variants
Arabic literature?
Writing conventions—to aid memory, used in business and administration
Orthography—some consonantal diacritics but no short vowels, and variability of use of long vowels
Ḥijāzi scripts
Surah order variants
Discourse length variants
Synonyms/word length variants
Orthographic variants

PERIOD 2	15 +	Companions' Collections	632–653

Oral milieu predominantly, writing being used more
Writing conventions—to aid memory
Orthography—some consonantal diacritics but no short vowels
Ḥijāzi scripts
Companions' codices
Palimpsests *inferior* scripts?
Surah order variants
Discourse length variants
Synonyms/word length variants
Orthographic variants
Consonantal diacritical mark variants

PERIOD 3	1	'Uthmān and al-Ḥājjāj	653–705

Basic Consonantal line standardized but with incomplete diacritics and no vocalization
Al-Ḥiajjāj's revision, consonantal changes, consonantal line now found in great majority of manuscripts
Imposed by force
Orthography—some cons. diacritics but no short vowels
Ḥijāzi and Kufic scripts?
Companions codices suppressed, but some continue in use
Surah order variants
Orthographic variants
Consonantal diacritical mark variants
No consonant Ḥamza, though sometimes represented by long vowels
Continuation of strong oral transmission, but tied to incomplete consonantal text
Palimpsest superior text?
Shi'ite variants start to develop?

PERIOD 4	50+	Reading Systems[1]	705–936

Surah order standardized
Consonantal line standardized, non-'Uthmānic ones prohibited and suppressed
Orthography—some cons. diacritics but no short vowels; cons. Diacritics removed in Kufic MSS (700s)
Ḥijāzi and Kufic scripts, Kufic comes to supersede Ḥijāzi (700s); other scripts develop (8–900s)

PERIOD 4	50+	Reading Systems[1]	705–936

Companions' codices suppressed, but at least three still in use[2]
Shi'ite variants develop
Qur'ān sciences literature develops with various views of *qirā'āt* and *ahruf.* Flexibility and personal choice in how reading systems are constructed
Ḥamza introduced as a letter (800s)
Colored dot systems introduced to distinguish reading systems and variants (7–900s)
Current complete phonetic system developed (8–900s)(Ibn Muqlah Chancery reforms)
Official suppression of Companions codices continues, but some still in use
Orthographic variants
Consonantal diacritical mark variants
Reading systems develop that have same basic consonantal line but with different consonantal diacritics and short vowels
Shi'ite view of Qur'ān variants develops
Qur'ān sciences literature develops with various views of *qirā'āt* and *ahruf*
During this period (Abbasid) under Muslim rule both the Arabic text of the Qur'ān and the Hebrew text of the Hebrew Bible (Old Testament) were developed to their phonetically complete scripts that are still in use today.

PERIOD 5	10 (7+3) → 80	Ibn Mujāḥid	936–1924

50 systems narrowed to 7 through application of 4 criteria:[3]
1) 'Uthmān's (?) consonantal text,
2) representation of versions used in great metropolitan centers,
3) must have sound isnads,
4) must conform to/ support the meaning of the existing standard text.
3 additional systems gain same status for fulfilling criteria.
4 additional systems almost gain same status, but at least one has notable consonantal variants (Ḥasan al-Baṣrī's[4])
These 10 (7+3) come to acquire 8 approved transmissions each.[5]
Complete phonetic orthography introduced into manuscripts about 900–1000
Variants with short vowels
Some minor consonantal variants between *Qirā'āt*
Suppression of variant readings effective (Companions' versions finally completely suppressed)

PERIOD 6	1	Primacy of the Ḥafṣ text	1924–Now

Egypt authorizes printing of a new text using Ḥafs reading of 'Āṣim's version that came to prominence in the Ottoman Empire.[6] Because of its wide distribution, this has become in effect the modern standard Qur'ān text.
Warsh text also comes into print, though does not acquire same prominence and distribution as Ḥafs.
Other readings are being discovered in manuscripts in various collections:
Abū Amr's, via the transmission of al-Dūri- Leeds MS. 619[7]
Ibn 'Āmir's, BN Arabe 328a[8]
Ḥimṣi, BL Or. 2165[9]
Variants with short vowels[10]
Some minor consonantal variants[11]

PERIOD 6	1	Primacy of the Ḥafṣ text	1924–Now
Marks added for aids in reciting Some editing since 1924 Regional variations in minor editing and readers' helps			

[1] Jeffery, *Materials*, x, page 2 footnote 3.
[2] Dodge, *Fihrist.* 53–63.
[3] These criteria come from Adrian Alan Brockett, "The Value of the Hafs and Warsh Transmissions for the Textual History of the Qur'an," Adrian Alan Brockett, *Approaches to the History of the Interpretation of the Qur'an.* Oxford: Clarendon, 1988, 31-45, 37, and Peter Riddell, *Transferring a Tradition.* Berkeley, California: 1990, 242.
[4] Michael Cook, *The Koran: A Very Short Introduction.* Oxford: OUP, 2000, 118-119.
[5] as-Said, *Koran.*
[6] Cook, *Koran.* 74-75.
[7] Adrian Alan Brockett, "Aspects of the physical transmission of the Qur'ān in 19th-century Sudan: Script, decoration, binding and paper," *Manuscripts of the Middle East,* 2, 45-67, 45.
[8] Dutton, "Notes," 43.
[9] Intisar A. Rabb, "Non-Canonical Readings of the Qur'an: Recognition and Authenticity (the Himsî Reading)," *Journal of Qur'anic Studies,* VIII, 2, 84-127.
[10] Mark, *Qur'an,* as seen in Hafs and Warsh texts.
[11] Mark, *Qur'an,* as seen in Hafs and Warsh texts.

STANDARDIZATION

In view of this survey of the Qur'ān text's history, certain issues require further comment. The Qur'ān manuscripts show a precise standardization of the text within the somewhat flexible conventions of orthography used in the early period. A very high standard of concern for precise verbal accuracy is demonstrated in the manuscripts examined, even without the texts possessing extensive consonantal diacritical marks and short vowel marks. The complete lack of word, phrase, and transposition variants also provides evidence of a strong measure of intentional textual stabilization. The variants that can be observed in extant manuscripts are relatively minor revolving around a consonantal text that even at the time of the earliest manuscripts, including the palimpsests, shows a remarkable degree of fixation. One might attribute this to a precisely transmitted *Ur-text*, except for this historical testimony of such editing projects with 'Uthmān and al-Ḥajjāj, and the extensive testimony in the secondary literature that a much broader scope of variants were once part of the Qur'ān's transmission history.

The palimpsests demonstrate this fixation to a high but lesser degree in that the material they contain is recognizably Qur'ānic, but they do also contain variants involving different words and phrases. A level of standardization is evident in their *scriptio inferiors* that appears to have then been more carefully brought into line with what is found in the rest of the early manuscript tradition. A degree of textual variation similar to that in the palimpsests is also found in non-Qur'ānic Arabic papyri from this early period.[35] Conversely, with non-palimpsest Qur'ān manuscripts from the same era and in the same script style, instead of such a list being easily amplified, one is hard put to find even single examples.

When the initial standardizations of the consonantal text of the Qur'ān were made, certain features of Arabic script were undeveloped and unsystematic. Intentional development and experimentation then made Arabic script a more precise and consistent vehicle for reproducing all the phonetic features of Arabic. Within three centuries, an initially variable use of long vowels was standardized. The consonantal form for the glottal stop *ḥamza* was invented and introduced. Also, a consistent and unified system for designating consonantal diacritical marks and then the short vowels were developed, introduced, and became standard features of the manuscript tradition.

In large measure the strong standardization of the text was to be expected, but what this study brings out is the precision and scope of the stabilization of the text. The small size of the zones of variable spelling is striking, being limited to names and orthographic conventions concerning the long vowels and *ḥamza*. The contrast provided by the few palimpsests that are known is also striking, since word, phrase, and transposition variants do occur in them. In other words, the most significant variants, the ones that had the most bearing on the meaning of the text, were the ones found the least in the manuscripts. The kinds of variant that affected only pronunciation and recitation of the text were found in greater numbers and apparently with a greater tolerance of variability.

Some might take this as confirmation that the original text has been remarkably preserved. If so, then it is difficult to make sense of all of the records of variants in the hadith and early Islamic literature. If there was just one original text, then these records must be regarded as either untrustworthy or inventions.

The Qur'ān's Consonantal Text was Standardized Early in its Textual History

Related to the degree of textual standardization is the issue of when the stabilization process took place. If the generally accepted dates to the early seventh/late first century for the earliest Qur'ān manuscripts are accurate, then these observations support the view that the major standardizations of the basic consonantal text took place between 653/30 and 705/86. Also, while there may have been a longer period of flexibility of the order of surahs in collected Qur'āns, it appears that the basic content of the surahs that are represented in early manuscripts is the same as what is observed today. The questions remaining concern those portions of the Qur'ān that do not survive in the earliest manuscripts.

Also, this is not asserting that the Qur'ān material was yet in a fixed order, even if the contents of individual surahs were decided. Overall, there is evidence that though the consonantal text was fixed within surahs, the exact number and order of surahs may have still been flexible well into Umayyad times, and possibly into the early Abbasid era.

The paleographical evidence that the consonantal text within surahs was fixed at an early date also corresponds to this conclusion reached from a linguistic approach. Blau states his view in response to those who would argue a very late date for the fixation of the consonantal text of the Qur'ān:[36]

> In my opinion, indeed, a *ne varietur* text of the Islamic revelation existed in the middle of the seventh century. I consent to the general opinion that the consonantal text of the Qur'ān became sacred very quickly. If, in fact, the text of the Qur'ān had been revised according to the rules of Classical Arabic at the end of the eighth century, one would expect it fully to conform to them. Yet, as is well known, this is not the case. . . . Indeed, the deviations of Qur'ānic orthography from Classical spelling . . . are sufficient proof for the traditional view that the consonantal text of the Qur'ān in its present form became sacred quite early.

If the dates assigned to the manuscripts surveyed are correct, then they could confirm this, but they could also confirm a slightly later date of the late seventh/early eighth century, and possibly a little later for the entire content of the Qur'ān as it now stands. Blau's position and the one he is addressing are not the only two alternatives. The palimpsests also provide evidence that details in the text itself were still being worked out in the late seventh/mid-late first century though the general material was possibly in place.

It would be difficult to attribute such a high degree of uniformity of text to anything less than the involvement of a strong, centralized religious authority. This is especially true when one considers the kind of texts that are reported to have existed prior to the efforts to unify the text. According to Islamic tradition, there were various collections of Qur'ānic material all being read and recited as authoritative scriptural texts. There was not one initial, original text from the period of Muḥammad's career which was preserved with this high degree of precision. Instead, at best, one of the collections from among the various versions available was chosen to be the one text everyone would use. It was then edited heavily, and the others were forcibly suppressed, not because they were less authentic per se, but because they presented rivals to the one chosen text and could provide a basis for political and religious competition. This seems to be a role the collection of material attributed to Ibn Mas'ūd played in the first three Islamic centuries until it was finally suppressed in the wake of Ibn Mujāhid's reforms. It was a competing Authoritative text-form to the Canonical text-form attributed to 'Uthmān.

Informal vs. Formal Standardization

From what one can tell from the palimpsests, other forms of the text would not have been radically different, but they are a very insufficient sampling of what different forms of the text may have once existed. In the 1930s, one scholar made the general comparative statement concerning the Qur'ān text,[37]

> But while it may be true that no other work has remained for twelve centuries with so pure a text, it is probably equally true that no other has suffered so drastic a purging.

Other ancient literatures seem to have gone through less formal processes of standardization. The Greek and Latin classics come to us in a form largely influenced by the accidents of history. The text is reconstructed from the few examples that survive. With the New Testament, accidents of history, in spite of the destruction of Christian books in the Diocletian persecution of CE 306–315, as well as a lively unregulated culture of scribal copying have left many manuscripts available for research. Though there are not as many from the earliest period as one might like, hundreds of New Testament texts that do survive show that the forms of the text before and after Diocletian's action were largely the same, differing only within the normal parameters of scribal practice then in use. The Hebrew Bible in the Masoretic period (800s C.E.) is perhaps the closest model to the Qur'ān's with it undergoing a form of formal standardization, but in the centuries before there was a larger degree of variation, similar to the degree and kinds of variation found in the New Testament tradition.[38]

All manuscript traditions share certain features because they use a certain set of shared materials, forms, and paleographical requirements for preserving and transmitting written texts. Scriptural traditions, because of their dogmatic concerns and high devotional regard for the text, also share particular features. Within the additional overriding effort at standardization, there was also the normal and strong evidence of careful copying to preserve the meaning and form of their chosen text.

INTENTIONALITY AND NON-INTENTIONALITY WITH VARIANTS

Both intentional and unintentional variants were observed in the manuscripts surveyed. The unintentional variants were the many copyist errors observed. Most of the intentional variants related to the flexible orthography and development of more precise orthographic conventions. Others were corrections to the text, grammatical variants, and word variants. Two intentional variants were perhaps doctrinally related, or at least could be put at the service of dogmatic views.

Perhaps the greatest underlying issue related to intentionality is that a unified Canonical text-form was maintained in these manuscripts. The corrections of the text demonstrate this kind of intentional action.

The palimpsests, together with the background of a partially controlled manuscript tradition in the early part of Qur'ānic textual history, indicate that the very shape of the consonantal text, and later, the completely vocalized text of the Qur'ān are in effect intentional variants and Interpretive text-forms of the Consonantal text-form in their own right. They are also versions that were made at the expense of more original versions that were purposefully suppressed. This is especially true viewing the palimpsests and/or the stories of suppression against the backdrop of Ehrman's assertion that scribes introducing variants that improve the text prevent access to the precise form of the original text.[39]

The precise, uniform state of the text is testimony to an extensive, detailed, and prolonged effort to unify the manuscript tradition. It is noteworthy that in spite of this, intentional variants that affected the meaning of the text were still found, as well as minor variants that match what was reported for existing in the Codices of the Companions. Substantial portions of text that have been erased and rewritten were also observed. Jeffery's contention that what has survived is what was considered "not too unorthodox" looks very plausible.[40] Also, there appears to have been a degree of flexibility allowed in how precisely the consonants were pointed.

Rezvan noted that the development of Arabic orthography in Qur'ān manuscripts "was largely due to the need to precisely interpret Qur'ānic texts."[41] The orthographic development observed in the collated Qur'ān manuscripts made the script both a script that could be precisely pronounced for a unified recitation and a script that could be precisely interpreted for instruction and dogma.

A CRITICAL TEXT OF THE QUR'ĀN?

In the Introduction, the aim of establishing a critical text of the Qur'ān was discussed and some further comments would be helpful. The Islamic records of variants are remarkable in their extensiveness in regard to the entire text of the Qur'ān, and that in addition to generating a genre of *qirā'āt* literature, they permeate the early and medieval commentaries and grammatical literature as well. In spite of this, there are two basic problems which make the construction of a critical text of the Qur'ān impossible at this time. The first problem concerns the lack of suitable primary source materials. The second problem concerns the reliability of the available secondary sources, that is, the records of textual variants for the Qur'ān found in early Islamic literature.

First, the available sources do not provide the necessary information for reconstructing the original text of the Qur'ān from the time of Muḥammad. Neither do they yet provide the necessary information for reconstructing the text from the time immediately after Muḥammad's death until the first official edition of the Qur'ān attributed to have been ordered by the Caliph 'Uthmān in c. 653/30. Even an edition with a consistent placement of consonantal diacritical marks is not available from this period.

The second problem is the qualitative difference in the nature of the records of early textual variants which have come down to us compared to what is found in the manuscripts themselves. Though discrepancies are present, it is thought that the records contain an incomplete though authentic memory of a more variable situation. The variants in the palimpsests and other manuscripts that are not mentioned in the literature, however, are not radically different from what are found in the literature, merely more of the same kind. There may be more word variants and some phrase variants, but they present the same basic kinds of texts in regard to themes, form, and content.

Gilliot mentions two forms of textual reconstruction that are appropriate for the available Qur'ānic materials.[42] His deductive reconstruction based on extant manuscripts and the secondary records of variants could potentially provide the earliest form of the Canonical text-form from the era of 'Uthmān-to-al-Ḥajjāj as a partially pointed consonantal text and, depending on how the palimpsests are interpreted, possibly with glimpses into prior Authoritative text-forms. The different schemes of how the consonantal text is partially pointed would need to be indicated, since the same letters are not always pointed in the earliest texts. The later schemes of adding colored dots would provide the data for indicating later Interpretive text-forms as would the later well-defined systems of the Seven, Ten, and Fourteen. The later texts that have fully or almost fully pointed and vocalized texts would provide another layer indicating further Interpretive text-forms, some of which have taken on an authority that is almost canonical through widespread dissemination and printing. What cannot be reconstructed with precision are any of the Companions' Collections or a precise vocalization of the accepted consonantal text from before 1000/391.

ONE VERSION GOING BACK TO MUḤAMMAD?

One issue that has stood in the background of the centuries of study of Qur'ān variants is whether or not the idea of one precise version of the Qur'ān going back to Muḥammad can be supported from all available evidence. The belief in such a text is a mainstay of popular Islamic discourse.[43] In Western scholarship, this issue has factored into discussions of the existence of an *Ur-text* of the Qur'ān. Donner helpfully observes that even though there is an early form of a consonantal *textus receptus*, there has never been one single, identifiable textual specimen or manuscript that has been universally accepted as representing that text.[44] If one relies on Islamic traditions, a pedigree of such a text can be constructed (not the text itself), but it must be done selectively at the expense of material that contradicts the idea. If manuscript evidence is included, the idea becomes even more difficult to maintain because of the amount of editing done after Muḥammad's death. That the consonantal form of the Canonical text-form attributed to 'Uthmān contains authentic material dating back to Muḥammad does not seem to be in doubt. What is in doubt is the original form of the material, how this material was originally pronounced, and how its meaning was understood, since both the Autographic text-forms and the Authoritative text-forms are missing. It is impossible to quantify how much material has been lost through the various efforts to standardize the text. Also, the meaning of any text can be drastically altered in the editing process by the selective inclusion and omission of words, phrases, and portions. How much the meaning of the text of the Qur'ān was changed by this editing is impossible to quantify one way or the other. The idea of one precise version of the Qur'ān going back to Muḥammad cannot be substantiated in this situation.

One version of the consonantal text going back to either 'Uthmān or al-Ḥajjāj is more possible to conceive, but the task of recovering it is complicated by two problems: internal contradictions in the Islamic traditions, and the fact that the earliest extant manuscripts have differing diacritical point patterns and no vocalization marks. The contents of the manuscripts available from this period also do not fully represent the text of the Qur'ān in 114 surahs as it is found today. They are partial and fragmentary with especially the latter portions of the Qur'ān missing.[45] This is not to say that those parts did not exist or were not used. There are other lines of evidence that can be pursued to support their existence. But their general or precise forms cannot be established from extant manuscripts.

Since it cannot be demonstrated that there was one version going back to Muḥammad, it also cannot be demonstrated that seven or ten recitations went back to him. What can be maintained is that one form of the consonantal text has been very well preserved from the seventh/first century, and that oral traditions have developed which reinforce a particular understanding of, and a set number of recitals of, that one consonantal text. These recitals do perhaps survive from an early time in Islamic history, but not to before the fixing of the Canonical text-form or to Muḥammad himself. Also, there is no available method of testing how early their precise features were practiced, other than the very few consonantal markers that some of these systems contained. Some have sought to argue that all of these versions were somehow present in or contained by the flexibility of this orthography.[46] A more accurate way of stating this is to say that the flexibility and ambiguity inherent in the unpointed text allowed their development, and the development of other systems as well; the text contained a ready-to-be-tapped potential to generate new readings. The oral transmission was as static as the written text required, and as organic and creative as the ambiguous orthography and recitation conventions permitted. At this point, the earliest that precise and complete versions of the Seven or Ten reading systems can be documented is to when the script was written with full consonantal diacritics and vocalization symbols in the fourth/tenth century.

Though Muslims may take pride in the fidelity of the preservation of this text, it does not reproduce precisely what was originally considered to be the Qur'ān in the early seventh century. Because of the standardizations of the text in 653–705/33–86 and 936/324, together with the constant pressure throughout Islamic history to have one text match their dogma, many texts which had equally good claims to containing authentic readings were suppressed and destroyed. And, because of the emphasis on oral transmission and the vagaries of Arabic as it developed, the written text was constantly vocalized in new ways which did not preserve the original vocalization. The original vocalization must have been lost very early on if it did indeed exist.

While bearing testimony to the careful preservation of one particular consonantal text, the history of the transmission of the text of the Qur'ān is at least as much a testament to the destruction of Qur'ān material as it is to its preservation. It is also testimony to the fact that there never was one original text of the Qur'ān.

A PARALLEL ORAL TRADITION?

Another issue requiring some final comments is the role of oral tradition in the preservation of the text. That an oral tradition of the recital of the Qur'ān exists from the earliest period of the text is not in question. What is contested is how complete and strong this tradition was to preserve a precise pronunciation of the text as it was received. That a written version was produced within decades of Muḥammad's death demonstrates that a strictly oral transmission was not considered enough of a safeguard to preserve the text.[47] The manuscript evidence best supports a view that though it was a necessary feature accompanying the written text, an oral tradition of the precise pronunciation of the text was never strong enough or developed enough to unify the earliest Muslim community on one standard recitation of the text. The mechanics and systems were not in place to establish and maintain an indisputably precise oral pronunciation of the ambiguous consonantal text of the Qur'ān. The textual mechanics were not in place in that there were multiple Authoritative text-forms after Muḥammad's death which would have each required a separate strong oral tradition. Otherwise, a written recension, like the one attributed to 'Uthmān, would not have been needed. 'Uthmān's collection, in being an exercise to limit written variety of the text, was also as much a deliberate effort to limit oral recitation to a single written version of the text.

Second, there seems to have been in this period an attitude of flexibility of oral pronunciation that matched the flexibility of the written text. With the standardization of the Canonical text-form and the suppression of the Authoritative text-forms, the oral traditions for those text-forms would have also been suppressed or conformed to the new standard. Also, though this early standardization of the consonantal text did provide a basis of unity that still exists in Islam, it was not precise enough to prevent the development of rival recitation systems, even of its own consonantal text, nor did it completely displace the use of different recitation systems based on other forms of the consonantal text attributed to other companions of Muḥammad, which can be viewed as competing Authoritative text-forms. The most comprehensive explanation for the complexity of the records of textual variants and the Companions' collections is that a historical situation of competing recitals and written versions of the Qur'ān did in fact exist. If these variant versions were real, then the oral tradition was not strong enough to keep them completely in check.

Then, after the Canonical text-form was in place, there was a degree of flexibility allowed concerning its precise pointing and pronunciation that grew into the multiplicity of recitation systems that were being practiced two hundred and fifty years later when Ibn Mujāhid found it necessary to try to limit them to seven. Some of these other systems were possibly tied to Authoritative text-forms that preceded the Canonical one, but most of them seem to have been based on different ways of applying diacritical and vocalization marks to the Canonical consonantal text-form. The manuscripts from this period would have allowed this degree of flexibility, and the systems of colored dots for vocalizations confirm that more systems than the seven or ten were being practiced. Melchert makes an observation that in the era before Ibn Mujāhid there was growth in the reliance on and precision of the oral transmission.[48] In other words, it did not start out as the precise system it eventually became. As the oral tradition became more precise it advanced the need for a more precise Arabic script, and at the same time the more precise

Arabic script enabled the oral tradition to be recorded and maintained with greater precision. This oral transmission is not a separate parallel transmission that has been kept separate and pristine from the written transmission through the Qur'ān's history. Rather, the various oral recitation systems have always arisen from the written text and the ambiguities allowed by its basic consonantal form.[49]

Arguments that this entire edifice is a pious fabrication[50] cannot be maintained in that there are manuscripts that preserve discernible features of distinctive readings of the Qur'ān.[51] Also, there is a conspicuous lack of evidence of the survival of one form of recitation with a strong written and oral pedigree traced directly back to Muḥammad, which, if it ever existed, would have commanded a high degree of use and allegiance. Though political and religious motives may have been sufficient reasons for people to abuse a system and create recitations that served their sectarian purposes, these are not sufficient reasons to cause the creation of the entire edifice of the reading systems in the first place. More sufficient reasons are at hand, with the defective character of the Arabic script and the transition from an oral literary environment to one that operated according to the conventions of written literature.

Though the colored dot systems do give an indication that some of these recitation systems may have existed earlier, they do not present the short vowels with the precision required to record and transmit a complete reading system. The chains of names of transmitters of these systems are also not enough of a guarantee of the precise pronunciation of these systems. The growth represented by the development of the eight eventual versions of each of the Ten recitation systems occurred when the script was developed enough to contain and preserve a precise recitation of the text. If there was this amount of flexibility and growth with such a system in place, there could have been no guarantee strong enough to prevent similar growth of reading systems before such a system was invented.

Though an extensive oral tradition has been claimed for the Qur'ān, and there is excellent evidence for its existence, it was never strong enough to guard one precise form of pronunciation of the text, and the oral traditions that have existed have always been tied to particular versions of the written text, especially after orthographic improvements were added to the consonantal text to make it more precise syntactically and phonetically.

A COPPICED TRANSMISSION

A picture from forestry provides a useful illustration for the Qur'ān's textual history. Coppicing is a practice where certain kinds of small trees are regularly pruned back to the stumps so that they can grow again and provide a steady supply of material for crafts, building, and firewood.[52]

The Qur'ān in its earliest period was like many small trees sprouting from the same root, like a cluster of oak sprouts from a buried hoard of acorns. From these sprouts, a few grew into the authoritative text-forms of the Companions' collections. They were many trunks sharing the same root of material planted within Muḥammad's lifetime. At Muḥammad's death these trunks became independent trees still sharing the same root system. 'Uthmān attempted to prune these back to one trunk and was largely but not completely successful, and then he shaped this main trunk through grafts and pruning into a distinctive shape. Al-Ḥajjāj did some further shaping to the main trunk, and then this form became a strong tree, but the root continued to support the surviving shoots, and the main trunk continued to grow new branches so that within three hundred years there were fifty-plus trunks or major branches sharing the same root system. Ibn Mujāhid and others then pruned these back to ten major branches from the main trunk and trimmed away all of the other trunks or shoots coming independently from the root. These ten branches have been maintained but have also been allowed to sprout 8 branches each. Two of these eighty branches have been put into print in this last century.

For the Qur'ān, the original forms of the small trees cannot be recovered. One trunk survives which was heavily pruned and grafted onto at the outset. It has since been subject to two further major pruning exercises. Also, this metaphor breaks down in the complexity of the pruning/editing that was done. The earliest Canonical text-form that can be recovered is a consonantal text in its basic outline without diacritical dots or vocalization marks. The set patterns of diacritics, and the precise vocalization of the short vowels are later Interpretive text-forms. They were not fixed until the tenth /third century when Ibn Mujāhid legitimized the Seven reading systems. The two forms of text in print today are Interpretive text-forms of two of the seven readings. These two text-forms might date back to before the time of Ibn Mujāhid to the lives of Ḥafṣ (d. 796/180) and Warsh (d. 812/197), but this cannot be confirmed by manuscripts of those early dates. Instead, we have only the indirect testimony from later tradition that the oral versions attributed to them started within their lifetimes.

IMPLICATIONS FOR FURTHER STUDY

In Qur'ānic studies there is tremendous scope for textual criticism to trace the history of the development of the text. For periods one through three, establishing a more precise earliest text-form incorporating palimpsests and corrections in manuscripts would provide a better basic text for form and source critical studies. This would also improve the precision of the timetable of the Qur'ān's codification. In manuscripts without vowels this can be done only by examining their specific consonantal features where these have been recorded in writing, as has been done by Dutton[53] and Rabb.[54] This can also be done to a degree in manuscripts that have dots for voweling systems, as has been done by Dutton.[55] This also needs to be done in more fully vocalized manuscripts as has been done by Brockett.[56] A particular task in this enterprise needing attention is isolating reading systems in addition to the Seven, Ten, and Fourteen that were in use up until the time of Ibn Mujāḥid (936/324). For instance, more study is needed on how the Seven, Ten, and Fourteen recitation systems came to hold their positions of prominence, and how the Ten developed further into eighty recitation systems. Tracing these reading systems in extant manuscripts would be a useful step towards this.

The physical corrections in extant Qur'ān manuscripts need examination for the presence and percentages of dogmatic corrections, orthographical updating, and conforming the text to standard text-forms. This would help bring greater precision to our understanding of the chronological development of Arabic orthography as well as give historical data for the times when outside pressure was brought to bear on the text to standardize it to a particular reading. Qur'ānic palimpsests should be sought and used especially for this kind of study.

Also, more work is needed tracing the transition from a predominantly oral literary environment in early Islam to one dominated by written literary conventions. Changes in orthography, the standardization of spelling of names and other words, and detailed examination of the palimpsests could all contribute to this goal. This also would provide historical data to chart the encounter of early Islam with the more literate cultures of late near eastern antiquity.

CLOSING THOUGHTS

Instead of the pure autographic text-forms being preserved, what has been preserved and transmitted for the Qur'ān is a text-form that was chosen from amidst a group of others, which was then edited and canonized at the expense of these others, and has been improved upon in order to make it conform to a desired ideal. Altogether, the transmission of the text of the Qur'ān in early manuscripts shows evidence of editing, control, correction, and preservation. The textual tradition shows fidelity to a standard form of the text that within the flexible conventions of orthography for the time represents a very high degree of precision. Though they are few in number, textual variants that show intentionality and that affect the meaning of the text can be found. Evidence of readings attributed to the Companions of Muḥammad can also be found. However, what cannot be determined are the Autographic text-forms of what the earliest Muslims considered to be the full corpus of revelations given through Muḥammad and left at his death or the Authoritative text-forms of his Companions. Instead, a strongly edited version of one corpus has been preserved and transmitted, made between twenty and one hundred years after Muḥammad's death. It is impossible to know how much material was left out or changed in order to make this edited version, though from all indications it was material of a similar nature to what was preserved.

The Qur'ān as it is preserved today is a book providing a glimpse into many eras of Qur'ān development. The consonantal text preserves much of what was considered Qur'ān material from at least the beginning of the eighth century. The diacritical marks on the consonants bear testimony to a period of development between the seventh and the tenth centuries. The vowel points also bear witness to developments in orthography in the ninth and tenth centuries. The pattern of recitation that is found in printed texts provides testimony to the eighty systems of the ten authorized reading systems of the Qur'ān that were standardized in the tenth century. The actual form of the printed text also bears witness to the twentieth century in that it was produced specifically for printing and wide acceptance to an international audience.

NOTES

1. This refers to Arabic business and administrative papyri dating into the seventh/first century. See Nabia Abbott, *Studies in Arabic Literary Papyri III, Language and Literature* (Chicago: University of Chicago Press, 1969), Adolf Grohmann, "The Problem of Dating Early Qur'âns," *Der Islam* 33: 213–231, and Simon Hopkins, *Studies in the Grammar of Early Arabic* (Oxford: Oxford University Press, 1984).

2. Alan Jones, "Orality and Writing in Arabia," in Jane Dammen McAuliffe, ed. *EQ* (Leiden: Brill, 2003), 587–93, 593.

3. Fred M. Donner, "The Historical Context," in Fred M. Donner, *The Cambridge Companion to the Qur'ān* (Cambridge: Cambridge University Press, 2006), 23–40, citing 32; Daniel A. Madigan, *The Qur'ân's Self-Image* (Oxford: Princeton University Press, 2001), 40.

4. Fred M. Donner, "The Qur'ān in Recent Scholarship: Challenges and Desiderata," in Fred M. Donner, *The Qur'ān in its Historical Context* (London: Routledge, 2008), 29–50, 31.

5. Günter Lüling, *A Challenge to Islam for Reformation* (Delhi: Motilal Banarsidass, 2003); B. M. Metzger, "Early Arabic Versions of the New Testament," in B. M. Metzger, *On Language, Culture, and Religion: In Honor of Eugene A. Nida* (The Hague: Mouton, 1974), 157–68, 49.

6. Beatrice Gruendler, "Arabic Script," in Jane Dammen McAuliffe, ed., *EQ* (Leiden: Brill, 2001), 135–42, 138.

7. Gregor Schoeler, "The Codification of the Qur'an: A Comment on the Hypotheses of Burton and Wansbrough," in Angelika Neuwirth, Nicolai Sinai, and Michael Marx, eds., *The Qur'ān in Context* (Leiden: Brill, 2010), 779–94, 780.

8. Efim A. Rezvan, "The Qur'ān: between *Textus Receptus* and Critical Edition," in Efim A. Rezvan, *Les problemes poses par l'edition critique des texts anciens et medievaux: Volume en collaboration internationale Institut d'Etudes Medievals* (Paris: 1992), 291–310, 297.

9. Ahmad Von Denffer, *'Ulūm al-Qur'ān* (Leicester: The Islamic Foundation, 1994), 46–52, and Arthur Jeffery, "Progress in the Study of the Qur'an Text," *MW* 25, 1: 4–16, 8.

10. Gerd-R. Puin, "Observations on Early Qur'an Manuscripts in San'ā'," in Stefan Wild, ed., *The Qur'an as Text* (Leiden: Brill, 1996), 107–11, 111.

11. Alfred-Louis de Premare, "'Abd al-Malik b. Marwān and the Process of the Qur'ān's Composition," in Karl-Heinz Ohlig and Gerd-R. Puin, eds., *The Hidden Origins of Islam* (New York: Prometheus Books, 2010), 189–224, 194–97.

12. Arthur Jeffery, *Materials for the History of the Text of the Qur'ān* (Leiden: Brill, 1937), v–vi.

13. Claude Gilliot, "Creation of a Fixed Text," in Jane Dammen McAuliffe, ed., *Cambridge Companion of the Qur'ān* (Cambridge: Cambridge University Press, 2006), 41–58, 47.

14. Aliza Shnizer, "Sacrality and Collection," in Jane Dammen McAuliffe, ed., *The Blackwell Companion to the Qur'ān* (London: Blackwell Publishing, 2006), 159–71, 169.

15. Rizwi Faizer, "The Dome of the Rock and the Qur'ān," in Khaleel Mohammed and Andrew Rippin, eds., *Coming to Terms with the Qur'ān* (North Haledon: Islamic Publications International, No date), 77–106, 89; Omar Hamdan, "The Second Masāhif Project: A Step Towards the Canonization of the Qur'anic Text," in Angelika Neuwirth, Nicolai Sinai, and Michael Marx, eds., *The Qur'ān in Context* (Leiden: Brill, 2010), 795–836, 807–9. See also Matthias Radscheit, "The Qur'ān—Codification and Canonization," in Stefan Wild, ed., *Self-Referentiality in the Qur'ān* (Weisbaden: Harrassowitz Verlag, 2006), 93–102, 98–99, and de Premare, "Process," de Premare, 205–11, for other views of al-Hajjāj's edition.

16. William Muir, "The Apology of Al-Kindy," www.bible.ca/islam/library/Al-Kindi/index.htm, 27 June 2007.

17. Bayard Dodge, *The Fihrist of Ibn al-Nadīm* (Chicago: Kazi Publications, 1970), 53, 57, 58, 62.

18. Alba Fedeli, "Early Evidences of Variant Readings in Qur'ānic Manuscripts," in Karl-Heinz Ohlig and Gerd-R. Puin, eds., *Die dunklen Anfänge* (Berlin: Hans Schiler, 2005), 293–316, citing 315. Alford T. Welch, "al-Kur'ān," in Alford T. Welch, *EI2* (Leiden: Brill, 1960), 400–29, citing 408.

19. Denffer, *'Ulūm,* 117.

20. Christopher Melchert, "The Relation of the Ten Readings to One Another," *JQS* 10 (2008):73–87.

21. M. M. Al-Azami, *The History of the Qur'anic Text* (Leicester: UK Islamic Academy, 2003), 140.
22. Jeffery, *Materials*, x, page 2 footnote 3.
23. Arthur Jeffery, "The Qur'an Readings of Ibn Miqsam," in Arthur Jeffery, *Ignace Goldziher Memorial Volume* (Budapest: 1948), 1–38, 2.
24. David S. Margoliouth, "Textual Variations in the Koran," *MW* 15: 334–44, 340.
25. Labib as-Said, *The Recited Koran* (Princeton, NJ: Darwin Press, 1975), 92–93.
26. For example, the identification of the British Library's Or. 2165 with the reading of Ibn ʿĀmir, fourth of the seven, in Yasin Dutton, "Some Notes on the British Library's 'Oldest Qur'an Manuscript' (Or. 2165)," *Journal of Qur'anic Studies* VI, 1: 43–71.
27. Adrian Alan Brockett, *Studies in Two Transmissions of the Qur'ān* (University of St. Andrews, Department of Arabic Studies, 1984), 9.
28. Denffer, *'Ulūm,* 65.
29. Brockett, *Studies,* 86.
30. G. Bergsträsser, "Koranlesung in Kairo," *Der Islam* XX, 1: 1–41, 5.
31. Brockett, *Studies,* 11.
32. Theodor Noldeke, Friedrich Schwally, G. Bergsträsser, and O. Pretzl, *Geschichte des Qorāns* (Hildesheim: Georg Olms Verlag, 2005), 3:249.
33. Brother Mark, *A "Perfect" Qur'an.* Privately published, 2000, 52–60.
34. as-Said, *Koran,* 95.
35. Hopkins, *Studies,* §58, 60–61.
36. Joshua Blau, *The Emergence and Linguistic Background of JUDAEO-ARABIC* (Jerusalem: Ben-Zvi Institute for the Study of Jewish Communities in the East, 1999), 222.
37. L. Bevan Jones, *The People of the Mosque* (London: Student Christian Movement Press, 1932), 62.
38. Paul D. Wegner, *Textual Criticism of the Bible* (Downers Grove: IVP Academic, 2006), 93–94.
39. Bart D. Ehrman, *The Orthodox Corruption of Scripture* (Oxford: Oxford University Press, 1993), 280.
40. Jeffery, *Materials,* 16–17.
41. E. Rezvan, "The First Qur'ans," in E. Rezvan, *Pages of Perfection* (St. Petersburg: ARCH Foundation, 1995), 108–17 citing 108–9.
42. Gilliot, "Creation," 52–53.
43. Donner, "Qur'ān," 31.
44. Donner, "Qur'ān," 74.
45. For example, in Sergio Noja-Noseda, "Note Esterne in Margine Al 1° Volume Dei 'Materiali per un'Edizione Critica Del Corano,'" *Rendiconti* 134, 1: 3–37. Pages 19–28 contain a list of the contents of the known Ḥijāzī manuscripts in the United States, European collections, the Middle East, and Istanbul. Surahs 77–114 are not represented in any of these manuscripts, 71–76 in only one, and with very sporadic coverage between 45 and 70.
46. Brockett, *Studies*, 94, 142.
47. François Déroche, "Written Transmission," in Andrew Rippin, ed., *The Blackwell Companion to the Qur'ān* (London: Blackwell Publishing, 2006), 172–86, 172.

48. C. Melchert, "Relation of the Ten Readings to One Another." Oxford: 2007. Lecture given at SOAS, University of London conference: The Qur'an: Text, Interpretation & Translation, 7–9 November 2007. Copy obtained from author.

49. Adrian Alan Brockett, "The Value of the Hafs and Warsh Transmissions for the Textual History of the Qur'an," in Andrew Rippin, ed., *Approaches to the History of the Interpretation of the Qur'an* (Oxford: Clarendon, 1988), 31–45, 44.

50. A. Fischer, "Grammatisch schweirige Schwur- und Beschwörungsformeln des Klassichen Arabisch," *Der Islam* 28: 1–105.

51. Yasin Dutton, "An Early *Mushaf* According to the Reading of Ibn 'Āmir," *Journal of Qur'anic Studies* III, 1: 71–90, Dutton, "Notes," Intisar A. Rabb, "Non-Canonical Readings of the Qur'an: Recognition and Authenticity (the Himsī Reading)," *Journal of Qur'anic Studies* VIII, 2: 84–127.

52. *Collins English Dictionary* (Glasgow: Harper Collins, 1991), "coppice." See www.coppicenorthwest.org.uk/ for information on coppicing methods.

53. Dutton, "Mushaf," and Dutton, "Notes,"

54. Intisar A. Rabb, "Non-Canonical Readings of the Qur'an: Recognition and Authenticity (the Himsī Reading)," *Journal of Qur'anic Studies* VIII, 2: 84–127.

55. Yasin Dutton, "Red Dots, Green Dots, Yellow Dots & Blue: Some reflections on the Vocalisation of Early Qur'anic Manuscripts—Part I," *Journal of Qur'anic Studies* I, I (1999): 115–40, Yasin Dutton, "Red Dots, Green Dots, Yellow Dots, Blue," *Journal of Qur'anic Studies* II, I (2000): 1–24.

56. Adrian Alan Brockett, "Aspects of the Physical Transmission of the Qur'ân in 19th-Century Sudan: Script, Decoration, Binding and Paper," *Manuscripts of the Middle East* 2: 45–67.

Bibliography

Abbott, Nabia. *The Rise of North Arabic Script and its Kur'anic Development*. Chicago: University of Chicago Oriental Publications, 1939.

———. *Studies in Arabic Literary Papyri III, Language and Literature*, O.I.P. LXXVII. Chicago: University of Chicago Press, 1969.

Abboud, Peter F., and Ernest N. McCarus, eds. *Elementary Modern Standard Arabic*. New York: Cambridge University Press, 1983.

Akimushkin, O. F. "Textological Studies and the 'Critical Text' Problem." *Manuscripta Orientalia* 1 (1995): 22–28.

Aland, Kurt, and Barbara Aland. *The Text of the New Testament*, Second edn. Leiden: Brill, 1989.

Ali, Muhammad Mohar. *The Qur'an and the Latest Orientalist Assumptions*. Suffolk: Jam'iat Ihyaa' Minhaaj Al-Sunnah, 1999.

Altikulaç, Dr. Tayyar, ed. *Al-Muṣḥaf al-Sharif: Attributed to 'Uthmān bin 'Affān (The copy at the Topkapi Palace Museum)*, Istanbul: IRCICA, 2007.

———. *Al-Mushaf al-Sharif: Attributed to Uthman bin Affan (The copy at al-Mashhad al-Huseyni in Cairo)*, Istanbul: IRCICA, 2009, 2 vols.

Ambros, Arne A., and Stephan Procházka. *A Concise Dictionary of Koranic Arabic*. Weisbaden: Reichert Verlag, 2004.

Arberry, Arthur J. *The Koran Illuminated*. Dublin: Hodges, Figgis & Co. Ltd., 1967.

al-Azami, M. M. *The History of the Qur'anic Text*, Leicester: UK Islamic Academy, 2003.

Baker, Colin F. *Qur'an Manuscripts*, London: British Library, 2007.

al-Bannā', *Ithāf fudalā' al-bashar fī'l-qirā'āt al-arba' 'ashr*, Beirut: Dar al-Kotob al-Ilmiyah, 2001.

Bar-Asher, M. M. "Variant Readings and Additions of the Imami-Si'a to the Qur'an," *Israel Oriental Studies* 13 (1993): 39–74.

Barr, James. *The Variable Spellings of the Hebrew Bible*. The Schweich Lectures of the British Academy 1986, Oxford: Oxford University Press, 1989.

Beeston, A. F. L., T. M. Johnstone, R. B. Serjeant, and G. R. Smith, eds. *Arabic Literature to the End of the Umayyad Period*. Cambridge History of Arabic Literature. Cambridge: Cambridge University Press, 1983.

Bell, Richard. *Introduction to the Qur'an*. Edinburgh: Edinburgh University Press, 1953.

Bellamy, James A. "Some Proposed Emendations to the Text of the Koran." *JAOS* 113 (1993): 562–73.

———. "Textual Criticism of the Koran." *JOAS* 121 (2001): 1–6.

Berg, Herbert. *The Development of Exegesis in Early Islam*. Curzon Studies in the Qur'an. Richmond, Surrey: Curzon, 2000.

Bergsträsser, G. "Koranlesung in Kairo." *Der Islam* XX (1932): 1–41.

———. *Nichtkanonische Koranlesarten im Muhtasab des ibn Ginni*. Munich: Sizungsberichte der Bayerischen Akad. D, Wiss., 1933.

———, ed. *Ibn Hālawaih's Sammlung Nichtkanonischer Koranlesarten*. Bibliotheca Islamica, Leipzig: BEI F.A. Brockhaus, 1934.

Blachère, Régis. *Introduction au Coran*, 2e édition partiellement refondue edn. Paris: Besson & Chantemerle, 1959.

———. *Le Coran*, 5th edn. Paris: Universitaires de France, 1977.

Blair, Sheila S. *Islamic Calligraphy*. Edinburgh: Edinburgh University Press, 2006.

Blau, Joshua. *The Emergence and Linguistic Background of JUDAEO-ARABIC*, Third edn. Jerusalem: Ben-Zvi Institute for the study of Jewish Communities in the East, 1999.

Blochet, E. *Catalogue des manuscrits arabes des nouvelles acquisitions*. Paris: Bibliothèque Nationale, 1925.

Bothmer, Hans-Caspar Graf von, Karl-Heinz Ohlig, and Gerd-R Puin. "Neue Wege der Koranforschung." *Magazin Forschung*. Saarland, GDR: University of Saarland, 1999. Vol. 2005.

British Library. *List of Oriental Manuscripts 1948–1964, Or. 11820–12898*. London: British Library, 1964.

Brockett, Adrian Alan. *Studies in Two Transmissions of the Qur'ān*. PhD thesis, University of St. Andrews, 1984.

———. "Aspects of the Physical Transmission of the Qur'ān in 19th-century Sudan: Script, Decoration, Binding and Paper." *Manuscripts of the Middle East* 2 (1987): 45–67.

———. "The Value of the Hafs and Warsh Transmissions for the Textual History of the Qur'an," in Andrew Rippin, ed., *Approaches to the History of the Interpretation of the Qur'an*. Oxford: Clarendon, 1988, pp. 31–45.

———. "Qur'an Readings in Kitab Sibawayhi." *University of St. Andrews School of Abbasid Studies: Occasional Papers of the School of Abbasid Studies* (1990): 129–206.

al-Bukhari. "WinHadith v. 1.5." London: Islamic Computing Centre, 1994.

Burton, John. *The Collection of the Qur'ān*, 1979 Paperback edn., Cambridge: Cambridge University Press, 1977.

———. “The Collection of the Qur’an,” in Jane Dammen McAuliffe, ed., *Encyclopaedia of the Qur’an*. Leiden: Brill, 2001, pp. 351–61.

Collins English Dictionary, third edn. Glasgow: Harper Collins, 1991.

Cook, Michael. “The Opponents of the WritingTradition in Early Islam.” *Arabica* 44 (1997): 457–530.

———. *The Koran: A Very Short Introduction*. Oxford: Oxford University Press, 2000.

Cureton, W., and C. Rieu. *Catalogus codicum manuscriptorum orientalium qui Museo Britannico asservantur*. London: British Museum, 1846–71.

ad-Dānī, *al-Muqni’ fī’ rasm masāhif al amsār*. Cairo: Maktab al-Kulīāt al-’Azhariyat, 1978.

Denffer, Ahmad Von. *‘Ulūm al-Qur’ān*, Revised edn. Leicester: The Islamic Foundation, 1994.

de Premare, Alfred-Louis. “‘Abd al-Malik b. Marwān and the Process of the Qur’ān’s Composition,” in Karl-Heinz Ohlig and Gerd-R. Puin, eds., *The Hidden Origins of Islam*. New York: Prometheus Books, 2010, pp. 189–224.

———. “The Qur’ān in Recent Scholarship: Challenges and Desiderata,” in Gabriel Said Reynolds, ed., *The Qur’ān in its Historical Context*. London: Routledge, 2008, pp. 29–50.

Déroche, François. *Catalogue des Manuscrits Arabes*. Paris: Bibliotheque Nationale, 1983.

———. *The Abbasid Tradition*. The Nasser D. Khalili Collection of Islamic Art. London: Nour Foundation, 1992.

———. *L’art du livre arabe*. Paris: Bibliothèque nationale de France, 2001.

———. “Manuscripts of the Qur’ān,” in Jane Dammen McAuliffe, ed., *Encyclopaedia of the Qur’ān*. Leiden: Brill, 2003, pp. 254–75.

———. *Le livre manuscrit arabe*. Paris: Bibliothèque nationale de France, 2004.

———. *Le Coran*. Paris: Presses Universitaires de France, 2005.

———. “Written Transmission,” in A. Rippin, ed., *The Blackwell Companion to the Qur’ān*. London: Blackwell Publishing, 2006, pp. 172–86.

———. *La transmission écrite du Coran dans les débuts de l’islam: Le codex Parisino-petropolitanus*. Text and Studies on the Qur’ān. Leiden: Brill, 2009.

Déroche, François, and Sergio Noja-Noseda. *Sources de la Transmission Manuscrite du Texte Coranique*. Projet Amari. Lesa, Italy: Fondazione Ferni Noja Noseda Studi Arabo Islamici, vol. 1, 1998.

———. *Sources de la Transmission Manuscrite du Texte Coranique*. Projet Amari. Lesa, Italy: Fondazione Ferni Noja Noseda Studi Arabo Islamici, vol. 2.1, 2001.

DeSlane, W. M. *Catalogue des manuscrits arabes*. Paris: Imprimerie Nationale, 1883–95.

Dodge, Bayard, ed. *The Fihrist of Ibn al-Nadīm*. Great Books of the Islamic World. Chicago: Kazi Publications, 1970.

Donner, Fred M. “The Historical Context,” in Jane Dammen McAuliffe, ed., *The Cambridge Companion to the Qur’ān*. Cambridge: Cambridge University Press, 2006, pp. 23–40.

———. “Quranic *Furqān*.” *JSS* 52 (2007): 279–300.

———. "The Qur'ān in Recent Scholarship: Challenges and Desiderata," in Gabriel Said Reynolds, ed., *The Qur'ān in its Historical Context*. London: Routledge, 2008, pp. 29–50.

Dutton, Yasin. "Red Dots, Green Dots, Yellow Dots & Blue: Some Reflections on the Vocalisation of Early Qur'anic Manuscripts—Part I." *JQS* I (1999): 115–40.

———. "Red Dots, Green Dots, Yellow Dots, Blue." *JQS* II (2000): 1–24.

———. "An Early *Mushaf* According to the Reading of Ibn 'Āmir," *JQS* III (2001): 71–90.

———. "Some Notes on the British Library's 'Oldest Qur'an Manuscript' (Or. 2165)." *JQS* VI (2004): 43–71.

———. "An Umayyad Fragment of the Qur'an and its Dating." *JQS* IX (2007): 57–87.

Ehrman, Bart D. *The Orthodox Corruption of Scripture*. Oxford: Oxford University Press, 1993.

Ellis, A. G., and E. Edwards. *Descriptive List of the Arabic Manuscripts Acquired by the Trustees of the British Museum since 1894*. London: British Museum, 1912.

Epp, Eldon Jay. "The Multivalence of the Term 'Original Text' in New Testament Textual Criticism." *HTR* 92 (1999): 245–81.

Esack, Farid. *The Qur'an: A Short Introduction*, 2004 Reprint edn. Oxford: Oneworld Publications, 2002.

Faizer, Rizwi. "The Dome of the Rock and the Qur'ān," in Khaleel Mohammed and Andrew Rippin, eds., *Coming to Terms with the Qur'ān*. North Haledon: Islamic Publications International, No date, pp. 77–106.

Fedeli, Alba. "Early Evidences of Variant Readings in Qur'ānic Manuscripts," in Karl-Heinz Ohlig and Gerd-R. Puin, eds., *Die dunklen Anfänge*. Berlin: Hans Schiler, 2005, pp. 293–316.

———. "Mingana and the Manuscript of Mrs. Agnes Smith Lewis, One Century Later." *MO* 11 (2005): 3–7.

———. "A.Perg.2: A Non-Palimpsest and the Corrections in Qur'ānic Manuscripts." *MO* 11 (2005): 20–27.

———. "The Interdiction of Fighting in the Holy Month: The Struggle for the Abolition of an Early Tradition in the Scriptio Inferior of a Qur'ānic Palimpsest." Jerusalem: 2006.

Fischer, A. "Grammatisch schweirige Schwur- und Beschwörungsformeln des Klassichen Arabisch." *Der Islam* 28 (1948): 1–105.

Fischer, Wolfdietrich. *A Grammar of Classical Arabic*, Third Revised edn. London: Yale University Press, 2002.

Fleisch, H. "Hamza," in *EI2*. Leiden: Brill, 1960, pp. 150–52.

Fraser, Marcus, and Will Kwiatkowski. *Ink and Gold: Islamic Calligraphy*. London: Museum für Islamische Kunst, Berlin, 2006.

Fogg, Sam. *Islamic Manuscripts*. London: Sam Fogg, 2000.

———. *Islamic Calligraphy*. London: Sam Fogg, 2003.

Gacek, Adam. "Technical Practices and Recommendations Recorded by Classical and Post-Classical Arabic Scholars Concerning the Copying and Correction of

Manuscripts," in François Déroche, ed., *Actes du Colloque d'Istanbul*. L'Institut Français d'Études Anatoliennes d'Istanbul la Bibliothèque Nationale de Paris, Istanbul, Turkey: 1986, 51–59.

———. "Taxonomy of Scribal Errors and Corrections in Arabic Manuscripts," in Judith Pfeiffer and Manfred Kropp, eds., *Theoretical Approaches to the Transmission and Edition of Oriental Manuscripts*. Beirut: Ergon Verlag Würzburg, 2007, pp. 217–35.

Gibson, Margaret Dunlop, ed. *An Arabic Version of the Epistles of St. Paul to the Romans, Corinthians, Galatians with Part of the Epistle to the Ephesians from a Ninth Century MS. in the Convent of St. Catherine on Mount Sinai*. Studia Sinaitica, London: C. J. Clay and Sons, 1894.

Gilliot, Claude. "Un Verset Manquant du Coran ou Réputè Tel," in Marie-Thérèse Urvoy, ed., *En Hommage au Père Jacques Jomier, O.P.* Paris: CERF, 2002, pp. 73–100.

———. "Creation of a Fixed Text," in Jane Dammen McAuliffe, ed., *The Cambridge Companion to the Qur'an*. Cambridge: Cambridge University Press, 2006, pp. 41–58.

Griffith, Sidney H. "Disputing with Islam in Syriac: The Case of the Monk of Bêt Ḫālê." Washington, D.C.: Catholic University of America, 2005.

Grohmann, Adolf. "The Problem of Dating Early Qur'āns." *Der Islam* 33 (1958): 213–31.

Gruendler, Beatrice. *The Development of the Arabic Scripts*. Harvard Semitic Studies, Atlanta: Scholars Press, 1993.

———. "Arabic Script," in Jane Dammen McAuliffe, ed., *EQ*. Leiden: Brill, 2001, pp. 135–42.

Haleem, M. A. S. Abdel. "Qur'ānic Orthography: The Written Representation of the Recited Text of the Qur'ān." *The Islamic Quarterly* XXXVIII (1994): 171–92.

Hamdan, Omar. "The Second Masāhif Project: A Step Towards the Canonization of the Qur'anic Text," in Angelika Neuwirth, Nicolai Sinai, and Michael Marx, eds., *The Qur'ān in Context*. Texts and Studies on the Qur'ān. Leiden: Brill, 2010, pp. 795–836.

Helali, Asma. "The Sanaa Palimpsest: Introductory Remarks to Philological and Literary Aspects." Conference paper given 14 November at "The Qur'an: Text, History & Culture," 12–14 November 2009, SOAS, University of London, 2009.

al-Hilali, M. Taqi-ud-Din, and M. M. Khan. *Interpretation of the Meanings of the Noble Qur'ān*, Revised edn. Riyadh, Saudi Arabia: Darussalam, 2001.

Hobbs, Edward. "Prologue: An Introduction to Methods of Textual Criticism," in Wendy Doniger O'Flaherty, ed., *The Critical Study of Sacred Texts*. Berkeley: Berkeley Religious Studies Series, 1979, pp. 1–27.

Holmes, Michael W. "The Case for Reasoned Eclecticism," in David A. Black, ed., *Rethinking New Testament Textual Criticism*. Grand Rapids: Baker Academic, 2002, pp. 77–100.

Hopkins, Simon. *Studies in the Grammar of Early Arabic*. Oxford: Oxford University Press, 1984.

Horovitz, J. "Jewish Proper Names and Derivatives in the Koran." *Hebrew Union College Annual* (1925): 146–227.

Housman, A. E. "The Application of Thought to Textual Criticism." *Proceedings of the Classical Association* xviii (1922).

Hoyland, Robert. *Seeing Islam as Others Saw It.* Princeton, New Jersey: The Darwin Press, 1997.

Iman, Ahmad 'Ali al. *Variant Readings of the Qur'an.* Herndon, VA: International Institute of Islamic Thought, 1998.

James, David. *Qur'ans and Bindings from the Chester Beatty Library.* London: World of Islam Festival Trust, 1980.

Jeffery, Arthur. "Progress in the Study of the Qur'an Text." *MW* 25 (1935): 4–16.

———. "The Qur'an Readings of Zaid B. 'Ali." *Rivista Degli Studi Orientalia* XVI (1936): 40.

———. *Materials for the History of the Text of the Qur'ān.* Leiden: Brill, 1937.

———. *Foreign Vocabulary of the Qur'an.* Baroda: Oriental Institute, 1938.

———. "Abū 'Ubaid on the Verses Missing From the Qur'an." *MW* 28 (1938): 61–65.

———. "Review of 'The Rise of the North Arabic Script and its Kur'ānic Development' by Nabia Abbott." *MW* 30 (1940): 191–98.

———. "The Qur'an Readings of Ibn Miqsam," in Samuel Lowinger and Joseph Somogyi, eds., *Ignace Goldziher Memorial Volume.* Budapest: 1948, pp. 1–38.

Jeffery, Arthur, and Isaac Mendelsohn. "The Orthography of the Samarqand Qur'an Codex." *JAOS* 62 (1942): 175–95.

Jones, A. "The Qur'ān - II," in *Arabic Literature to the End of the Umayyad Period.* Cambridge History of Arabic Literature. Cambridge: Cambridge University Press, 1983.

Jones, Alan. "Orality and Writing in Arabia," in Jane Dammen McAuliffe, ed., *EQ.* Leiden: Brill, 2003, pp. 3:587–93.

Jones, L. Bevan. *The People of the Mosque.* London: Student Christian Movement Press, 1932.

Kathir, Ibn. *Stories of the Prophets.* Riyadh, Saudi Arabia: Darusslam. No date.

Khaldūn, Ibn. *The Muqaddimah.* New York: Bollingen Foundation, 1967.

Al-Khatīb, Abd al-Latīf. *Mu'jam al-Qirā'āt.* Damascus: Dār Sa'd al-Dīn, 1422/2002.

Kohlberg, Etan, and Mohammad Ali Amir-Moezzi. *Revelation and Falsification: The Kitāb al-qirā'āt of Ahmad b. Muhammad al-Sayyārī.* Text and Studies on the Qur'ān. Leiden: Brill, 2009.

Lawson, Todd. "Note for the Study of a 'Shī'ī Qur'ān." *JSS* 36 (1991): 279–95.

Leemhuis, Frederick. "From Palm Leaves to the Internet," in Jane Dammen McAuliffe, ed., *The Cambridge Companion to the Qur'ān.* Cambridge: Cambridge University Press, 2006, pp. 145–62.

"Libraries in the Desert." *The Economist,* 2 June 2007 edition, 63.

Lings, Martin, and Yasin Hamid Safadi, *The Qur'ān.* London: British Library, 1976.

Loth, O. *Catalogue of the Arabic Manuscripts in the Library of the India Office, vol. 1.* London: Secretary of State for India in Council, 1877.

Lüling, Günter. *A Challenge to Islam for Reformation.* Delhi: Motilal Banarsidass, 2003.

Madd al-Qamas. *An Arabic-English Lexicon* for Thesaurus Islamicus Foundation, 2003.

Madigan, Daniel A. *The Qur'ān's Self-Image*. Oxford: Princeton University Press, 2001.

Makram, Abd al-'Āl Sālim, and Ahmad Muktār 'Umar. *Mu'jam al-Qirā'āt al-Qurānīyah, Ma'a Maqaddimah fī Qirā'āt wa Ashhar al-Qurrā'*, Third edn. Cairo, Egypt: 'Ālam al-Kitab, 1997.

Mallalieu, Huon. "The Al-Sabah Collection in the Kuwait National Museum." *Arts of the Islamic World* 1 (1983): 7–12.

Marcinkowski, Muhammad Ismail. "Some Reflections on Alleged Twelver Shī'ite Attitudes Toward the Integrity of the Qur'ān." *Muslim World* 91 (2001): 137–53.

Margoliouth, David S. "Textual Variations in the Koran." *MW* 15 (1925): 334–44.

Mattson, Ingrid. *The Story of the Qur'an*. Oxford: Blackwell, 2008.

Mark, Brother. *A "Perfect" Qur'an*. Privately published, 2000.

McAuliffe, Jane Dammen, ed. *Encyclopaedia of the Qur'ān*. Leiden: Brill, 2001–2004.

McKenzie, D. F. *Bibliography and the Sociology of Texts*. The Panizzi Lectures, London: The British Library, 1986.

Melchert, Christopher. "Ibn Mujahid and the Establishment of Seven Qur'anic Readings." *Studia Islamica* 91 (2000): 5–22.

———. "Relation of the Ten Readings to One Another." Oxford: 2007. Printed copy of SOAS Conference lecture obtained from author.

Melchert, Christopher. "The Relation of the Ten Readings to One Another." *JQS* 10 (2008): 73–87.

Metzger, B. M. "Recent Trends in the Textual Criticism of the Iliad and the Mahabharata," in B. M. Metzger, ed., *Chapters in the History of New Testament Textual Criticism*. New Testament Tools and Studies. Grand Rapids: Eerdmans, 1963, pp. 142–54.

———. "Early Arabic Versions of the New Testament," in Matthew Black and William A. Smalley, eds., *On Language, Culture, and Religion: In Honor of Eugene A. Nida*. The Hague: Mouton, 1974, pp. 157–68.

Metzger, B. M. and Bart D. Ehrman. *The Text of the New Testament*, Fourth edn. New York: Oxford University Press, 2005.

Mihrān, Ibn. *al-Mabsūt fī'l-qirā'āt al-'ashr*. Damascus: Matyū'āt Majma' al-Lu'at al-'Arbayyat bi Damashiq, No date.

Mingana, Alphonse, and Agnes Smith Lewis, eds., *Leaves From Three Ancient Qur'āns, Possibly Pre-'Uthmānic*. Cambridge: Cambridge University Press, 1914.

Mingana, Alphonse. *An Ancient Syriac Translation of the Kur'ān Exhibiting New Verses and Variants*. Manchester: The University Press, 1925.

———. *Catalogue of the Arabic Manuscripts in the John Rylands Library*. Manchester: Manchester University Press, 1934.

———. "Syriac Influence on the Style of the Koran," in Ibn Warraq, ed., *What the Koran Really Says*. Amherst, NY: Prometheus Books, 2002, pp. 171–92.

Modarressi, Hossein. "Early Debates on the Integrity of the Qur'an." *Studia Islamica* 77 (1993): 5–39.
Motzki, Harald. "The Collection of the Qur'an: A Reconsideration of Western Views in Light of Recent Methodological Developments." *Der Islam* 78 (2001): 1–34.
Muir, William. "The Apology of Al-Kindy." 1886. Vol. 2005.
Mujāhid, Ibn. *Kitāb al-Sab'ah fi al Qirā'āt*. Cairo: Dar al-Mu'ārif, no date.
Mushaf Sharif. Istanbul: Dojan Kardes, 1967.
al-Mu'sirāwī, 'Ahmad 'Isā. *Al-Qirā'āt al-'Ashar*. Damascus: Dar al-Maarifah, 2007.
Nelson, Kristina. *The Art of Reciting the Qur'an*. Modern Middle East Series, Austin: University of Texas Press, 1985.
Neuwirth, Angelika. "Structural, Linguistic, and Literary Features," in Jane Dammen McAuliffe, ed., *The Cambridge Companion to the Qur'ān*. Cambridge: Cambridge University Press, 2006, pp. 97–113.
Neuwirth, Angelika, and Nicolai Sinai. "Introduction," in Angelika Neuwirth, Nicolai Sinai, and Michael Marx, eds., *The Qur'ān in Context*. Texts and Studies on the Qur'ān. Leiden: Brill, 2010, pp. 1–24.
Noja-Noseda, Sergio. "Book Review." *Annali* 58 (1998): 289–91.
———. "Note Esterne in Margine Al 1° Volume Dei 'Materiali per un'Edizione Critica Del Corano.'" *Rendiconti* 134 (2000): 3–37.
———. "La Mia Visita a Sanaa e il Corano Palinsesto." *Instituto Lombardo Rendiconti* 137 (2004): 43–60.
Noldeke, Theodor, Friedrich Schwally, G. Bergsträsser, and O. Pretzl. *Geschichte des Qorāns*. Hildesheim: Georg Olms Verlag, 2005.
O'Flaherty, Wendy Doniger, ed. *The Critical Study of Sacred Texts*. Berkeley: Berkeley Religious Studies Series, 1979.
Orwell, George. *Nineteen Eighty-Four*. 1971 reprint edn. Harmondsworth: Penguin, 1949.
Pakatchi, Ahmad. *The Orthographic Traditions in Early Arabic Writing as Reflected in Quranic Codices*. Berlin, 2005.
Penrice, John. *A Dictionary and Glossary of the Kor-ān*, New Edition. London: Curzon Press, 1975.
Peters, F. E. *The Monotheists*. Oxford: Princeton University Press, 2003.
Piotrovsky, Mikhail B., ed. *Heavenly Art, Earthly Beauty*. Amsterdam: Lund Humphries, 2000.
Pretzl, Otto. "Die Fortfuehrung des Apparatus Criticus zum Koran." *Sitzungsberichte der Bayerischen Akademie der Wissenshaften* Heft 5 (1934): 3–13.
Pissaref, S. Samarkandskii kuficheskii Koran. l'Institut Archéologique de St. Pétersbourg, 1905.
Powers, David S. *Muhammad is Not the Father of Any of Your Men: The Making of the Last Prophet*. Philadelphia: University of Pennsylvania Press, 2009.
Puin, Elisabeth. "Ein früher Koranpalimpsest aus San'ā' (DAM 01-27.1)," in Markus Groß and Karl-Heinz Ohlig, eds., *Schlaglichter*. Berlin: Hans Schiler, 2008, pp. 461–93.
Puin, Gerd-R. "Observations on Early Qur'an Manuscripts in San'ā'," in Stefan Wild, ed., *The Qur'an as Text*. Leiden: Brill, 1996, pp. 107–11.

———. "Vowel Letters and Ortho-epic Writing in the Qur'an." Saarbrücken: 2010.
al-Qabāqanī, Shams al-dīn Muhammad bin Khalīd. *'Īsanāh al-Rumūz wa Maftāh al-Kunūz*. Amman, Jordan: Amar House, 2003.
Qadhi, Yasir. *An Introduction to the Sciences of the Qur'aan*. Birmingham: Al-Hidaayah Publishing and Distribution, 1999.
Quaritch, Bernard. *The Qur'an and Calligraphy*. London: Bernard Quaritch, No Date.
Qur'ān Karīm. Hodeida, Yemen: Matbaghut al-Najār, 1989.
Rabb, Intisar A. "Non-Canonical Readings of the Qur'an: Recognition and Authenticity (The Himsī Reading)." *JQS,* VIII (2006): 84–127.
Rabin, Chaim. "The Beginnings of Classical Arabic," in Ibn Warraq, ed., *What the Koran Really Says*. Amherst, NY: Prometheus Books, 2002, pp. 211–27.
Radscheit, Matthias. "The Qur'ān—Codification and Canonization," in Stefan Wild, ed., *Self-Referentiality in the Qur'ān*. Diskurse der Arabistik, Weisbaden: Harrassowitz Verlag, 2006, pp. 93–102.
Ralston, Timothy J. *The Majority Text and Byzantine Texttype Development: The Significance of a Non-Parametric Method of Data Analysis for the Exploration of Manuscript Traditions*, PhD thesis, Dallas Theological Seminary University, 1994.
Reeve, John, ed. *Sacred*. London: British Library, 2007.
Rezvan, Efim A. "The Qur'ān: Between *Textus Receptus* and Critical Edition," in Jacqueline Hamesse, ed., *Les problemes poses par l'edition critique des texts anciens et medievaux: Volume en collaboration internationale Institut d'Etudes Medievals*. Paris: 1992, pp. 291–310.
———. "The First Qur'ans," in *Pages of Perfection*. St. Petersburg: ARCH Foundation, 1995, pp. 108–17.
———. "The Qur'ān and Its World: VI. Emergence of the Canon: The Struggle for Uniformity." *MO* 4 (1998): 13–54.
———. "The Qur'ān and Its World: VIII/2. *West-Östlichen Divans*." *MO* 5 (1999): 32–62.
———. "Orthography," in Jane Dammen McAuliffe, ed., *Encyclopaedia of the Qur'an*. Leiden: Brill, 2003, pp. 604–8.
———. *The Qur'ān of 'Uthmān*. St. Petersburg: St. Petersburg Centre for Oriental Studies, 2004.
———. "Mingana Folios: When and Why." *MO* 11 (2006).
Rezvan, M. E. "Qur'ānic Fragments From the A.A. Polotsov Collection at the St. Petersburg Branch of the Institute of Oriental Studies." *MO* 7 (2001): 20–35.
Riddell, Peter. *Transferring a Tradition*. Berkeley, California: 1990.
Rieu, Charles. *Supplement to the Catalogue of the Arabic Manuscripts in the British Museum*. London: British Museum, 1894.
Rippin, Andrew. "Qur'an 21:95: 'A Ban is Upon Any Town.'" *JSS* XXIV (1979): 43–53.
———. "Qur'ān 7.40: 'Until the Camel Passes through the Eye of the Needle.'" *Arabica* XXVII (1980): 107–13.
———. "Ibn Abbas's al-Lughat fi'l-Qur'an." *BSOAS* 44 (1981): 15–25.

———. *Approaches to the History of the Interpretation of the Qur'ān*. Oxford: Clarendon, 1988.

———. "Foreword," in *Quranic Studies*. Amherst: Prometheus, 2004, pp. ix–xix.

———. *Muslims: Their Religious Beliefs and Practices*, Second edn. London: Routledge, 2001.

———. *The Qur'an and its Interpretative Tradition*. Variorum Collected Studies, Burlington, VT: Ashgate, 2001.

Robinson, Neal. *Discovering the Qur'an*. London: SCM Press, 1996.

Roxburgh, David J., *Writing the Word of God: Calligraphy and the Qur'an*. Houston: Museum of Fine Arts, 2007.

Saeed, Abdullah. *The Qur'an: An Introduction*. London: Routledge, 2008.

as-Said, Labib. *The Recited Koran*. Princeton, NJ: Darwin Press, 1975.

"San'ā' Manuscripts." *Memory of the World*. Ed. UNESCO. Cairo, Egypt: Ritsec Cultureware. CD-ROM.

Schoeler, Gregor. "The Codification of the Qur'an: A Comment on the Hypotheses of Burton and Wansbrough," in Angelika Neuwirth, Nicolai Sinai, and Michael Marx, eds., *The Qur'ān in Context*. Texts and Studies on the Qur'ān. Leiden: Brill, 2010, pp. 779–94.

Shnizer, Aliza. "Sacrality and Collection," in A. Rippin, ed., *The Blackwell Companion to the Qur'ān*. London: Blackwell Publishing, 2006, pp. 159–71.

Small, Keith E. *Mapping a New Country: Textual Criticism and Qur'an Manuscripts*. PhD thesis, Brunel University, 2008.

———. "Textual Variants in the New Testament and Qur'anic Manuscript Traditions," in Markus Gross and Karl-Heinz Ohlig, eds., *Schlaglichter*. Berlin: Hans Schiler, 2008, pp. 572–93.

———. "UNESCO CD of San'ā' MSS: Qur'ān MSS Contents." *MO* 12 (2006): 65–72.

Small, Keith E., and Elisabeth Puin. "UNESCO CD of San'ā' MSS: Part III." *MO* 13(2007): 59–71.

Sotheby's. *Oriental Manuscripts and Miniatures*, Sale Catalogue 24 April 1996 edn., London: Sotheby's, 1996.

———. *Arts of the Islamic World*. London: Sotheby's, 2008.

———. *Arts of the Islamic World*. London: Sotheby's, 2010.

Spitaler, Anton. *Die Verszählung des Koran*. Sitzungsberichte der Bayerischen Akademie der Wissenchaften, München: Verlag der Bayerischen Akademie der Wissenschaften, 1935.

Storey, C. A. *Catalogue of the Arabic Manuscripts in the Library of the India Office*. London: Humphrey Milford, Oxford University Press, 1930.

Tabbaa, Yasser. "The Transformation of Arabic Writing: Part I, Qur'ānic Calligraphy." *Ars Orientalis* 21 (1991): 119–48.

———. "Canonicity and Control: The Sociopolitical Underpinnings of Ibn Muqla's Reform." *Ars Orientalis* XXIX (1999): 91–100.

Thackston, Wheeler M. *An Introduction to Koranic and Classical Arabic*. Bethesda: IBEX, 2000.

Tov, Emanuel. *Textual Criticism of the Hebrew Bible*. Minneapolis: Fortress Press, 1992.

Uri, J. *Bibliothecae Bodleianne codicum manuscriptorum orientalium catalogus, Part I*. Oxford: Oxonii e Typographea Clarendoniano, 1787.

Vajda, C. *Indes general des manuscrits arabes musulmans*. Paris: 1953.

Wansbrough, John. *Quranic Studies*. London Oriental Series. Oxford: Oxford University Press, 1977.

Warraq, Ibn, ed. *The Origins of the Koran*. Amherst, NY: Prometheus Books, 1998.

———, ed. *What the Koran Really Says*. Amherst, NY: Prometheus Books, 2002.

Wehr, Hans. *A Dictionary of Modern Written Arabic*, 1980 Reprint edn. Beirut: Libraire Du Liban, 1974.

Watt, W. M., and Bell, R. *Bell's Introduction to the Qur'ān*. Edinburgh: Edinburgh University Press, 1970.

Wegner, Paul D. *Textual Criticism of the Bible*. Downers Grove: IVP Academic, 2006.

Welch, Alford T. "al-Kur'ān," in *EI2*. Leiden: Brill, 1960, pp. 400–429.

———, ed. *Studies in Qur'an and Tafsir*. Journal of the American Academy of Religion Thematic Studies, Ann Arbor, MI: American Academy of Religion, 1979.

Wright, W. *A Grammar of the Arabic Language*. Cambridge: Cambridge University Press, 1986.

Qur'ān Manuscripts Index

Name and Subject Index

About the Author

Keith E. Small is a researcher and lecturer in early Qur'ān and New Testament manuscripts. He has a PhD in Islamics through the Centre for Islamic Studies and Christian Muslim Relations at the London School of Theology and a masters of theology from Dallas Theological Seminary. His research interests are textual criticism in early Christian and Islamic scriptural manuscripts, early Islamic history, and comparative Christian and Islamic theology. Though he has published articles on these topics, this is his first major book.

35479892R00146

Printed in Poland
by Amazon Fulfillment
Poland Sp. z o.o., Wrocław